Courtney Crumrin

VOLUME SIX

The Final Spell

Written & Illustrated by

—•❖ TED NAIFEH ❖•—

Colored by

WARREN WUCINICH

Original Series edited by

JILL BEATON

Collection edited by

ROBIN HERRERA

Designed by

KEITH WOOD & SONJA SYNAK

Published by Oni Press, Inc.

founder & chief financial officer, Joe Nozemack

publisher, James Lucas Jones

editor in chief, Sarah Gaydos

v.p. of creative & business development, Charlie Chu

director of operations, Brad Rooks

director of sales, Margot Wood

special projects manager, Amber O'Neill

director of design & production, Troy Look

digital prepress lead, Angie Knowles

senior graphic designer, Kate Z. Stone

graphic designer, Sonja Synak

senior editor, Robin Herrera

executive assistant, Michelle Nguyen

logistics coordinator, Jung Lee

Originally published as issues 6-10 of the Oni Press comic series
Courtney Crumrin.

1319 SE Martin Luther King Jr. Blvd.
Suite 240
Portland, OR 97214

onipress.com · tednaifeh.com
facebook.com/onipress · twitter.com/onipress
onipress.tumblr.com · instagram.com/onipress

First Edition: January 2020

ISBN 978-1-62010-683-9
eISBN 978-1-62010-056-1

1 3 5 7 9 10 8 6 4 2

Library of Congress Control Number: 2019939963

Printed in China.

For Carol Garcia

Chapter One

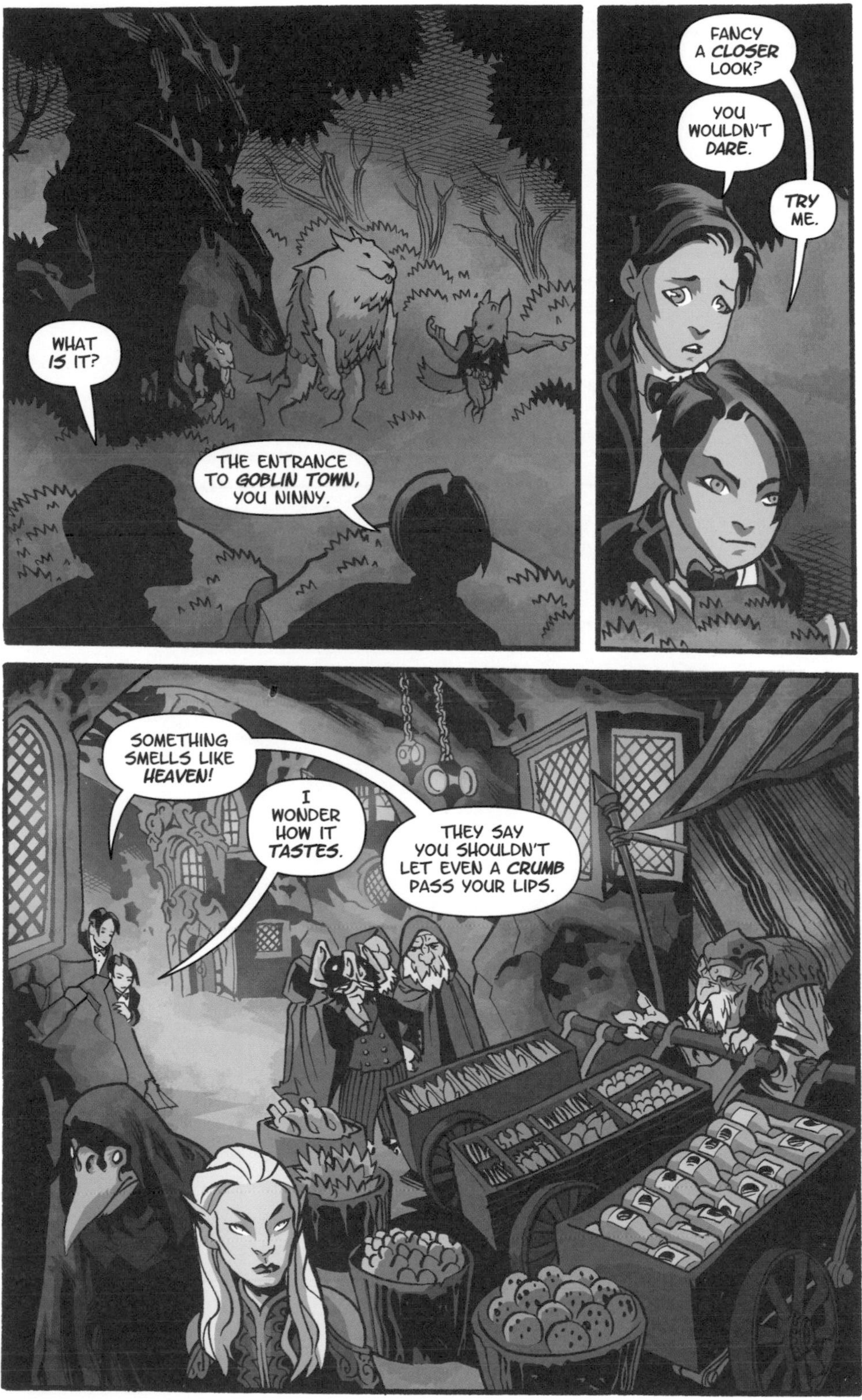
WHAT IS IT?
THE ENTRANCE TO GOBLIN TOWN, YOU NINNY.
FANCY A CLOSER LOOK?
YOU WOULDN'T DARE.
TRY ME.
SOMETHING SMELLS LIKE HEAVEN!
I WONDER HOW IT TASTES.
THEY SAY YOU SHOULDN'T LET EVEN A CRUMB PASS YOUR LIPS.

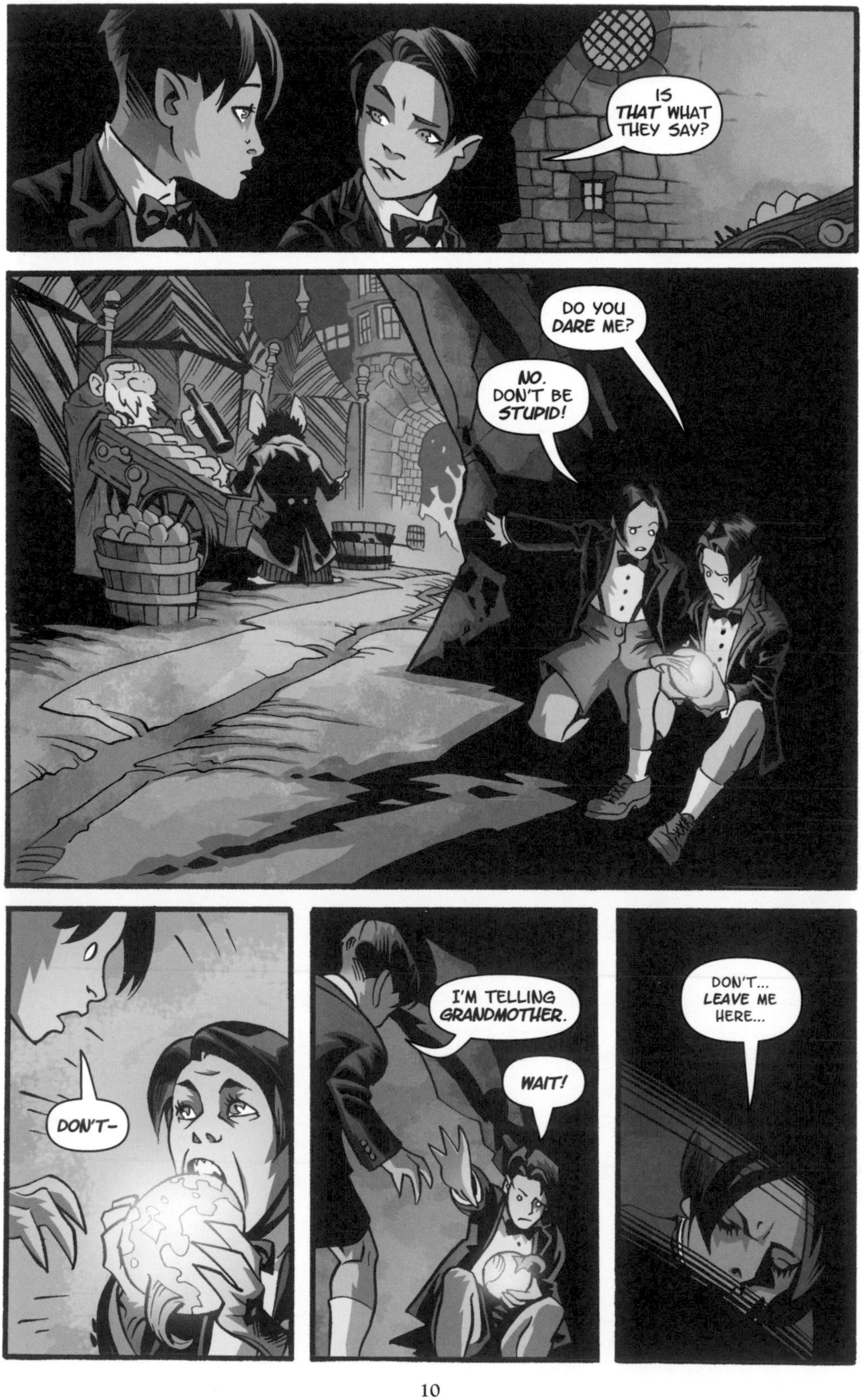
IS THAT WHAT THEY SAY?
DO YOU DARE ME?
NO. DON'T BE STUPID!
DON'T-
I'M TELLING GRANDMOTHER.
WAIT!
DON'T... LEAVE ME HERE...

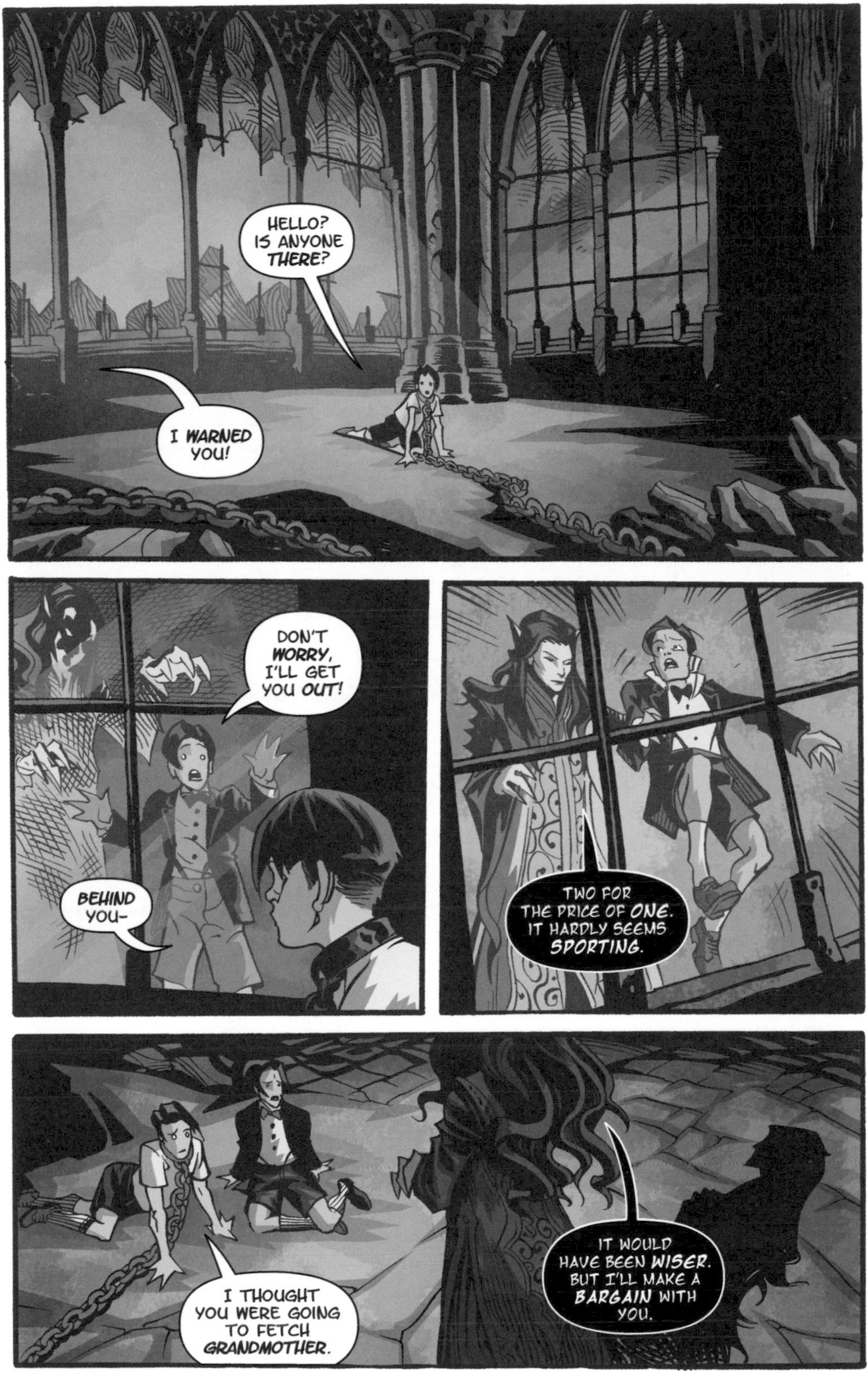
HELLO? IS ANYONE THERE?
I WARNED YOU!
DON'T WORRY, I'LL GET YOU OUT!
BEHIND YOU-
TWO FOR THE PRICE OF ONE. IT HARDLY SEEMS SPORTING.
I THOUGHT YOU WERE GOING TO FETCH GRANDMOTHER.
IT WOULD HAVE BEEN WISER. BUT I'LL MAKE A BARGAIN WITH YOU.

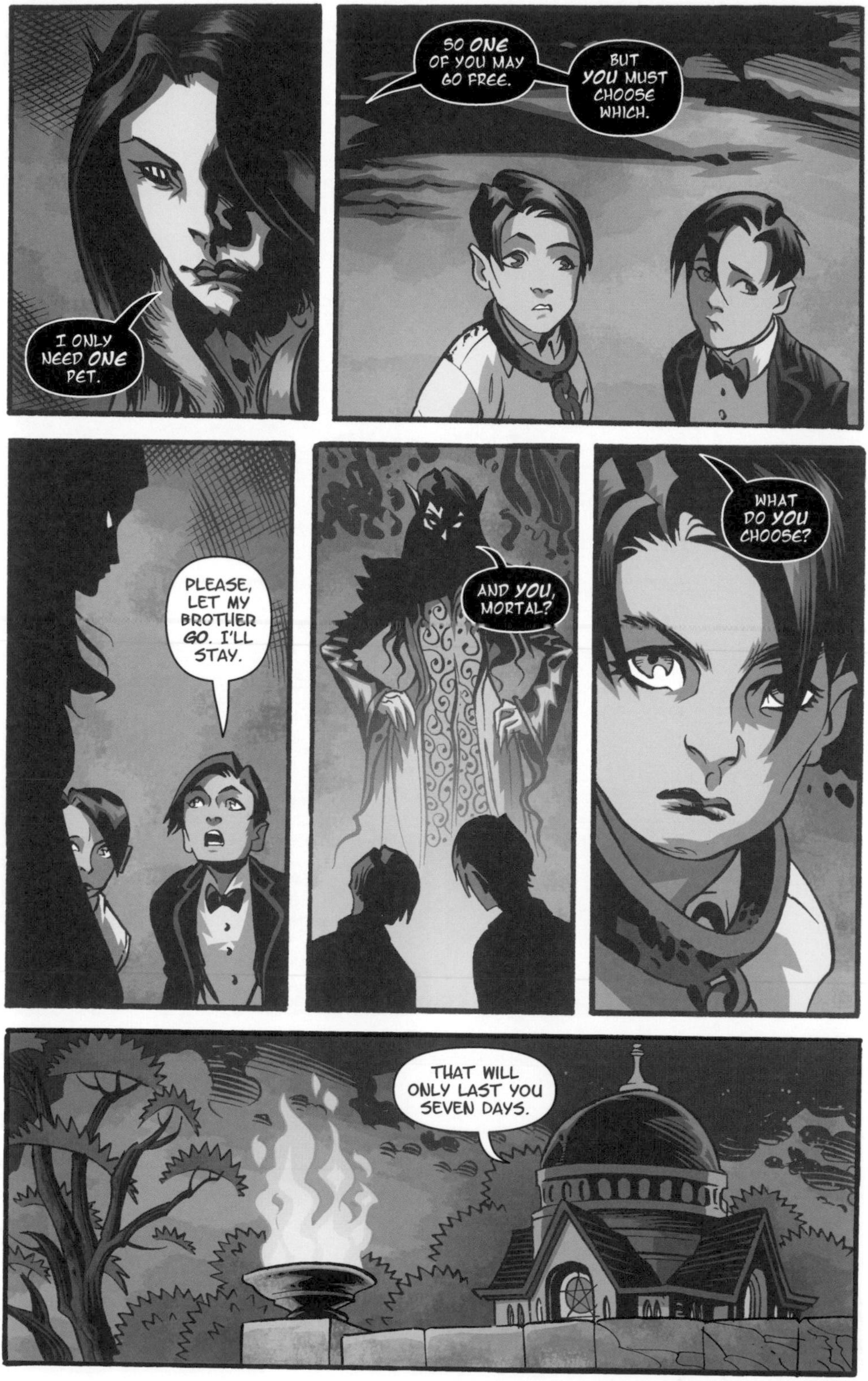
I ONLY NEED ONE PET.
SO ONE OF YOU MAY GO FREE.
BUT YOU MUST CHOOSE WHICH.
PLEASE, LET MY BROTHER GO. I'LL STAY.
AND YOU, MORTAL?
WHAT DO YOU CHOOSE?
THAT WILL ONLY LAST YOU SEVEN DAYS.

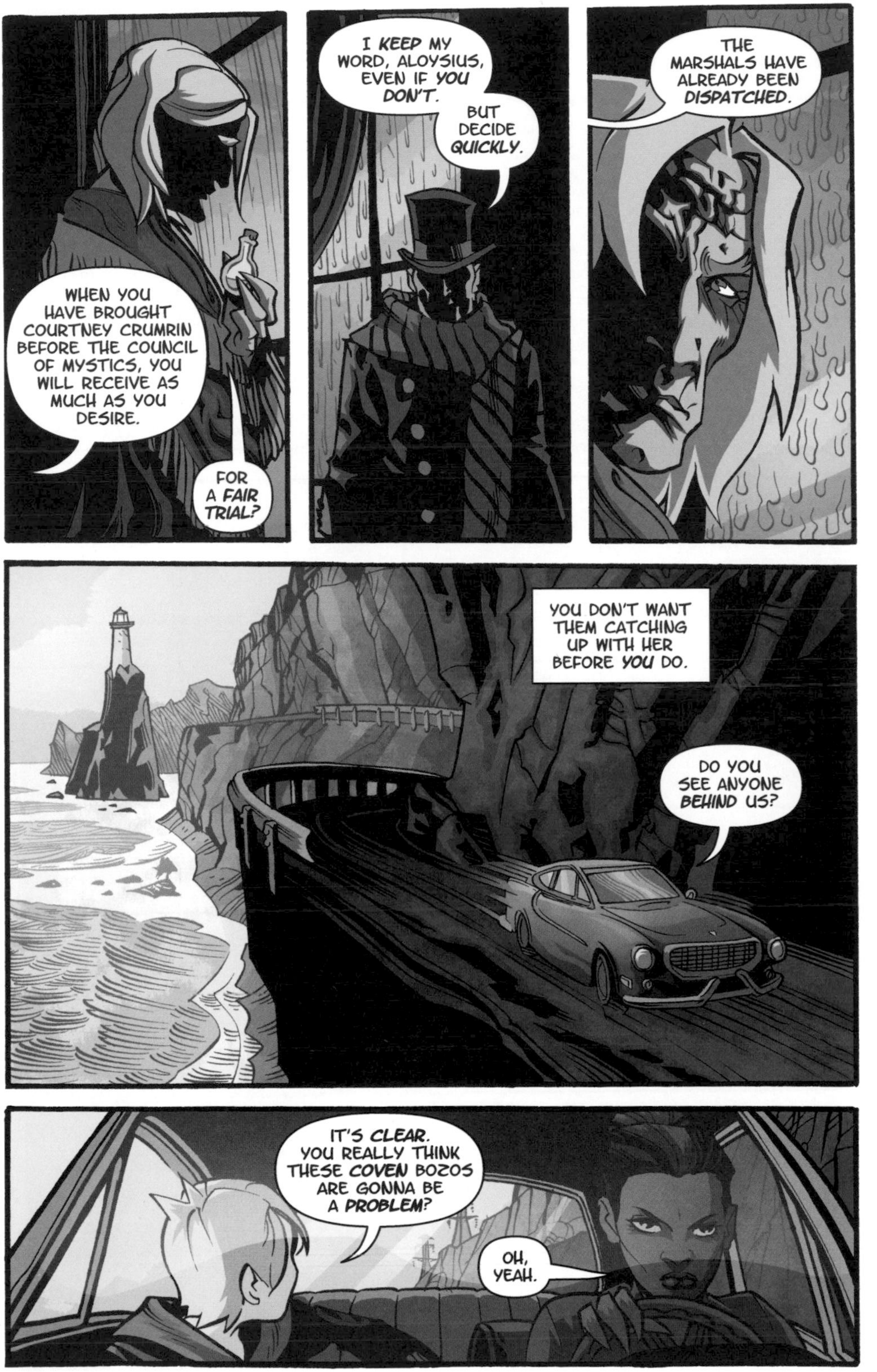
WHEN YOU HAVE BROUGHT COURTNEY CRUMRIN BEFORE THE COUNCIL OF MYSTICS, YOU WILL RECEIVE AS MUCH AS YOU DESIRE.
FOR A FAIR TRIAL?
I KEEP MY WORD, ALOYSIUS, EVEN IF YOU DON'T.
BUT DECIDE QUICKLY.
THE MARSHALS HAVE ALREADY BEEN DISPATCHED.
YOU DON'T WANT THEM CATCHING UP WITH HER BEFORE YOU DO.
DO YOU SEE ANYONE BEHIND US?
IT'S CLEAR. YOU REALLY THINK THESE COVEN BOZOS ARE GONNA BE A PROBLEM?
OH, YEAH.

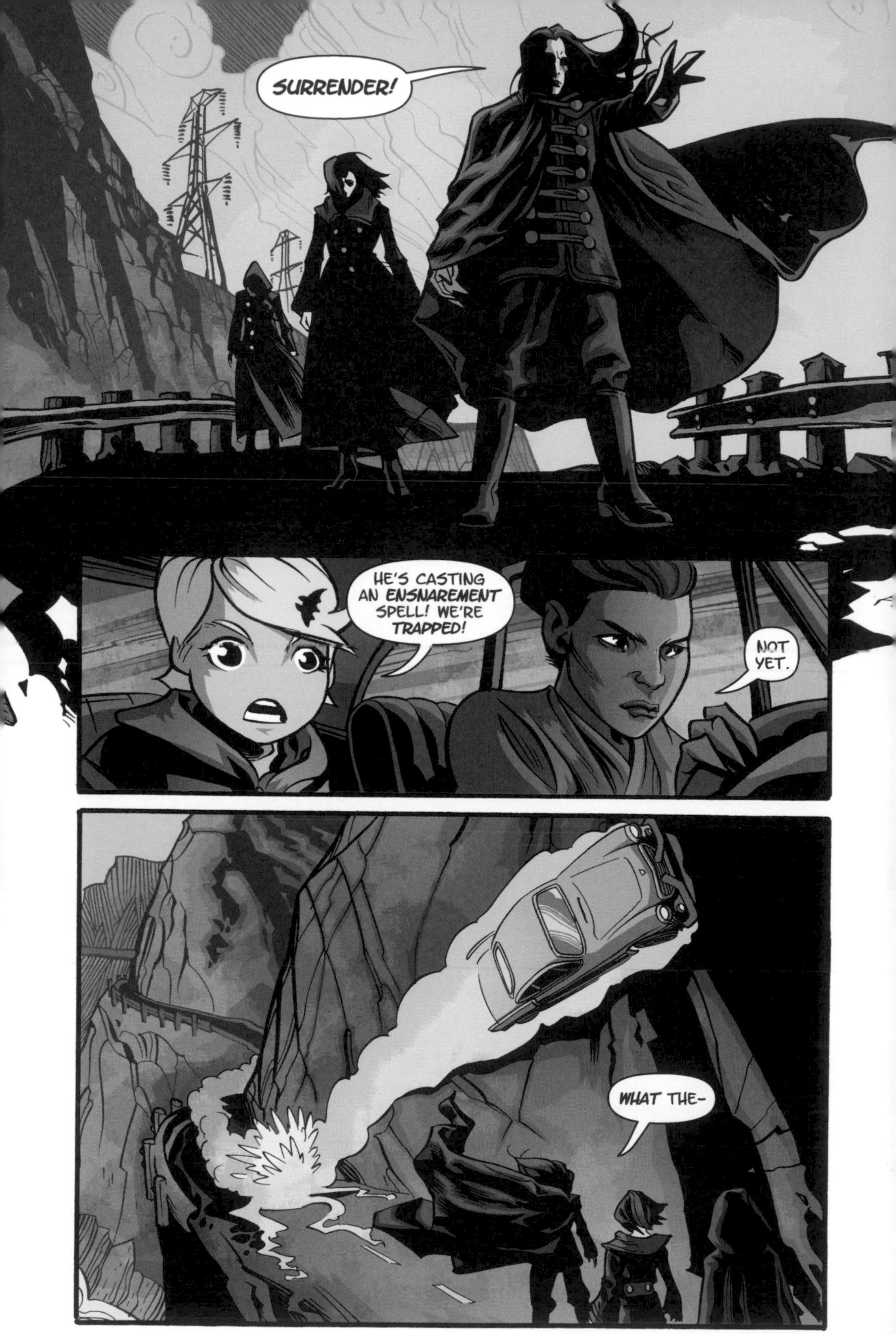
SURRENDER!
HE'S CASTING AN ENSNAREMENT SPELL! WE'RE TRAPPED!
NOT YET.
WHAT THE-

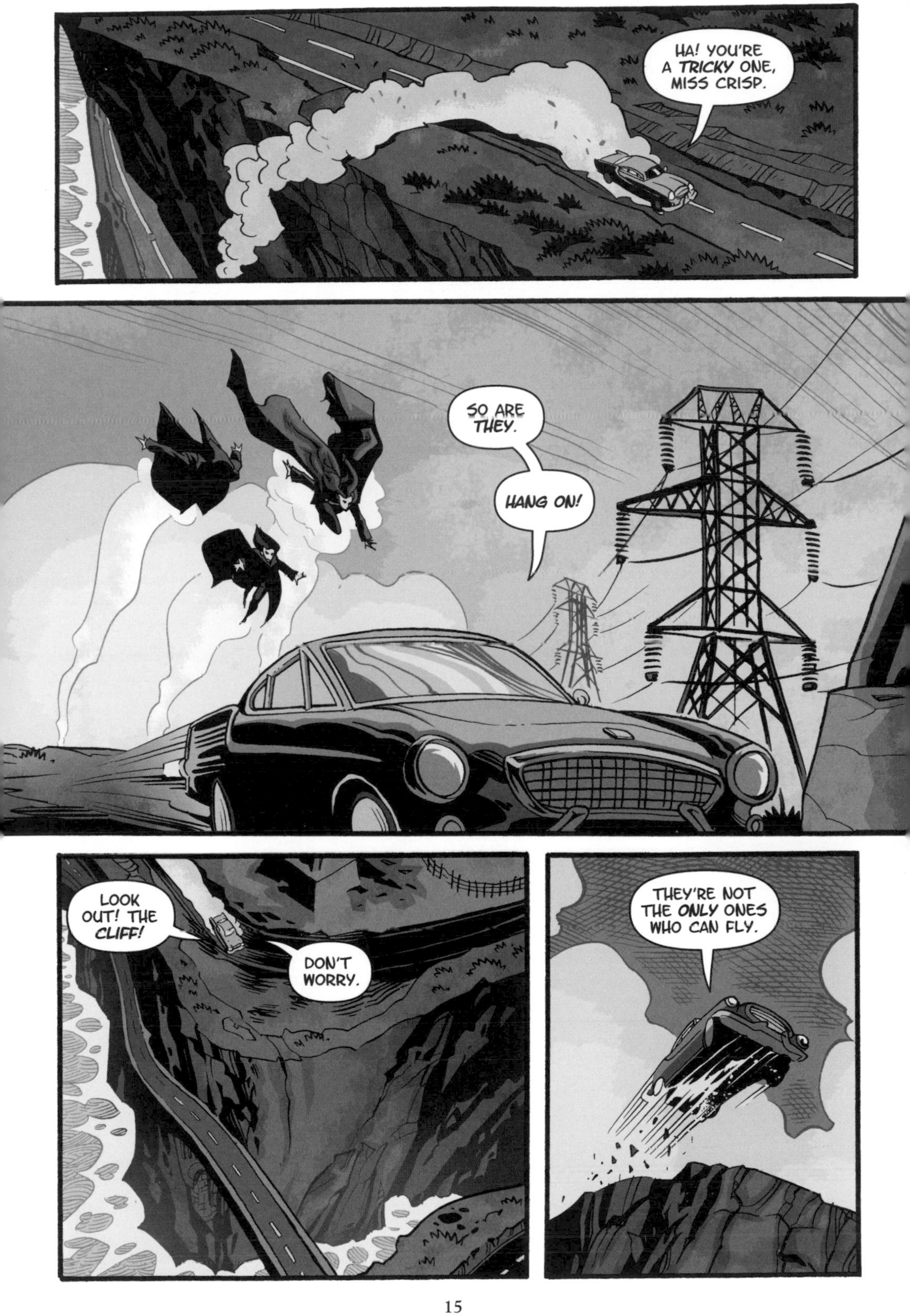
HA! YOU'RE A TRICKY ONE, MISS CRISP.
SO ARE THEY.
HANG ON!
LOOK OUT! THE CLIFF!
DON'T WORRY.
THEY'RE NOT THE ONLY ONES WHO CAN FLY.

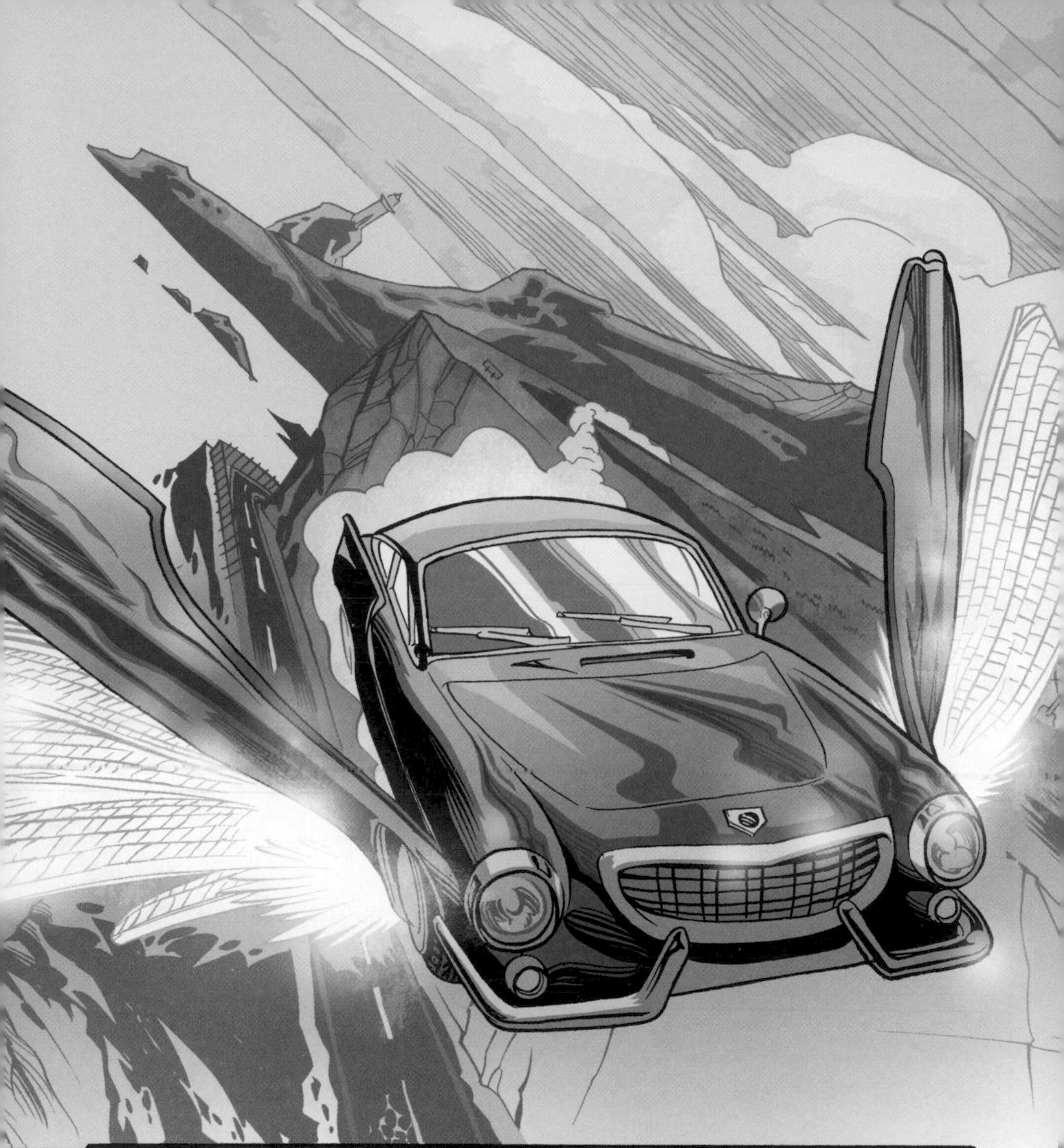

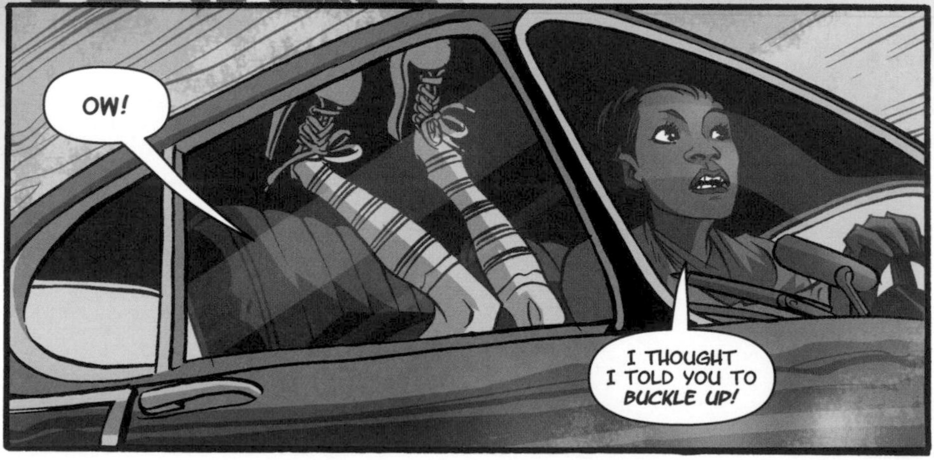
OW!
I THOUGHT I TOLD YOU TO BUCKLE UP!

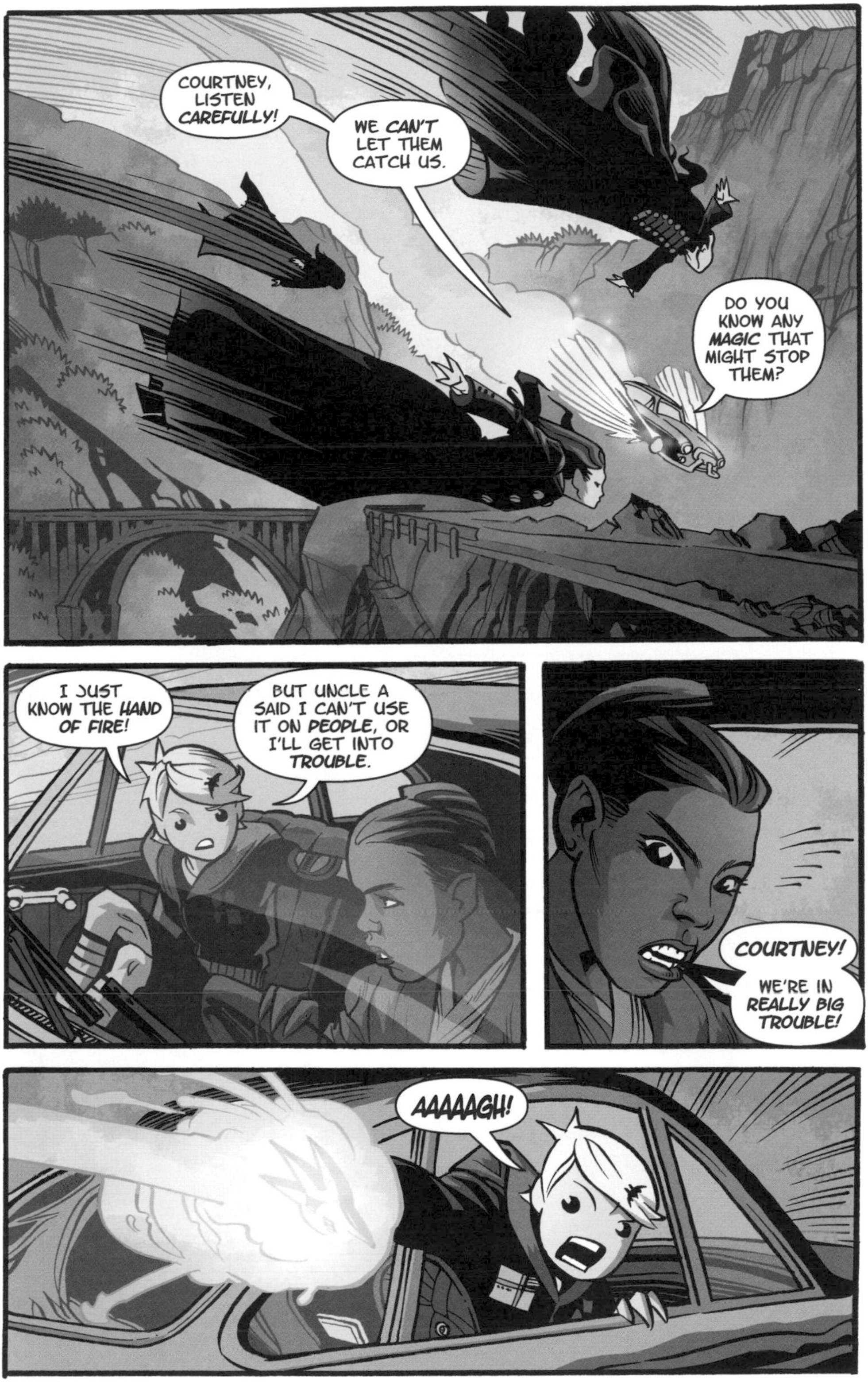
COURTNEY, LISTEN CAREFULLY!
WE CAN'T LET THEM CATCH US.
DO YOU KNOW ANY MAGIC THAT MIGHT STOP THEM?
I JUST KNOW THE HAND OF FIRE!
BUT UNCLE A SAID I CAN'T USE IT ON PEOPLE, OR I'LL GET INTO TROUBLE.
COURTNEY!
WE'RE IN REALLY BIG TROUBLE!
AAAAAGH!

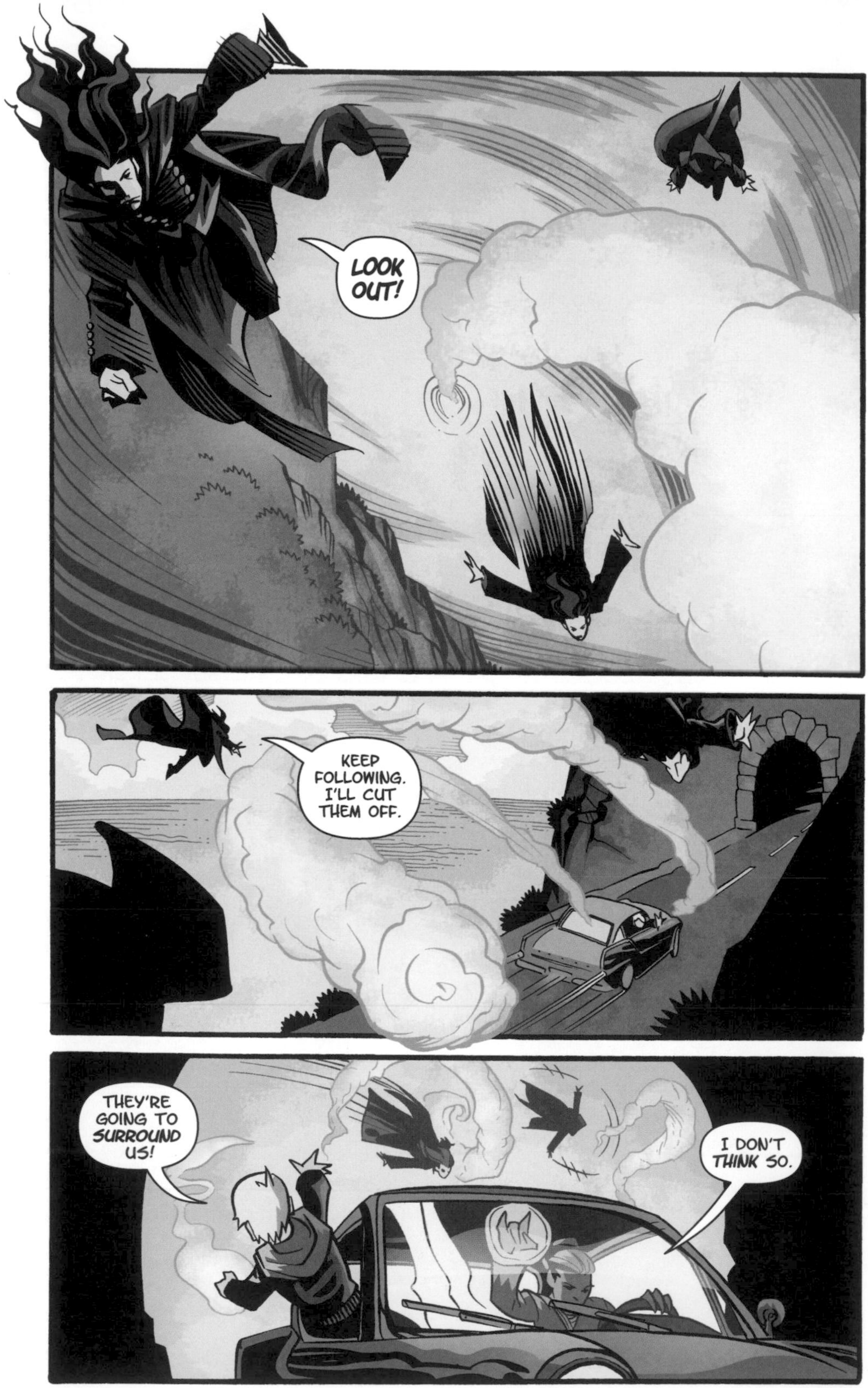
LOOK OUT!
KEEP FOLLOWING. I'LL CUT THEM OFF.
THEY'RE GOING TO SURROUND US!
I DON'T THINK SO.

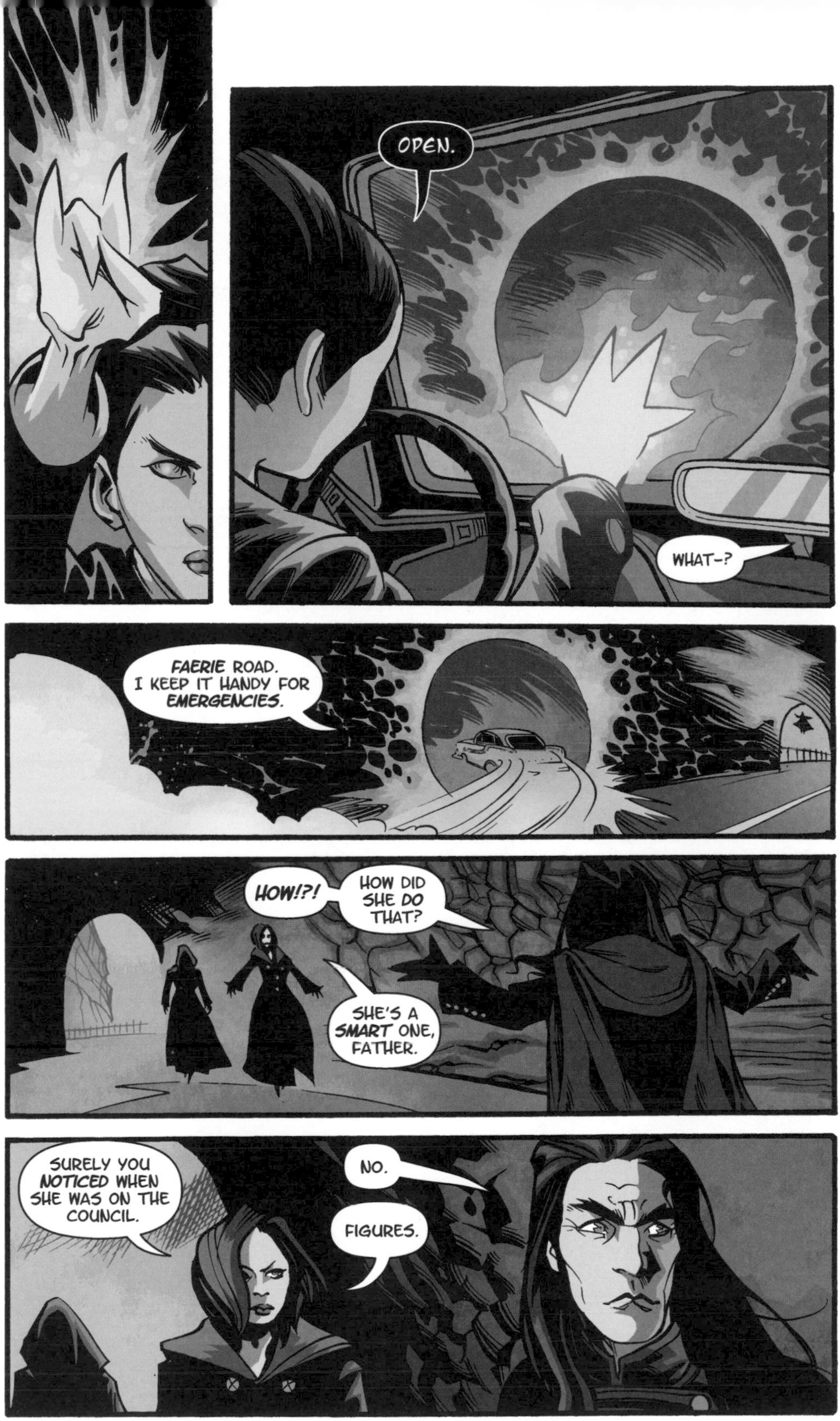
OPEN.
WHAT-?
FAERIE ROAD. I KEEP IT HANDY FOR EMERGENCIES.
HOW!?!
HOW DID SHE DO THAT?
SHE'S A SMART ONE, FATHER.
SURELY YOU NOTICED WHEN SHE WAS ON THE COUNCIL.
NO.
FIGURES.

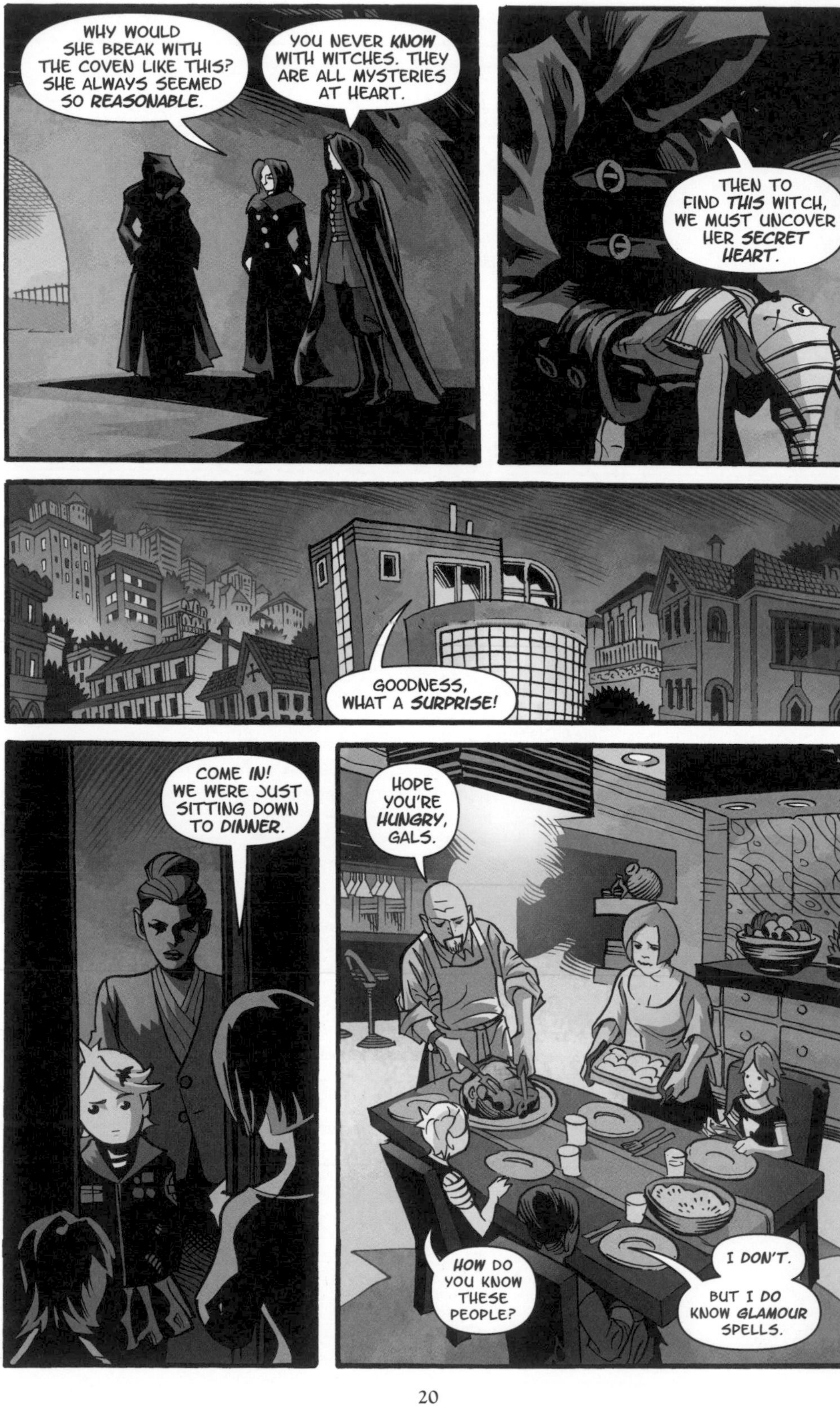
WHY WOULD SHE BREAK WITH THE COVEN LIKE THIS? SHE ALWAYS SEEMED SO REASONABLE.
YOU NEVER KNOW WITH WITCHES. THEY ARE ALL MYSTERIES AT HEART.
THEN TO FIND THIS WITCH, WE MUST UNCOVER HER SECRET HEART.
GOODNESS, WHAT A SURPRISE!
COME IN! WE WERE JUST SITTING DOWN TO DINNER.
HOPE YOU'RE HUNGRY, GALS.
HOW DO YOU KNOW THESE PEOPLE?
I DON'T.
BUT I DO KNOW GLAMOUR SPELLS.

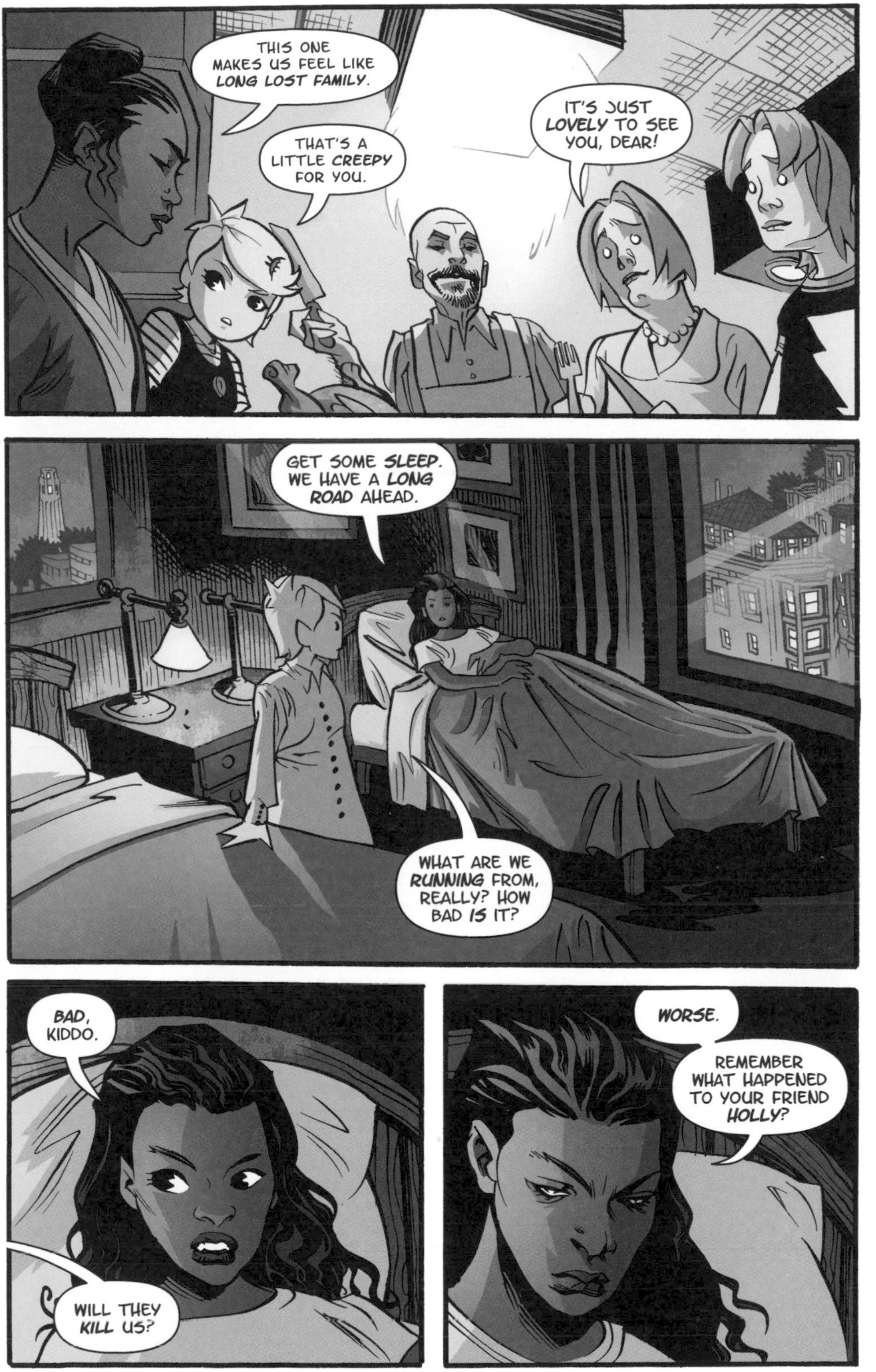
THIS ONE MAKES US FEEL LIKE LONG LOST FAMILY.
THAT'S A LITTLE CREEPY FOR YOU.
IT'S JUST LOVELY TO SEE YOU, DEAR!
GET SOME SLEEP. WE HAVE A LONG ROAD AHEAD.
WHAT ARE WE RUNNING FROM, REALLY? HOW BAD IS IT?
BAD, KIDDO.
WILL THEY KILL US?
WORSE.
REMEMBER WHAT HAPPENED TO YOUR FRIEND HOLLY?

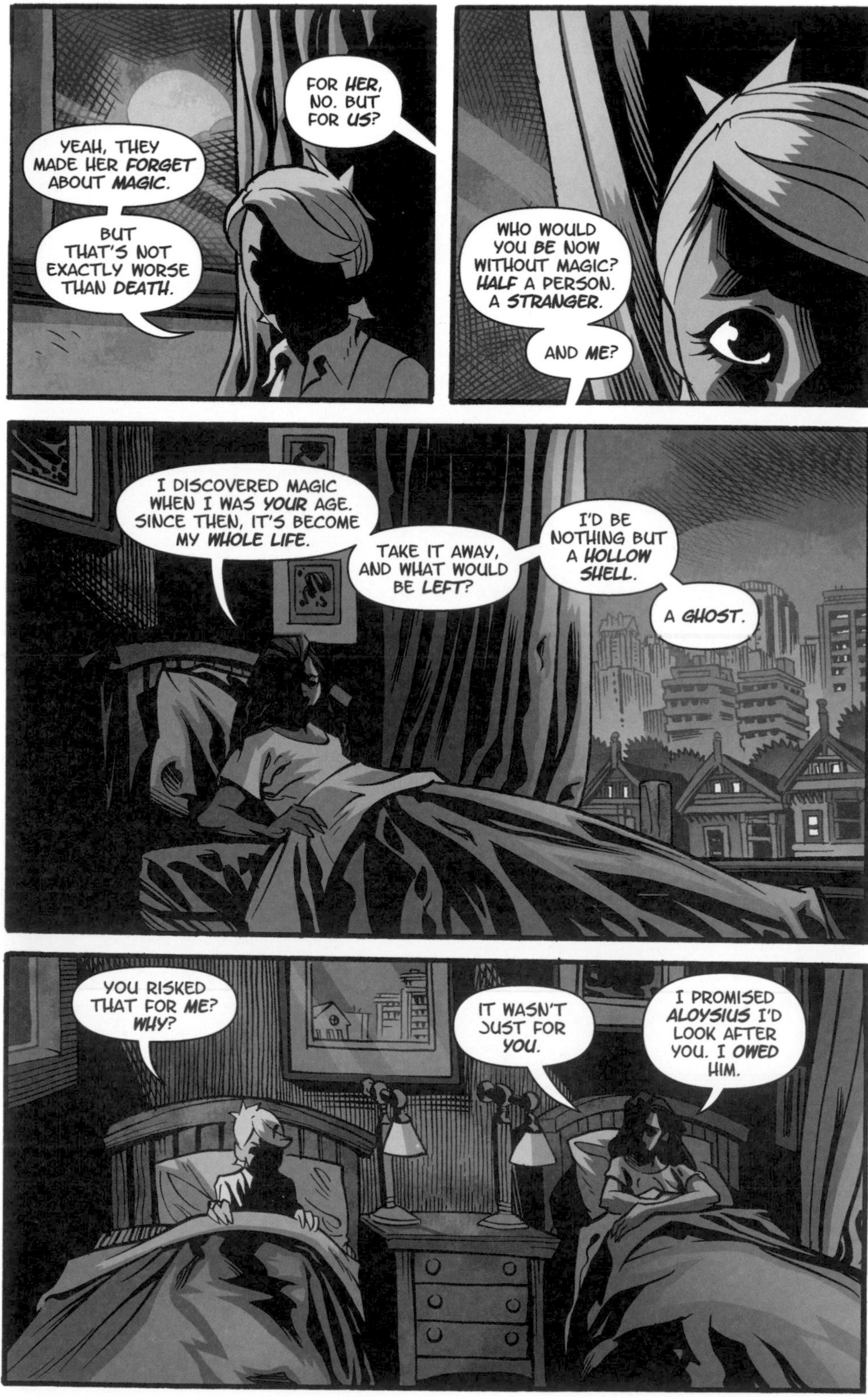
FOR HER, NO. BUT FOR US?
YEAH, THEY MADE HER FORGET ABOUT MAGIC.
BUT THAT'S NOT EXACTLY WORSE THAN DEATH.
WHO WOULD YOU BE NOW WITHOUT MAGIC? HALF A PERSON. A STRANGER.
AND ME?
I DISCOVERED MAGIC WHEN I WAS YOUR AGE. SINCE THEN, IT'S BECOME MY WHOLE LIFE.
TAKE IT AWAY, AND WHAT WOULD BE LEFT?
I'D BE NOTHING BUT A HOLLOW SHELL.
A GHOST.
YOU RISKED THAT FOR ME? WHY?
IT WASN'T JUST FOR YOU.
I PROMISED ALOYSIUS I'D LOOK AFTER YOU. I OWED HIM.

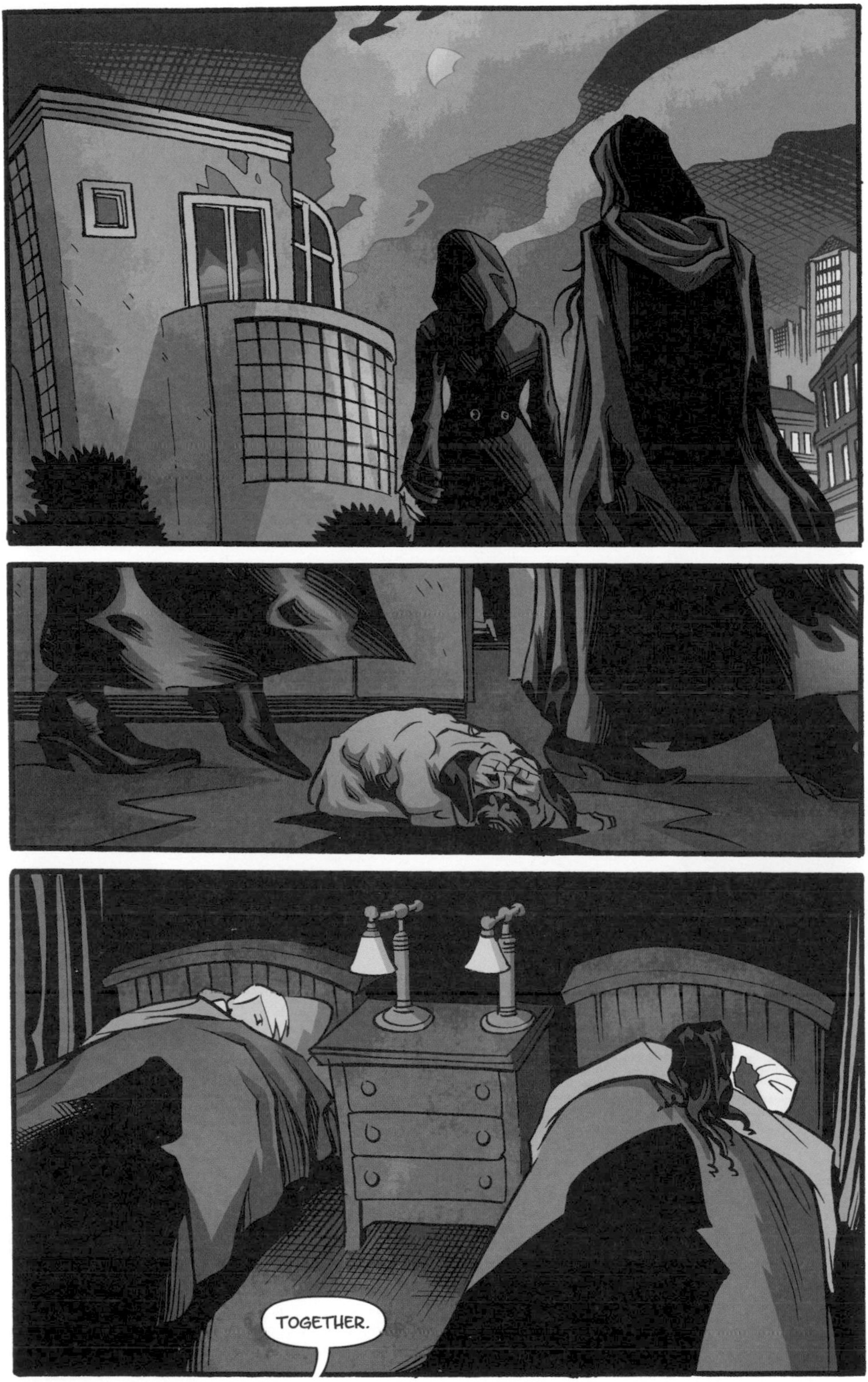
TOGETHER.

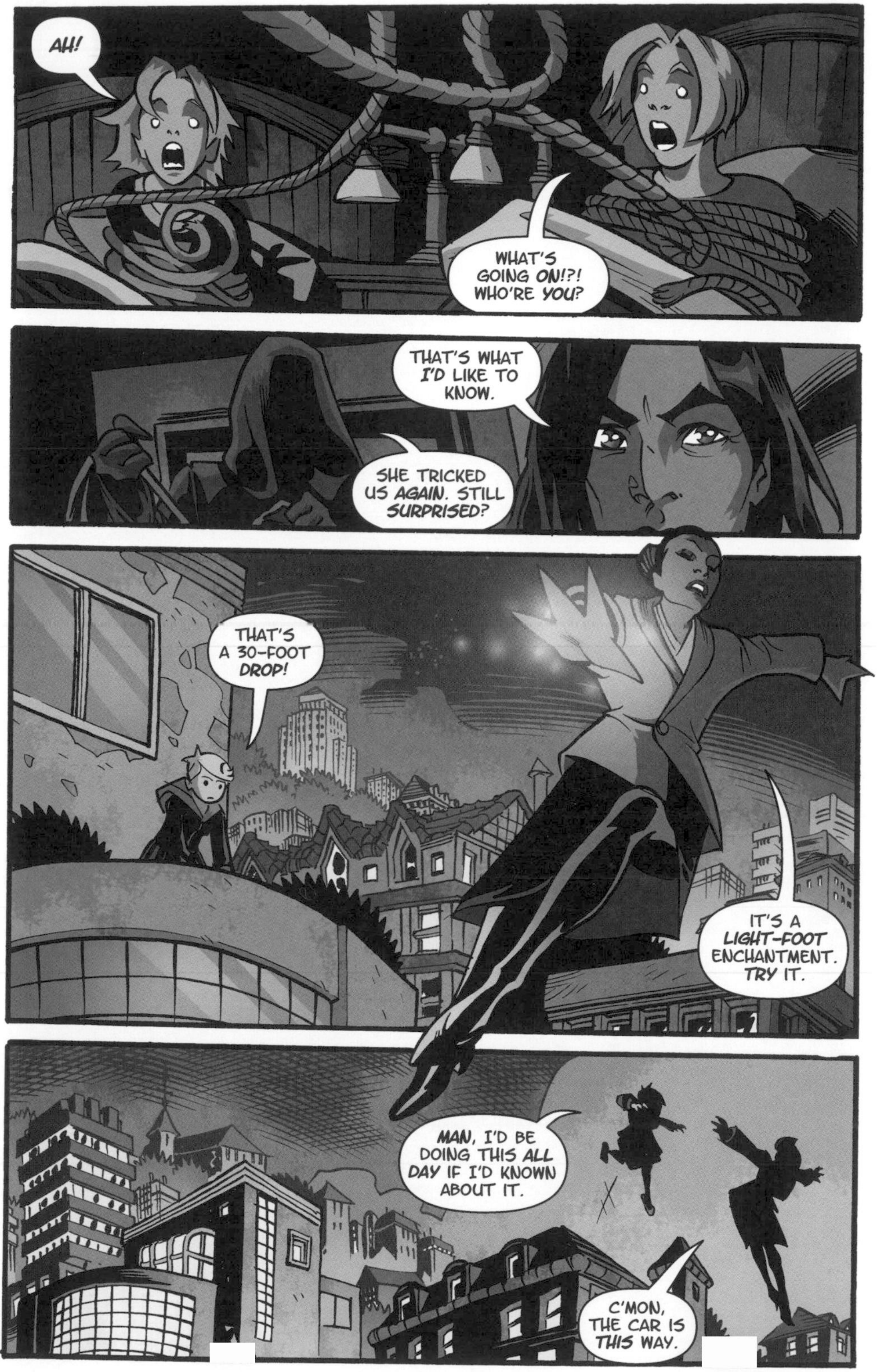
AH!
WHAT'S GOING ON!?! WHO'RE YOU?
THAT'S WHAT I'D LIKE TO KNOW.
SHE TRICKED US AGAIN. STILL SURPRISED?
THAT'S A 30-FOOT DROP!
IT'S A LIGHT-FOOT ENCHANTMENT. TRY IT.
MAN, I'D BE DOING THIS ALL DAY IF I'D KNOWN ABOUT IT.
C'MON, THE CAR IS THIS WAY.

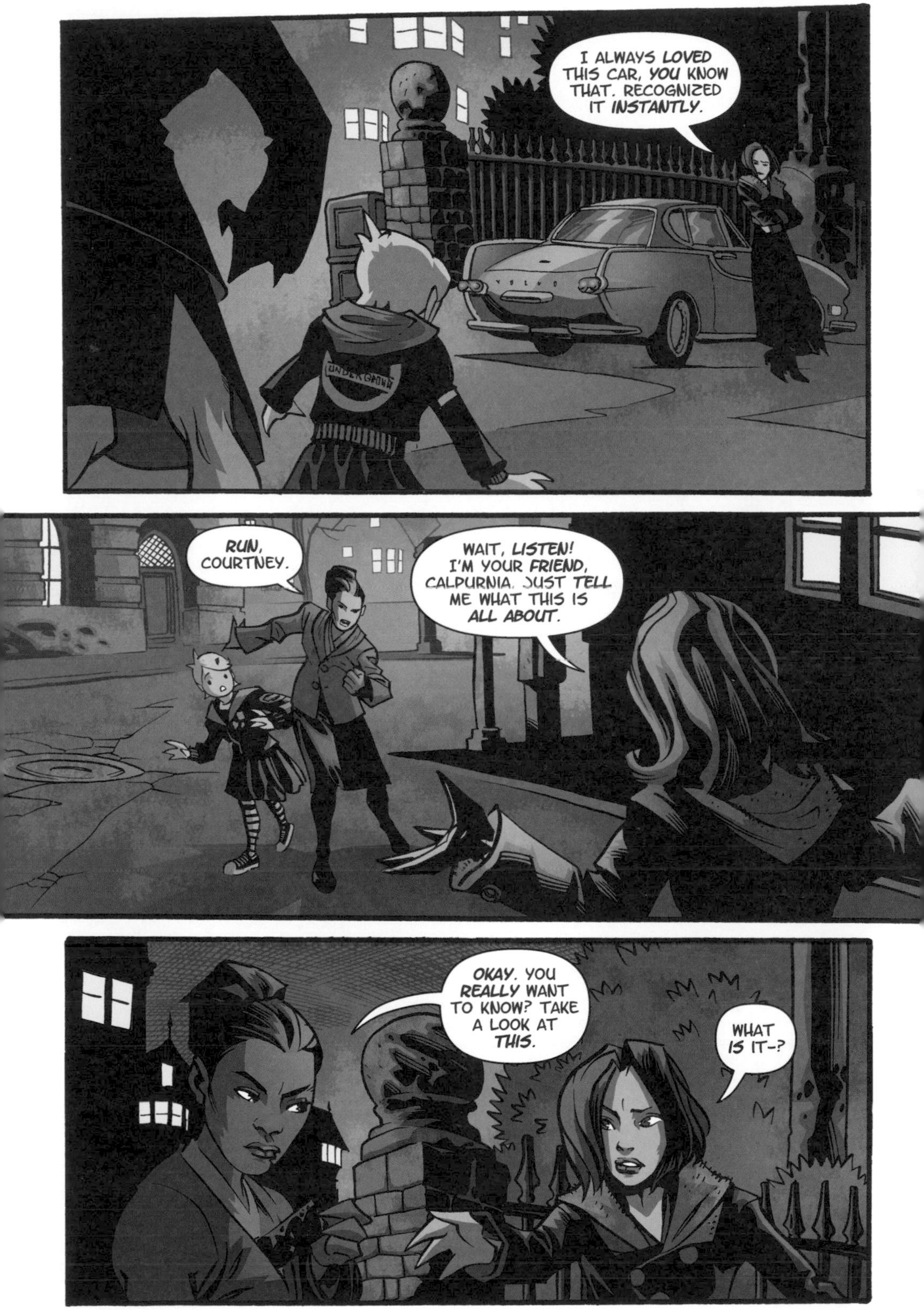
I ALWAYS LOVED THIS CAR, YOU KNOW THAT. RECOGNIZED IT INSTANTLY.
RUN, COURTNEY.
WAIT, LISTEN! I'M YOUR FRIEND, CALPURNIA. JUST TELL ME WHAT THIS IS ALL ABOUT.
OKAY. YOU REALLY WANT TO KNOW? TAKE A LOOK AT THIS.
WHAT IS IT-?

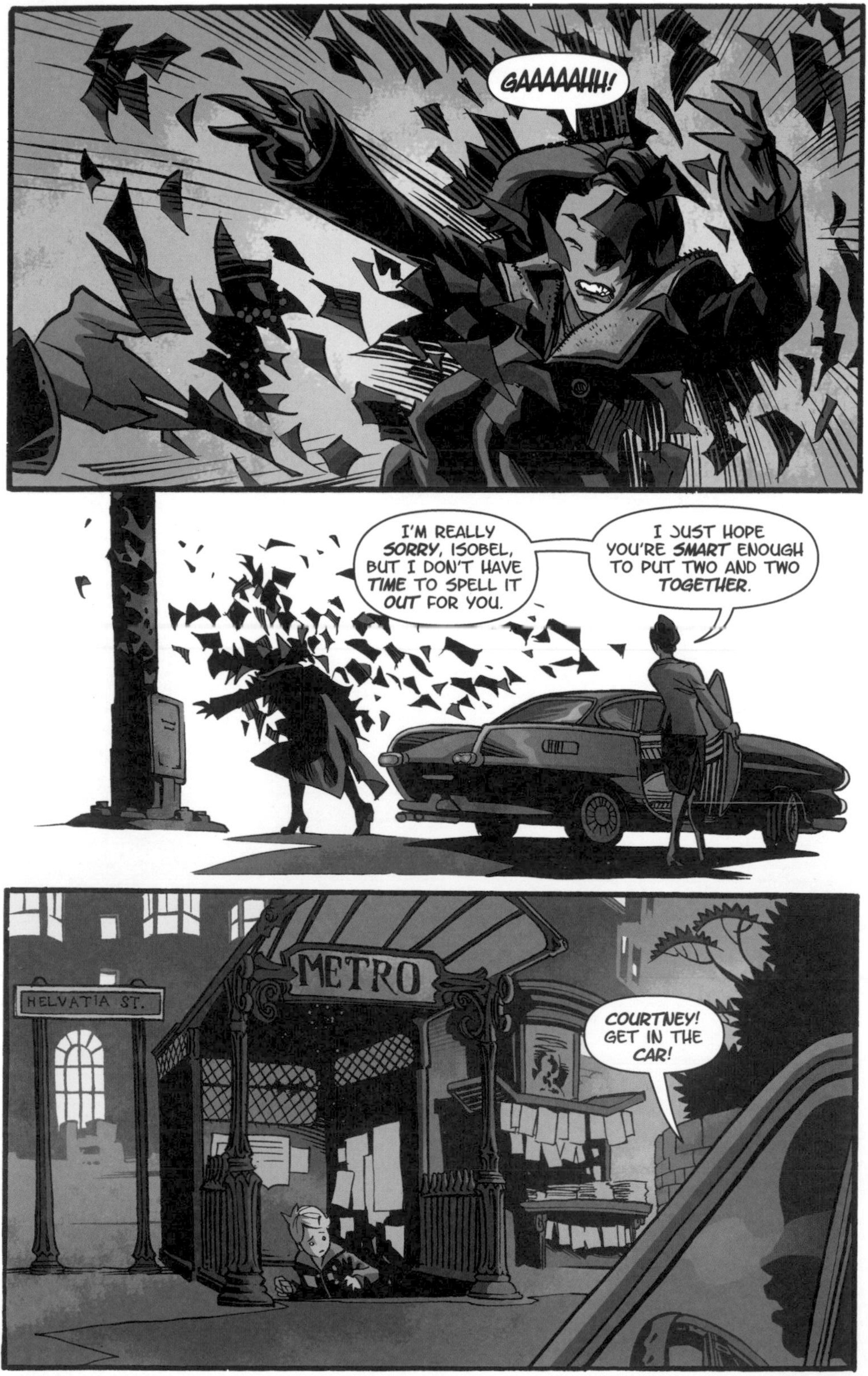
GAAAAAHH!
I'M REALLY SORRY, ISOBEL, BUT I DON'T HAVE TIME TO SPELL IT OUT FOR YOU.
I JUST HOPE YOU'RE SMART ENOUGH TO PUT TWO AND TWO TOGETHER.
METRO
HELVATIA ST.
COURTNEY! GET IN THE CAR!

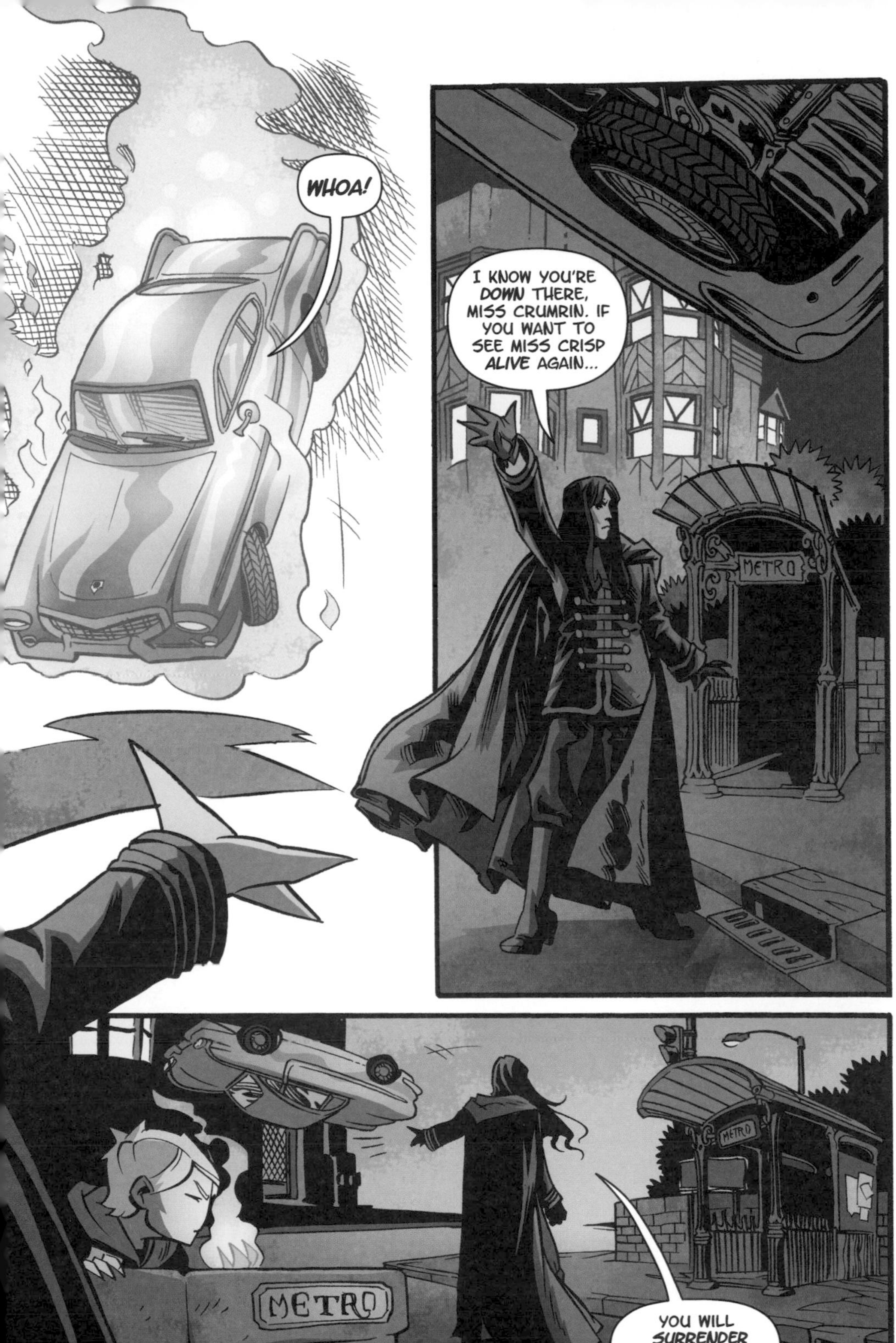
WHOA!
I KNOW YOU'RE DOWN THERE, MISS CRUMRIN. IF YOU WANT TO SEE MISS CRISP ALIVE AGAIN...
METRO
METRO
METRO
YOU WILL SURRENDER YOURSELF TO ME IMMEDIATELY.

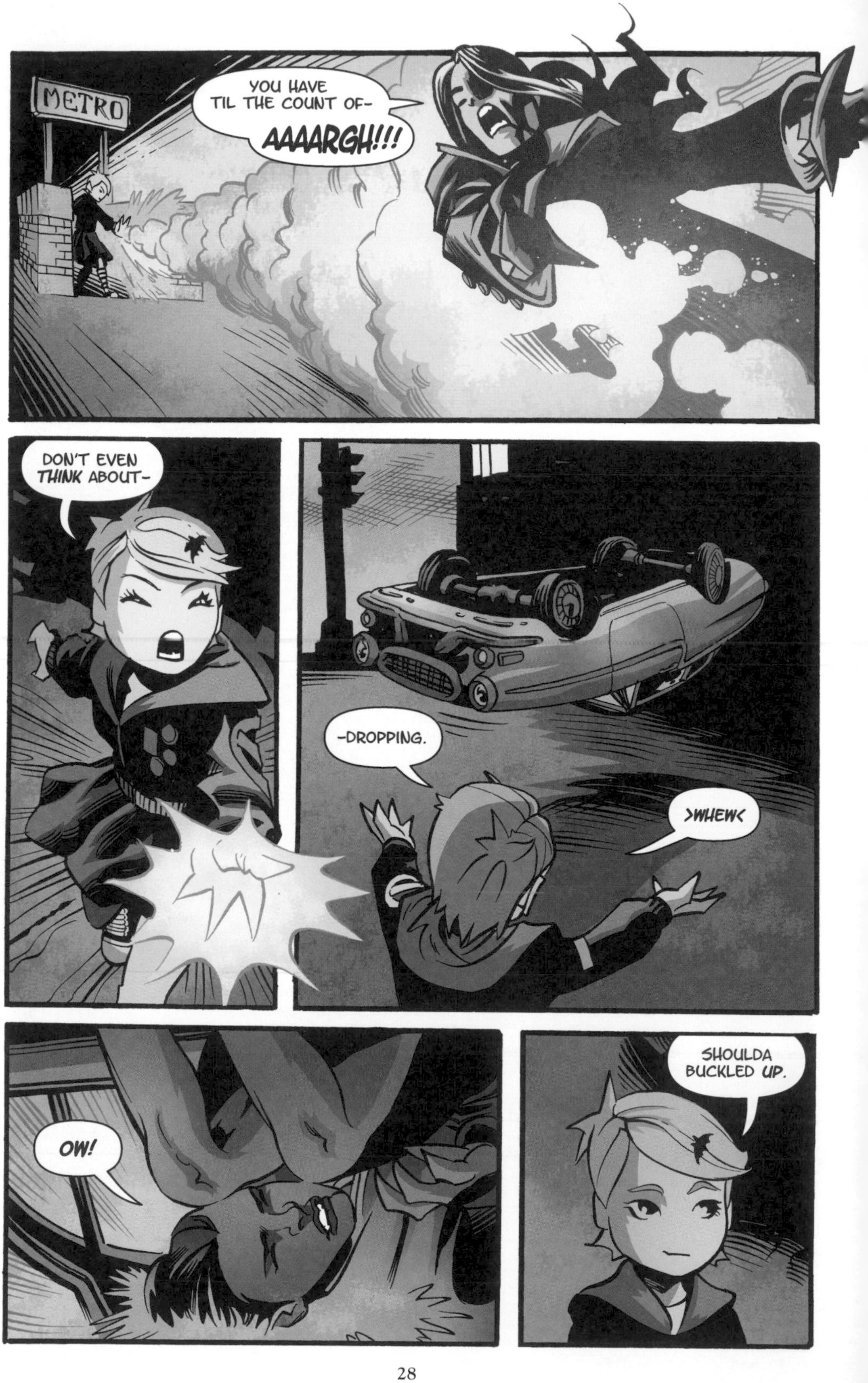
METRO
YOU HAVE TIL THE COUNT OF-
AAAARGH!!!
DON'T EVEN THINK ABOUT-
-DROPPING.
>WHEW<
OW!
SHOULDA BUCKLED UP.

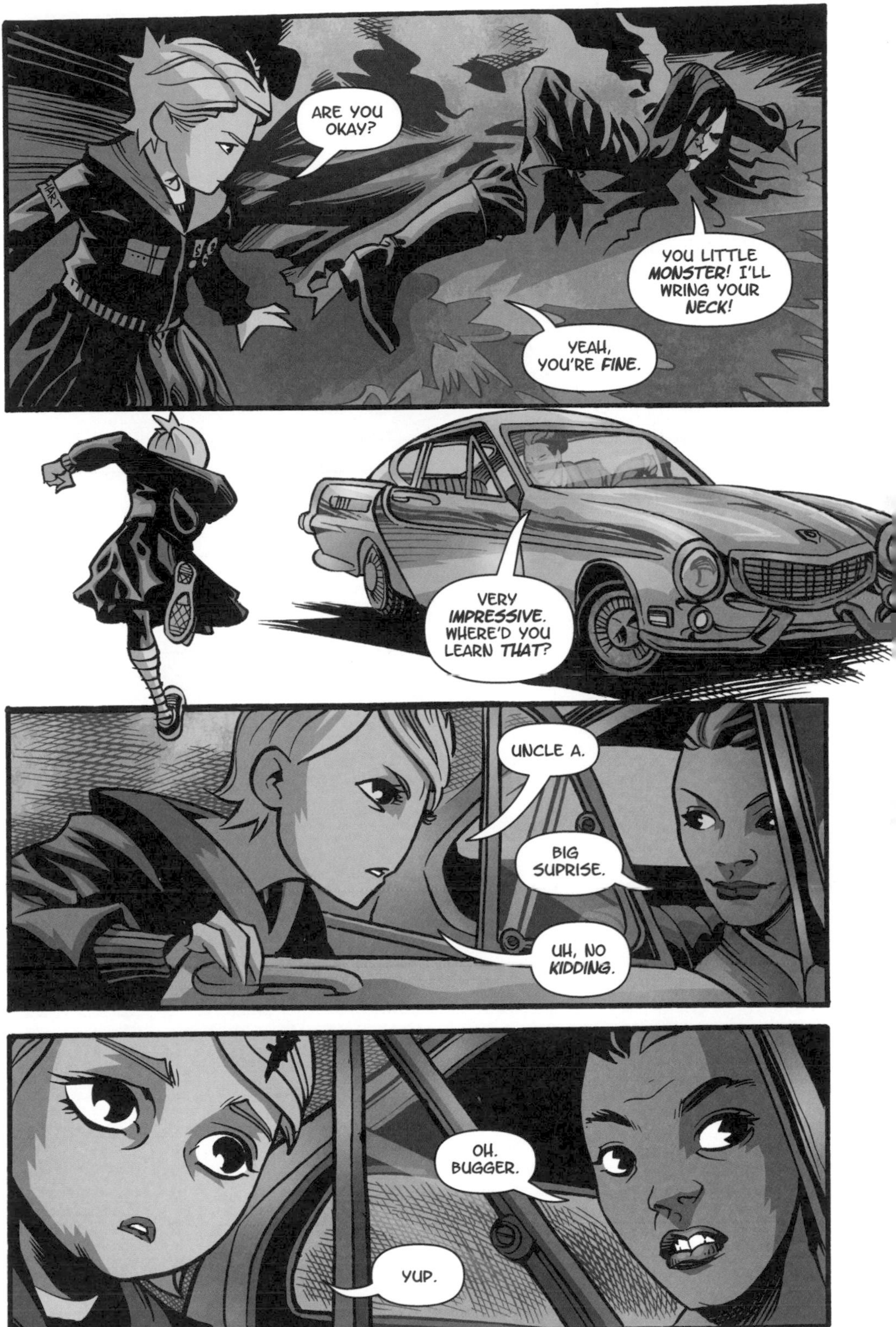
ARE YOU OKAY?
YOU LITTLE MONSTER! I'LL WRING YOUR NECK!
YEAH, YOU'RE FINE.
HART
VERY IMPRESSIVE. WHERE'D YOU LEARN THAT?
UNCLE A.
BIG SUPRISE.
UH, NO KIDDING.
OH. BUGGER.
YUP.

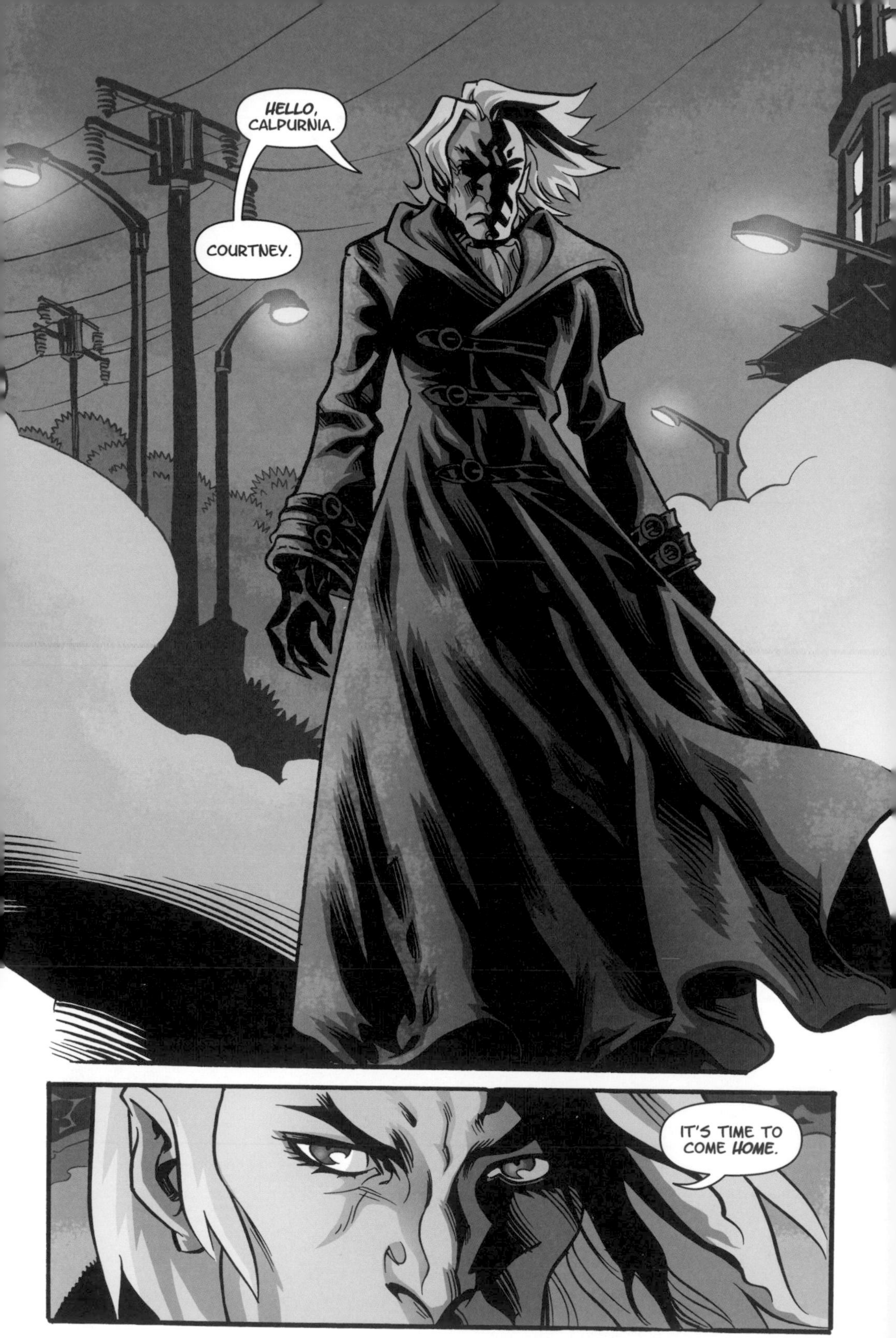
HELLO, CALPURNIA.
COURTNEY.
IT'S TIME TO COME HOME.

Chapter Two

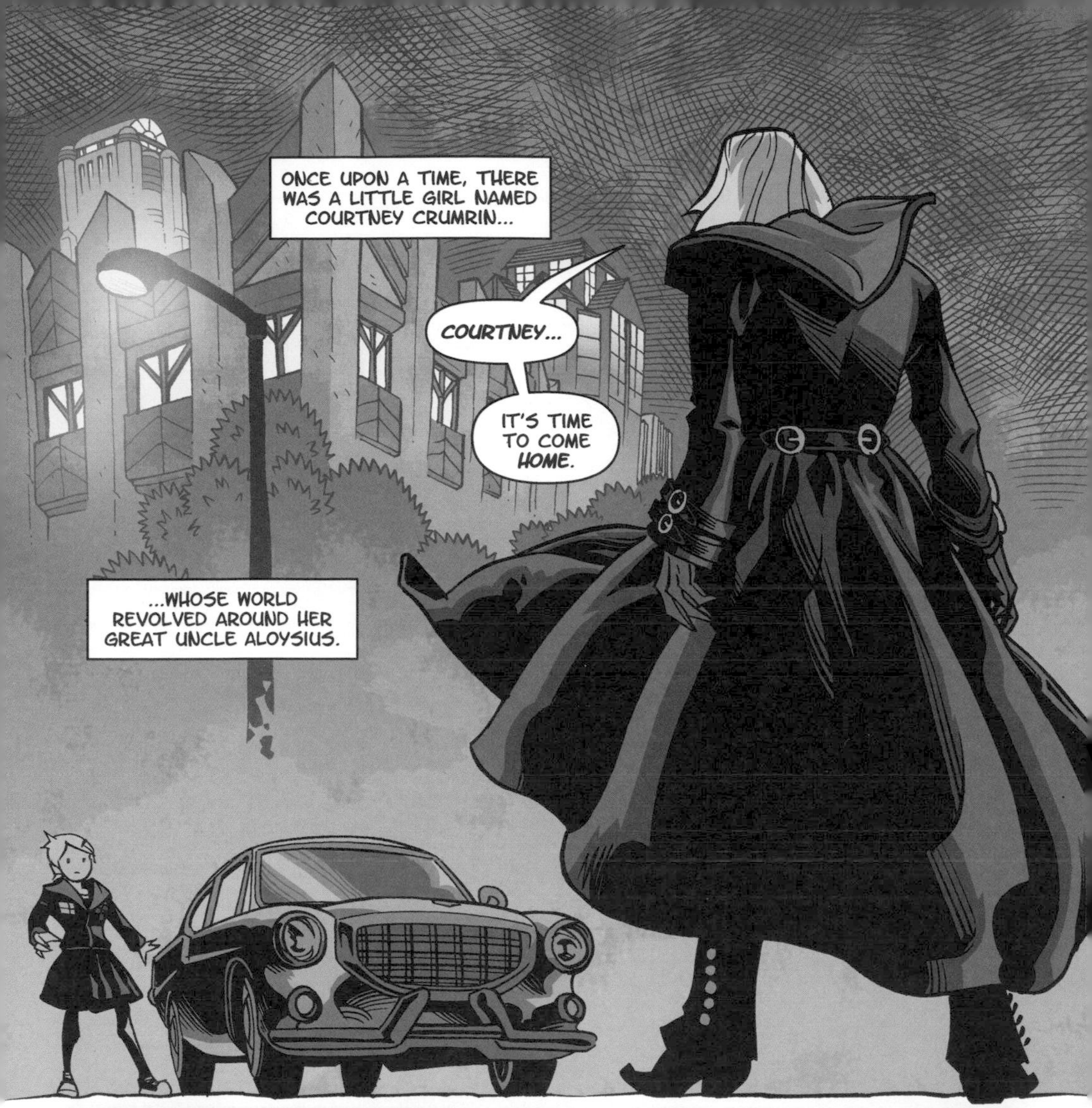
ONCE UPON A TIME, THERE WAS A LITTLE GIRL NAMED COURTNEY CRUMRIN...
COURTNEY...
IT'S TIME TO COME HOME.
...WHOSE WORLD REVOLVED AROUND HER GREAT UNCLE ALOYSIUS.

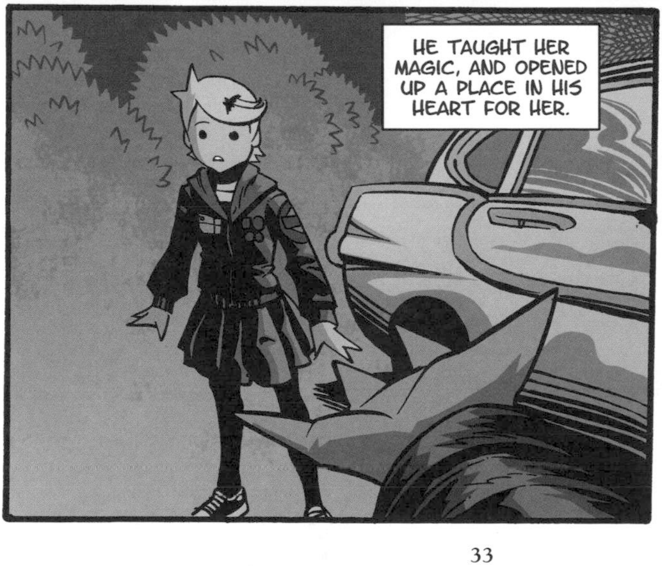
HE TAUGHT HER MAGIC, AND OPENED UP A PLACE IN HIS HEART FOR HER.

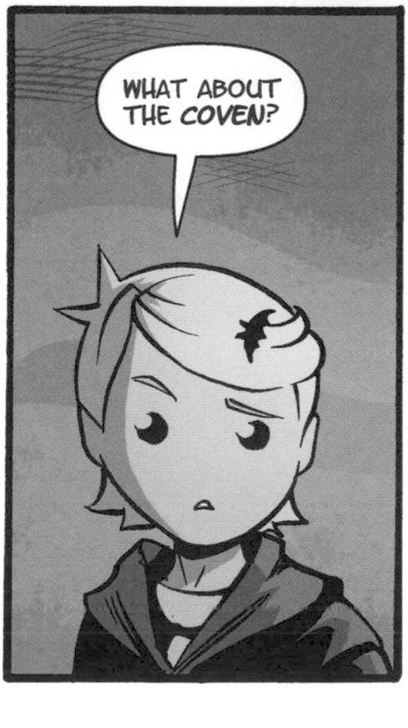
WHAT ABOUT THE COVEN?

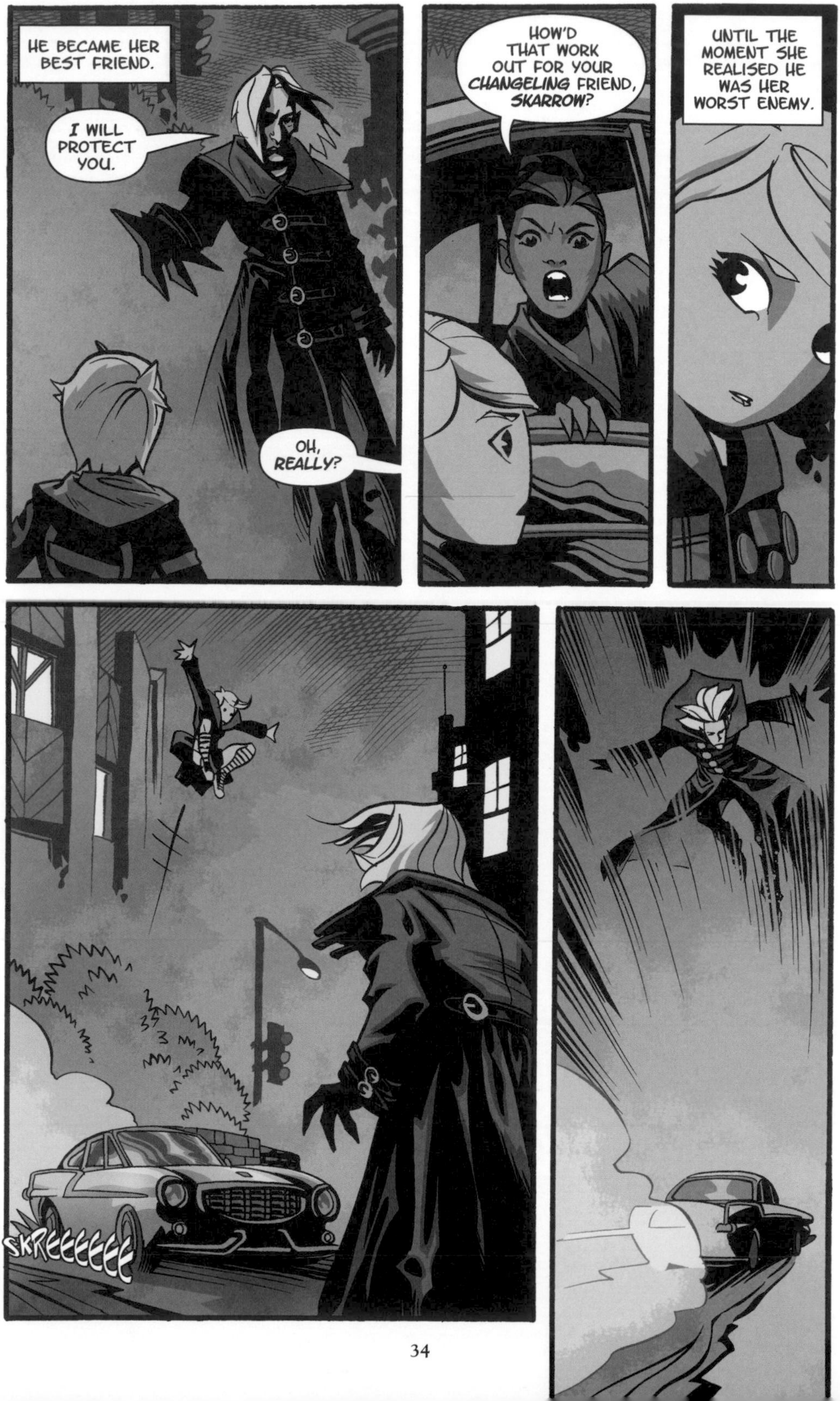
HE BECAME HER BEST FRIEND.
I WILL PROTECT YOU.
OH, REALLY?
HOW'D THAT WORK OUT FOR YOUR CHANGELING FRIEND, SKARROW?
UNTIL THE MOMENT SHE REALISED HE WAS HER WORST ENEMY.
SKREEEEEEE

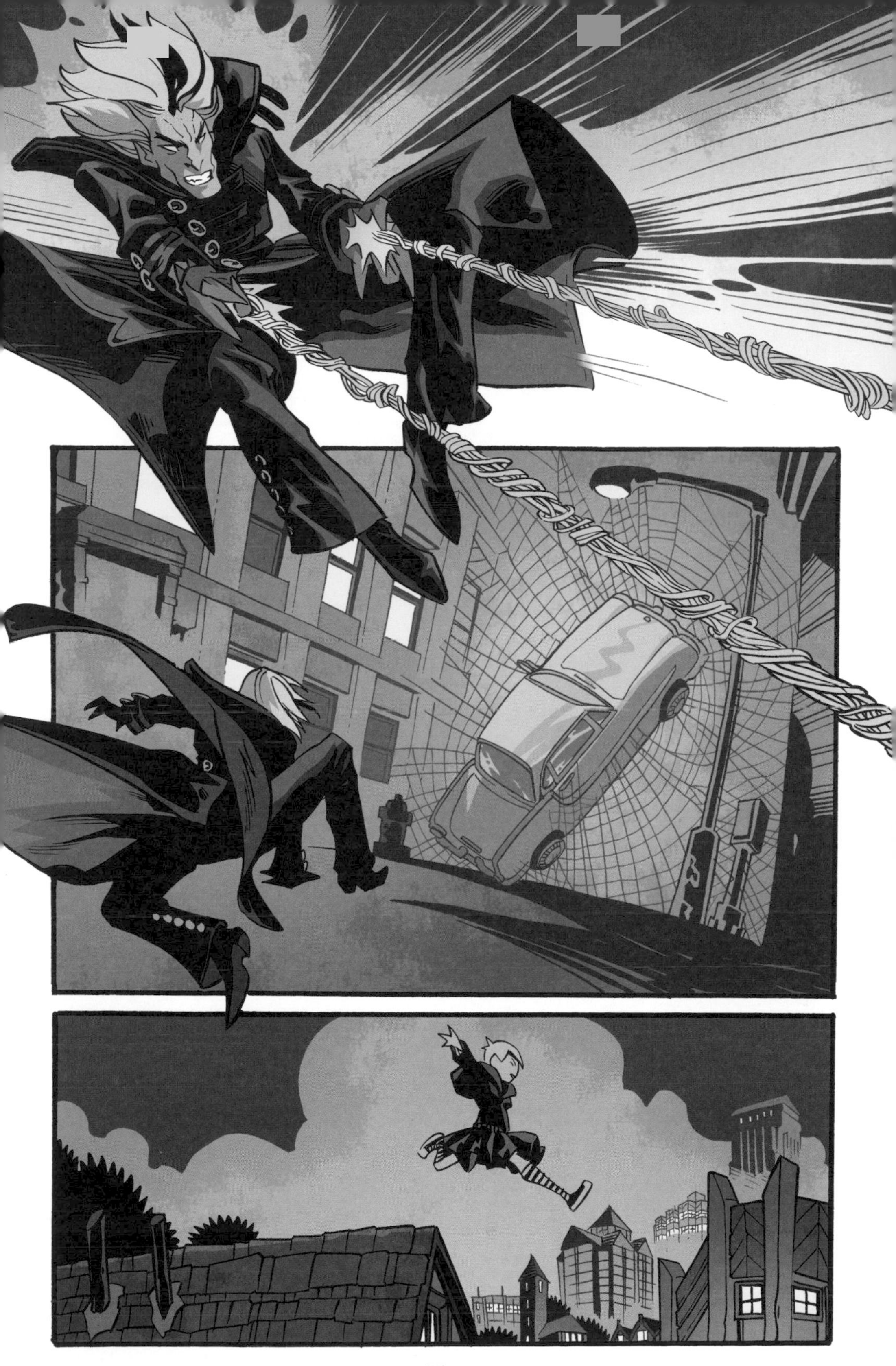

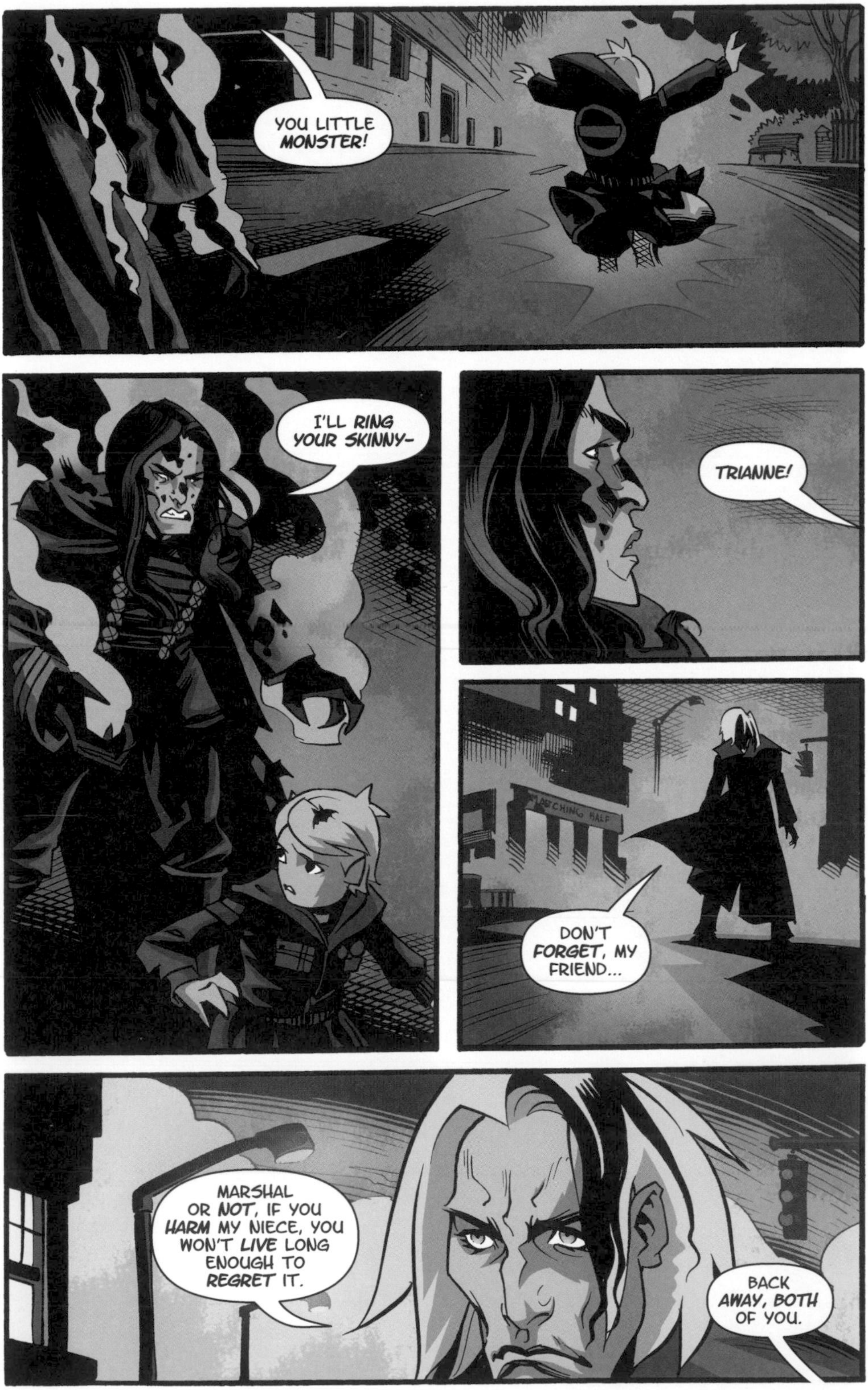
YOU LITTLE MONSTER!
I'LL RING YOUR SKINNY-
TRIANNE!
MATCHING HALF
DON'T FORGET, MY FRIEND...
MARSHAL OR NOT, IF YOU HARM MY NIECE, YOU WON'T LIVE LONG ENOUGH TO REGRET IT.
BACK AWAY, BOTH OF YOU.

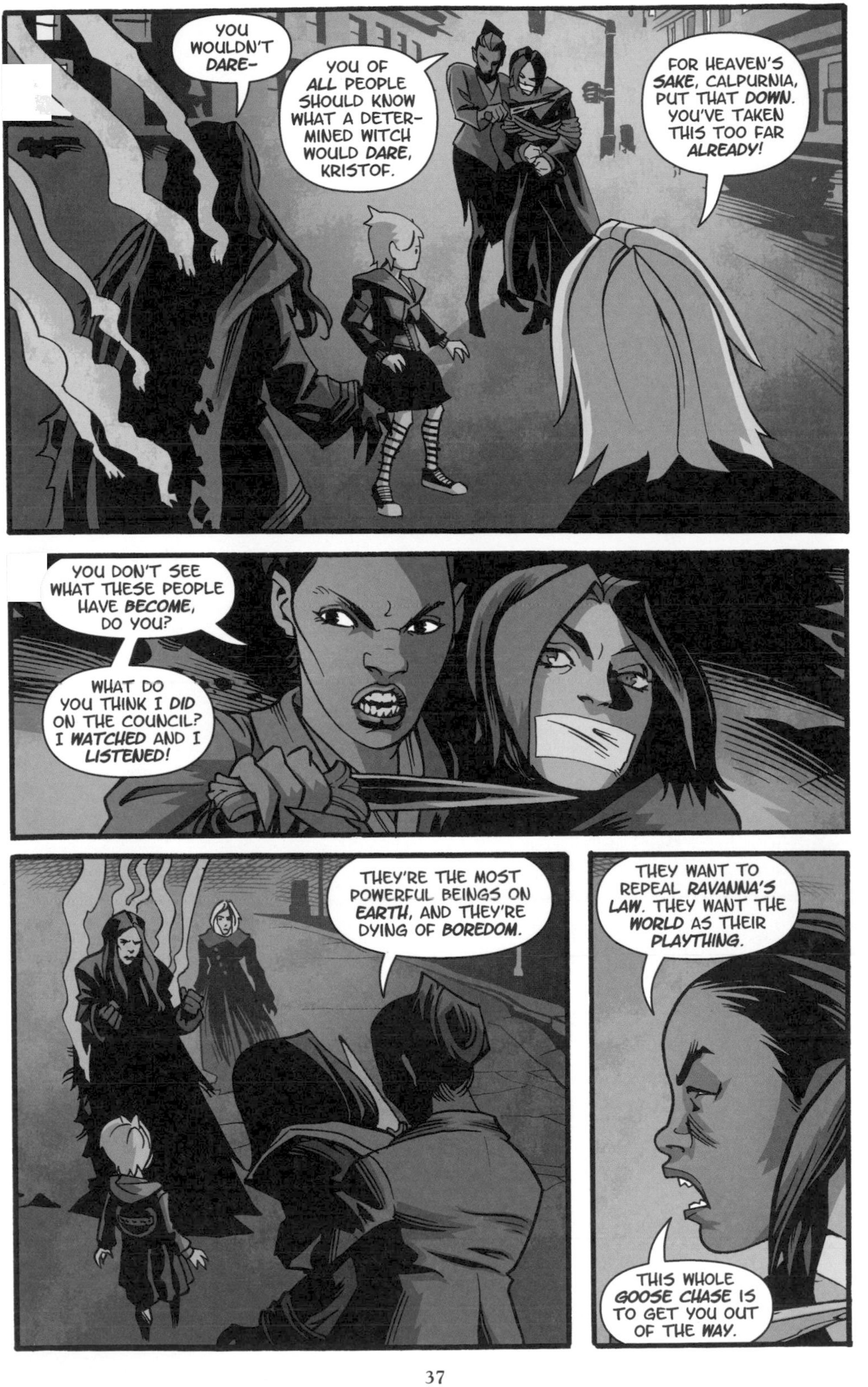
YOU WOULDN'T DARE-
YOU OF ALL PEOPLE SHOULD KNOW WHAT A DETERMINED WITCH WOULD DARE, KRISTOF.
FOR HEAVEN'S SAKE, CALPURNIA, PUT THAT DOWN. YOU'VE TAKEN THIS TOO FAR ALREADY!
YOU DON'T SEE WHAT THESE PEOPLE HAVE BECOME, DO YOU?
WHAT DO YOU THINK I DID ON THE COUNCIL? I WATCHED AND I LISTENED!
THEY'RE THE MOST POWERFUL BEINGS ON EARTH, AND THEY'RE DYING OF BOREDOM.
THEY WANT TO REPEAL RAVANNA'S LAW. THEY WANT THE WORLD AS THEIR PLAYTHING.
THIS WHOLE GOOSE CHASE IS TO GET YOU OUT OF THE WAY.

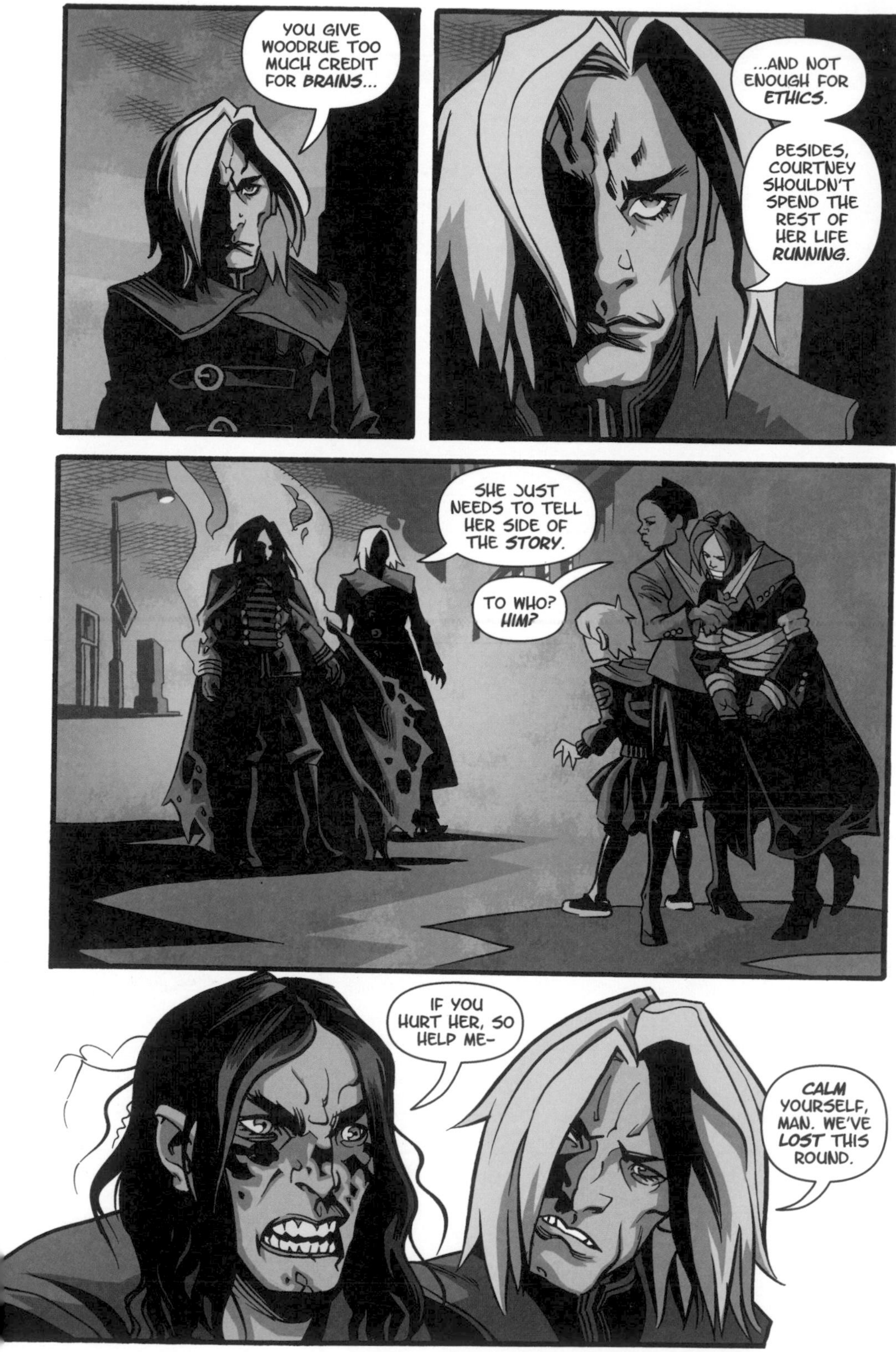
YOU GIVE WOODRUE TOO MUCH CREDIT FOR *BRAINS*...
...AND NOT ENOUGH FOR *ETHICS*.
BESIDES, COURTNEY SHOULDN'T SPEND THE REST OF HER LIFE *RUNNING*.
SHE JUST NEEDS TO TELL HER SIDE OF THE *STORY*.
TO WHO? *HIM?*
IF YOU HURT HER, SO HELP ME-
CALM YOURSELF, MAN. WE'VE *LOST* THIS ROUND.

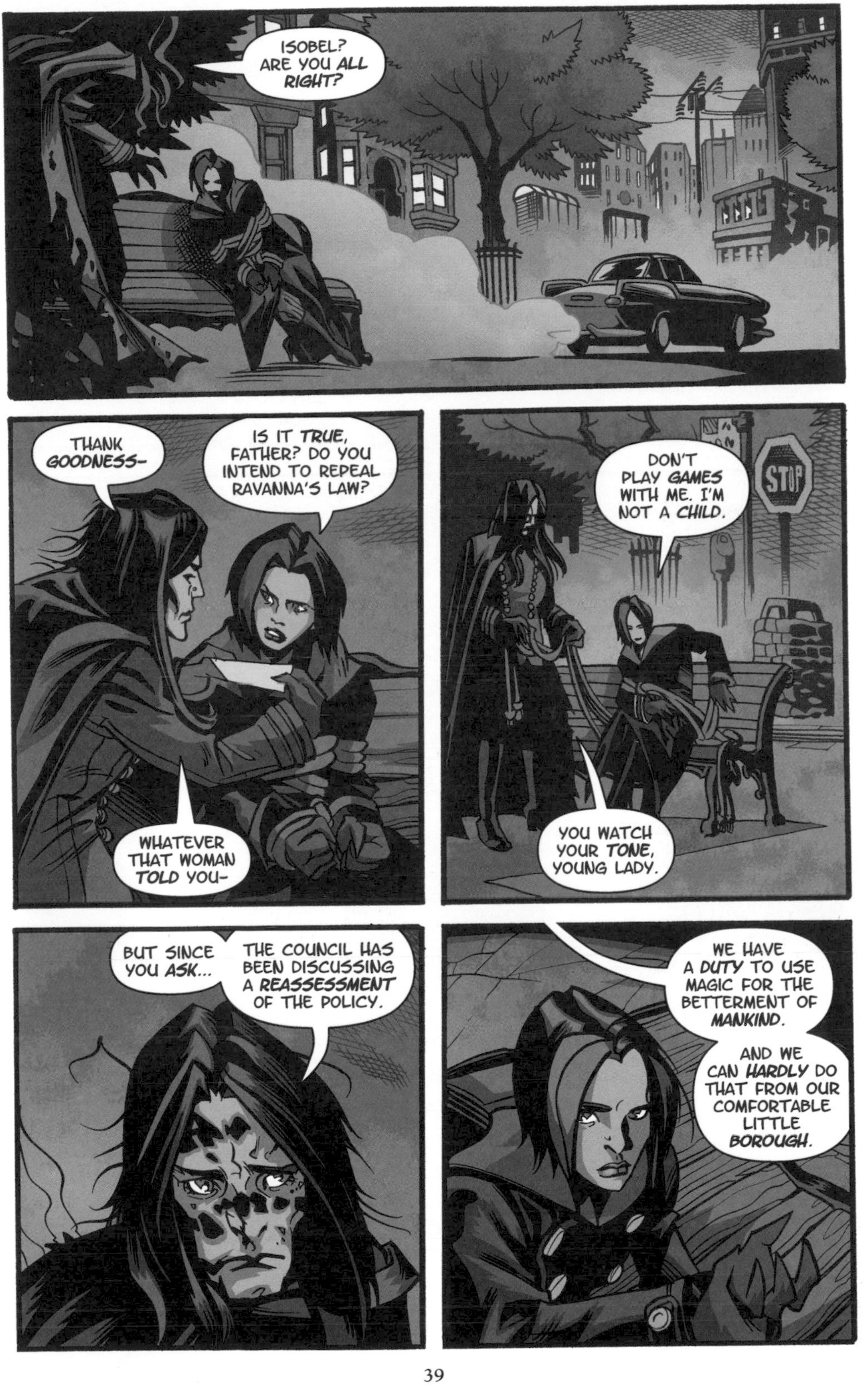
ISOBEL? ARE YOU ALL RIGHT?
THANK GOODNESS-
IS IT TRUE, FATHER? DO YOU INTEND TO REPEAL RAVANNA'S LAW?
WHATEVER THAT WOMAN TOLD YOU-
DON'T PLAY GAMES WITH ME. I'M NOT A CHILD.
STOP
YOU WATCH YOUR TONE, YOUNG LADY.
BUT SINCE YOU ASK...
THE COUNCIL HAS BEEN DISCUSSING A REASSESSMENT OF THE POLICY.
WE HAVE A DUTY TO USE MAGIC FOR THE BETTERMENT OF MANKIND.
AND WE CAN HARDLY DO THAT FROM OUR COMFORTABLE LITTLE BOROUGH.

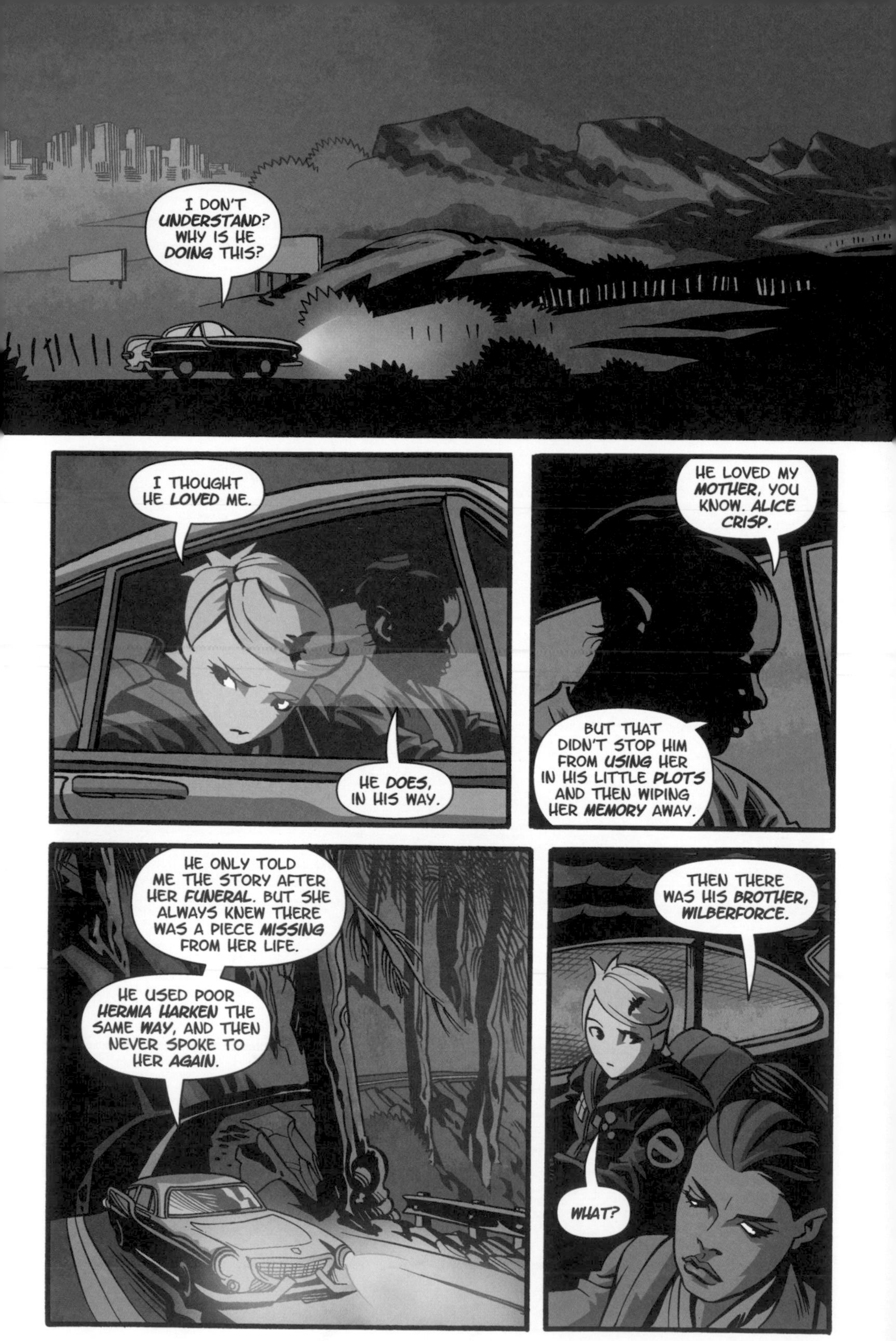
I DON'T UNDERSTAND? WHY IS HE DOING THIS?
I THOUGHT HE LOVED ME.
HE DOES, IN HIS WAY.
HE LOVED MY MOTHER, YOU KNOW. ALICE CRISP.
BUT THAT DIDN'T STOP HIM FROM USING HER IN HIS LITTLE PLOTS AND THEN WIPING HER MEMORY AWAY.
HE ONLY TOLD ME THE STORY AFTER HER FUNERAL. BUT SHE ALWAYS KNEW THERE WAS A PIECE MISSING FROM HER LIFE.
HE USED POOR HERMIA HARKEN THE SAME WAY, AND THEN NEVER SPOKE TO HER AGAIN.
THEN THERE WAS HIS BROTHER, WILBERFORCE.
WHAT?

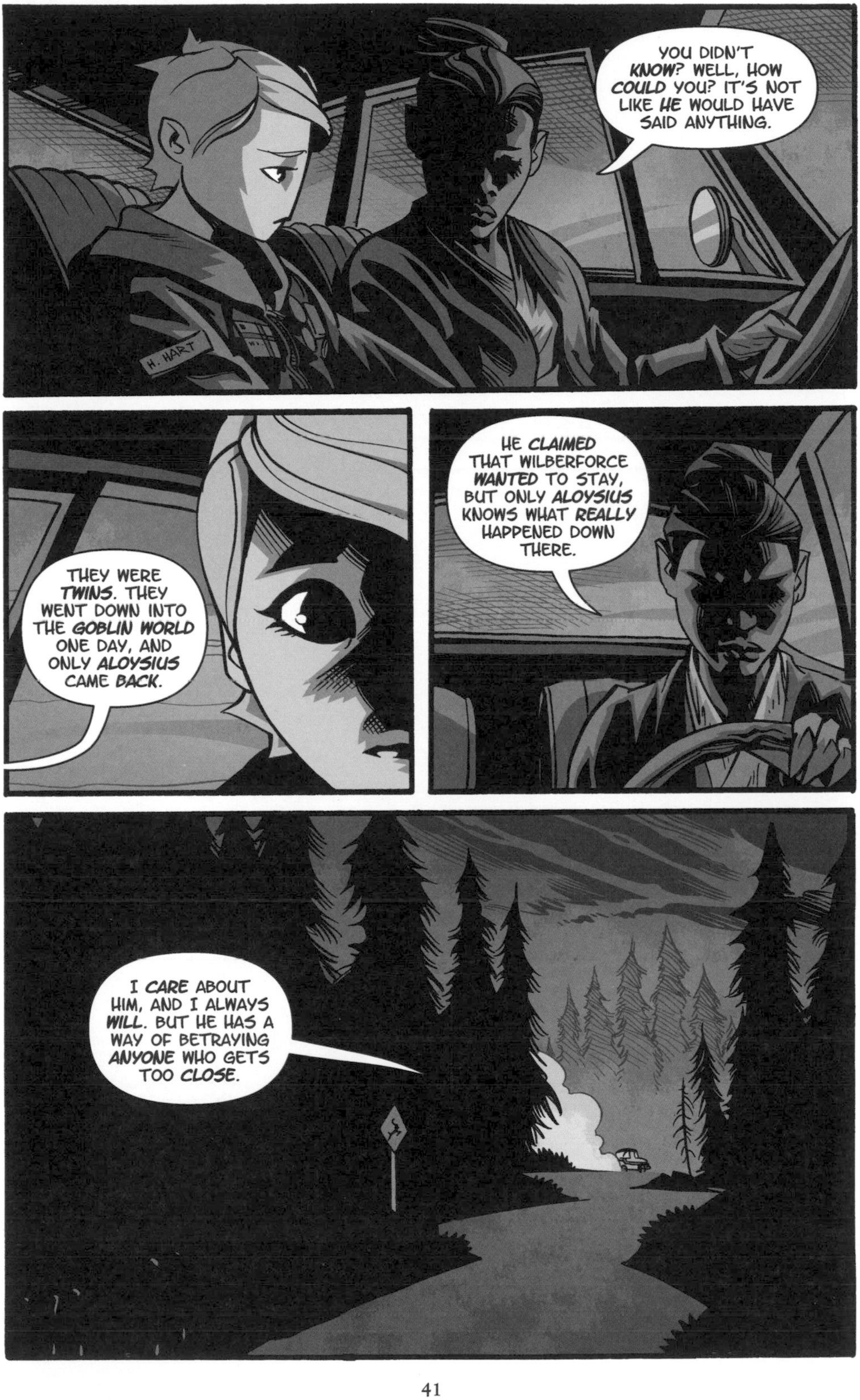
YOU DIDN'T KNOW? WELL, HOW COULD YOU? IT'S NOT LIKE HE WOULD HAVE SAID ANYTHING.
H. HART
THEY WERE TWINS. THEY WENT DOWN INTO THE GOBLIN WORLD ONE DAY, AND ONLY ALOYSIUS CAME BACK.
HE CLAIMED THAT WILBERFORCE WANTED TO STAY, BUT ONLY ALOYSIUS KNOWS WHAT REALLY HAPPENED DOWN THERE.
I CARE ABOUT HIM, AND I ALWAYS WILL. BUT HE HAS A WAY OF BETRAYING ANYONE WHO GETS TOO CLOSE.

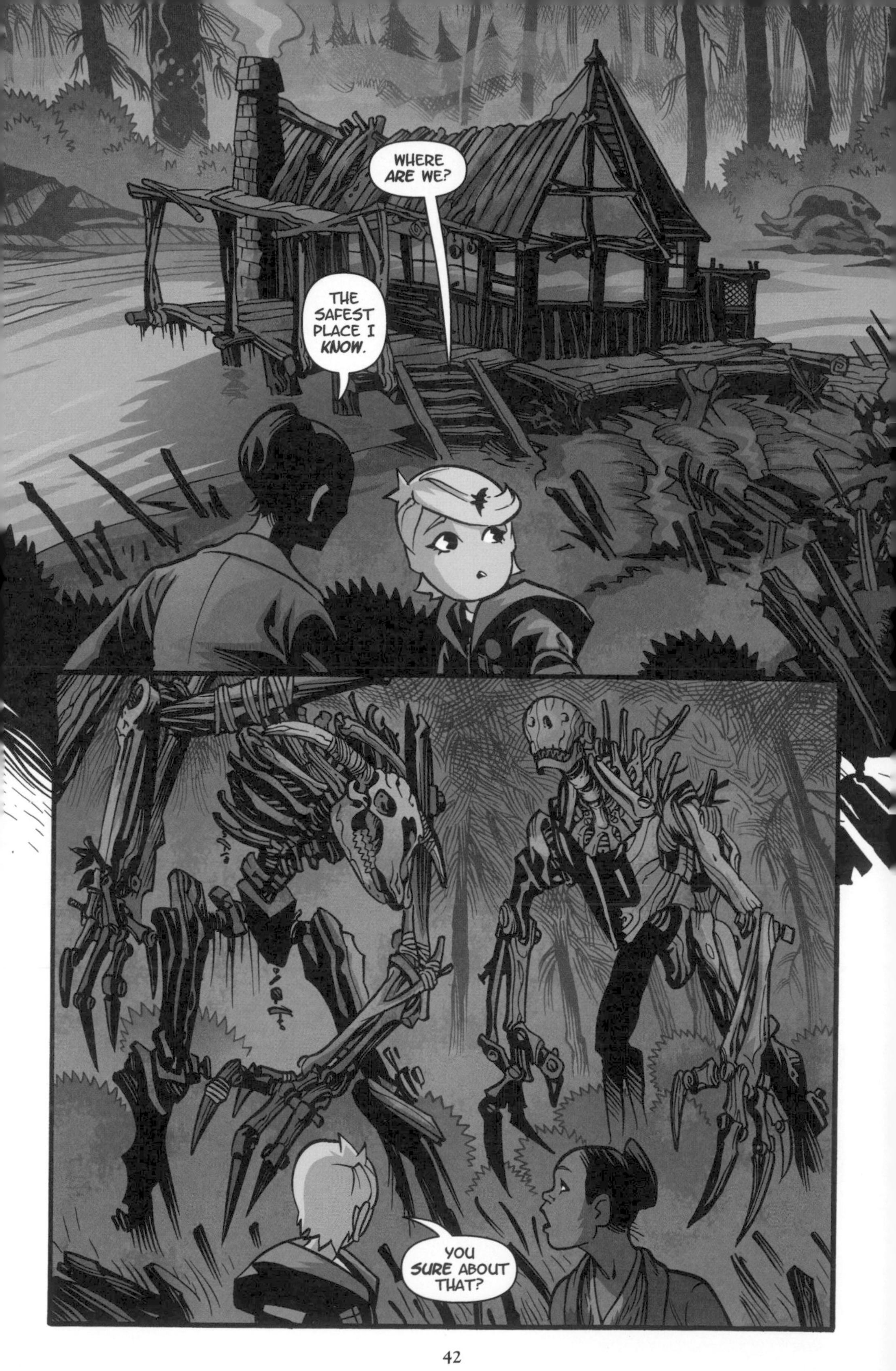
WHERE ARE WE?
THE SAFEST PLACE I KNOW.
YOU SURE ABOUT THAT?

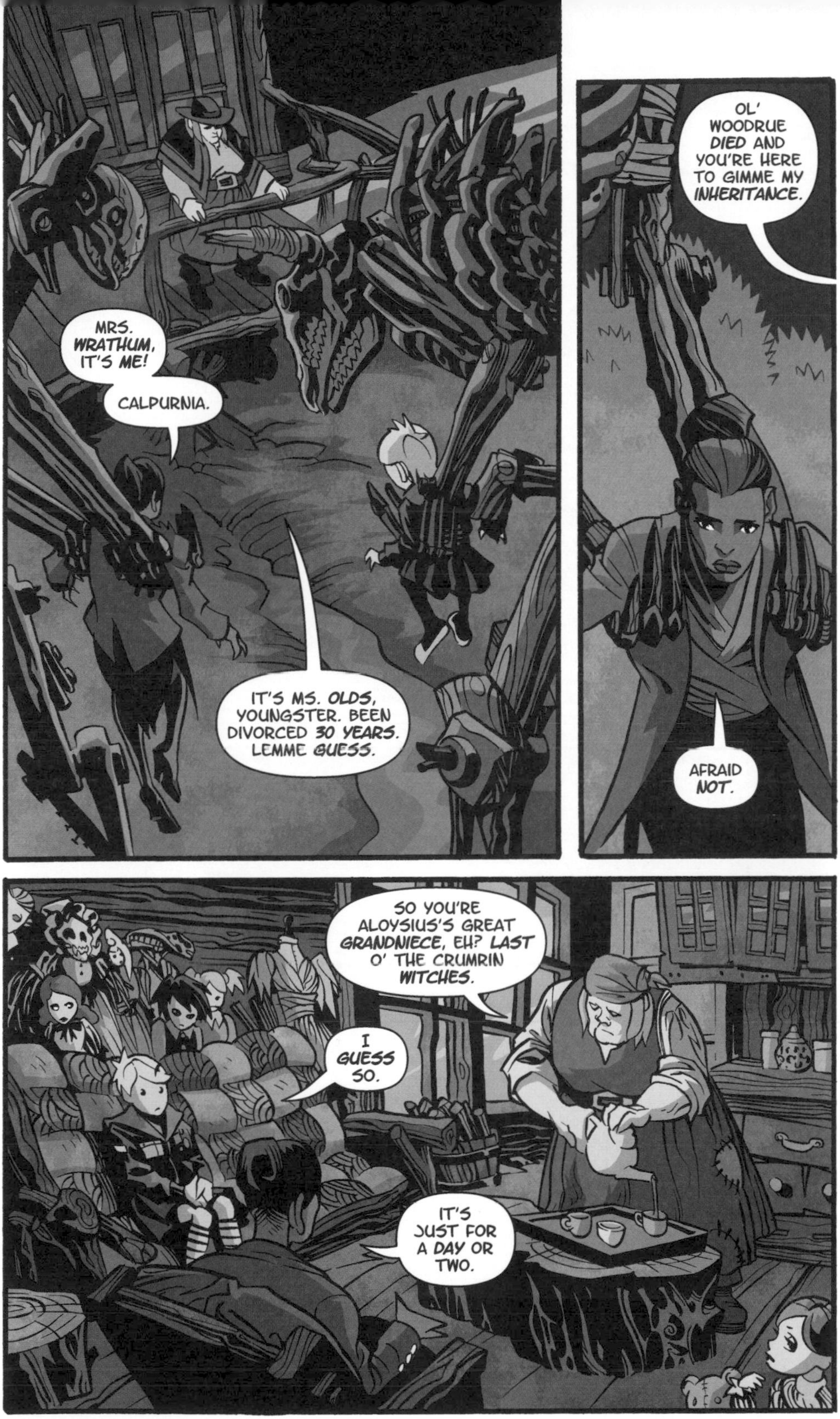
MRS. WRATHUM, IT'S ME!
CALPURNIA.
IT'S MS. OLDS, YOUNGSTER. BEEN DIVORCED 30 YEARS. LEMME GUESS.
OL' WOODRUE DIED AND YOU'RE HERE TO GIMME MY INHERITANCE.
AFRAID NOT.
SO YOU'RE ALOYSIUS'S GREAT GRANDNIECE, EH? LAST O' THE CRUMRIN WITCHES.
I GUESS SO.
IT'S JUST FOR A DAY OR TWO.

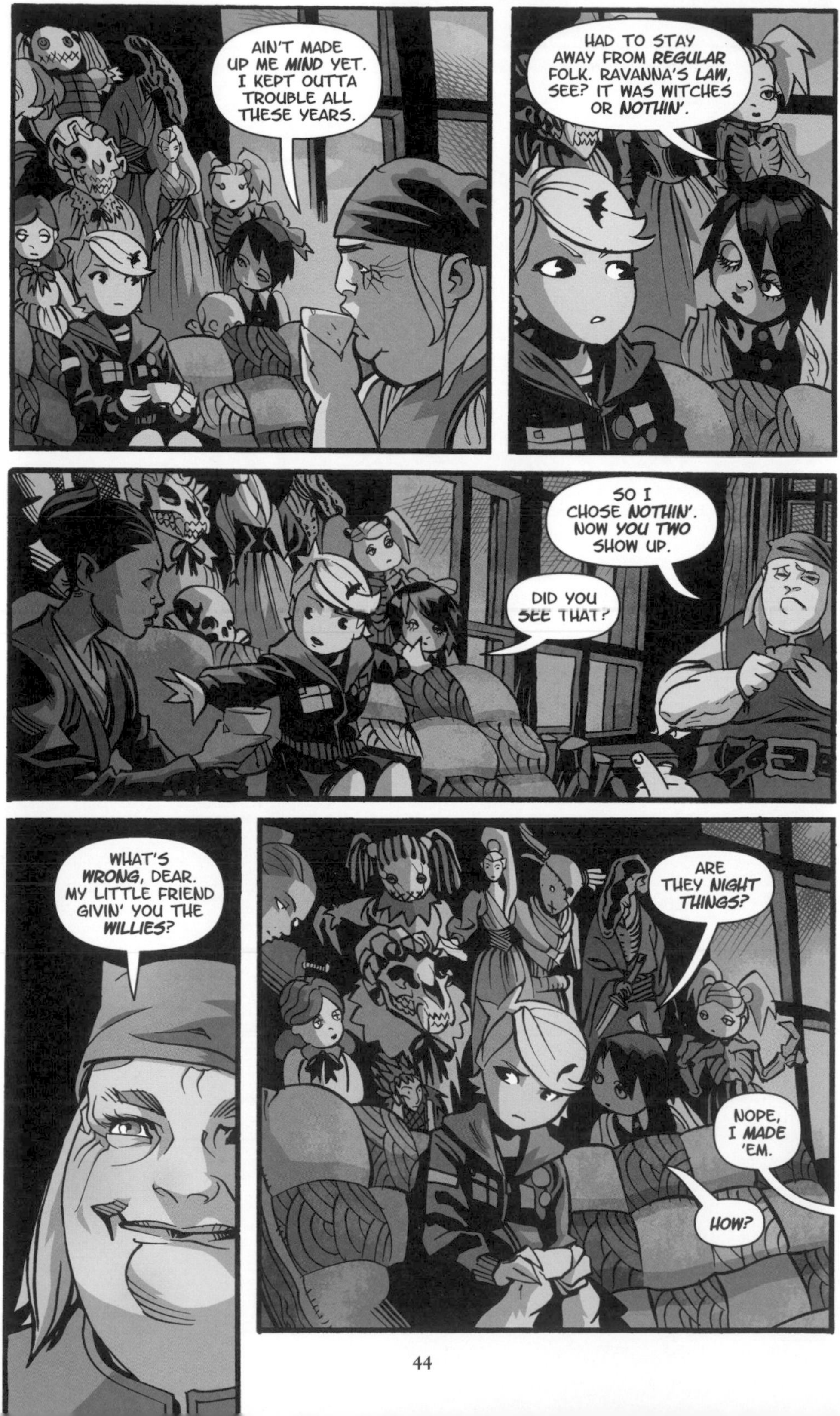
AIN'T MADE UP ME MIND YET. I KEPT OUTTA TROUBLE ALL THESE YEARS.
HAD TO STAY AWAY FROM REGULAR FOLK. RAVANNA'S LAW, SEE? IT WAS WITCHES OR NOTHIN'.
SO I CHOSE NOTHIN'. NOW YOU TWO SHOW UP.
DID YOU SEE THAT?
WHAT'S WRONG, DEAR. MY LITTLE FRIEND GIVIN' YOU THE WILLIES?
ARE THEY NIGHT THINGS?
NOPE, I MADE 'EM.
HOW?

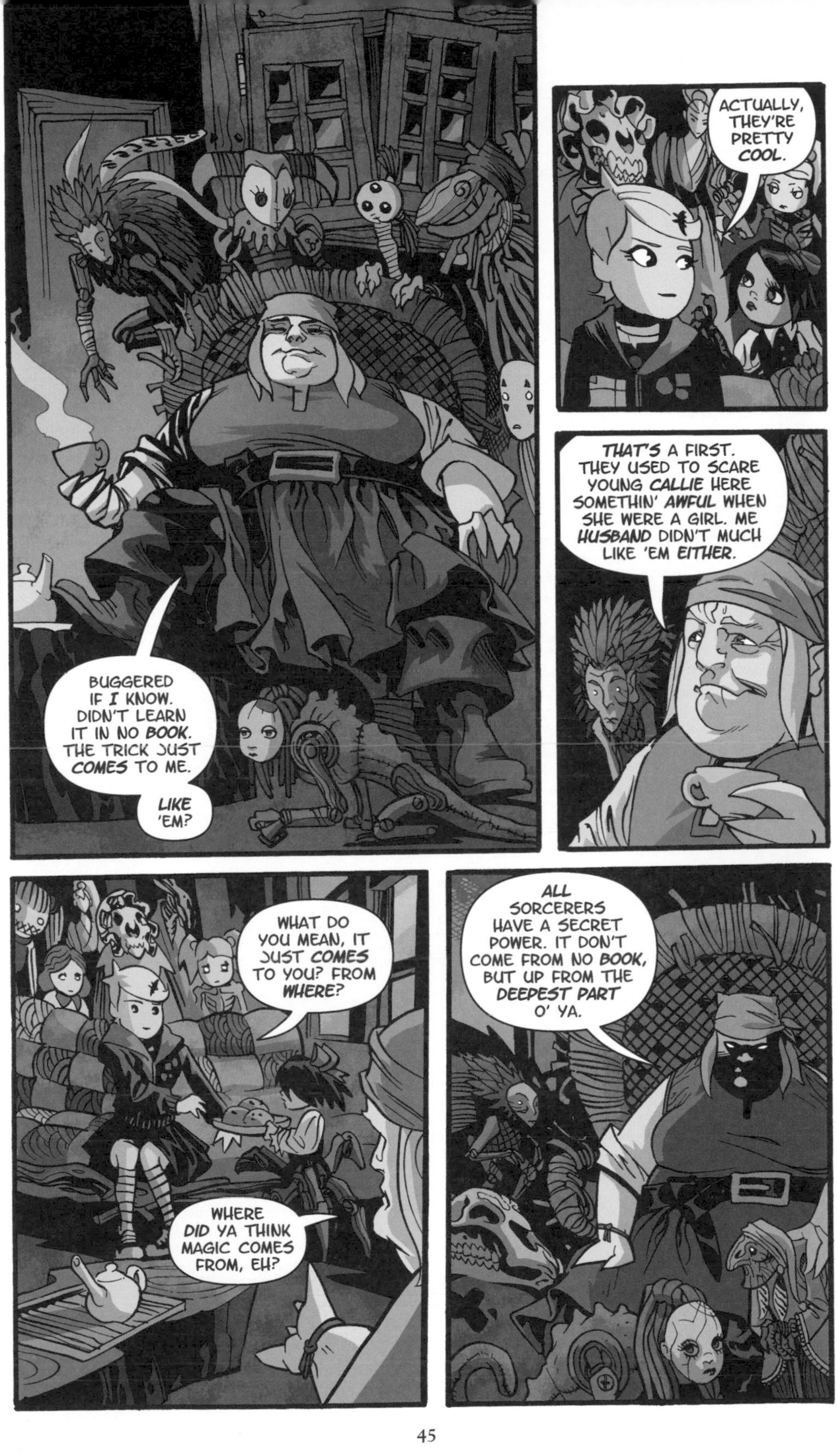
BUGGERED IF I KNOW. DIDN'T LEARN IT IN NO BOOK. THE TRICK JUST COMES TO ME.
LIKE 'EM?
ACTUALLY, THEY'RE PRETTY COOL.
THAT'S A FIRST. THEY USED TO SCARE YOUNG CALLIE HERE SOMETHIN' AWFUL WHEN SHE WERE A GIRL. ME HUSBAND DIDN'T MUCH LIKE 'EM EITHER.
WHAT DO YOU MEAN, IT JUST COMES TO YOU? FROM WHERE?
WHERE DID YA THINK MAGIC COMES FROM, EH?
ALL SORCERERS HAVE A SECRET POWER. IT DON'T COME FROM NO BOOK, BUT UP FROM THE DEEPEST PART O' YA.

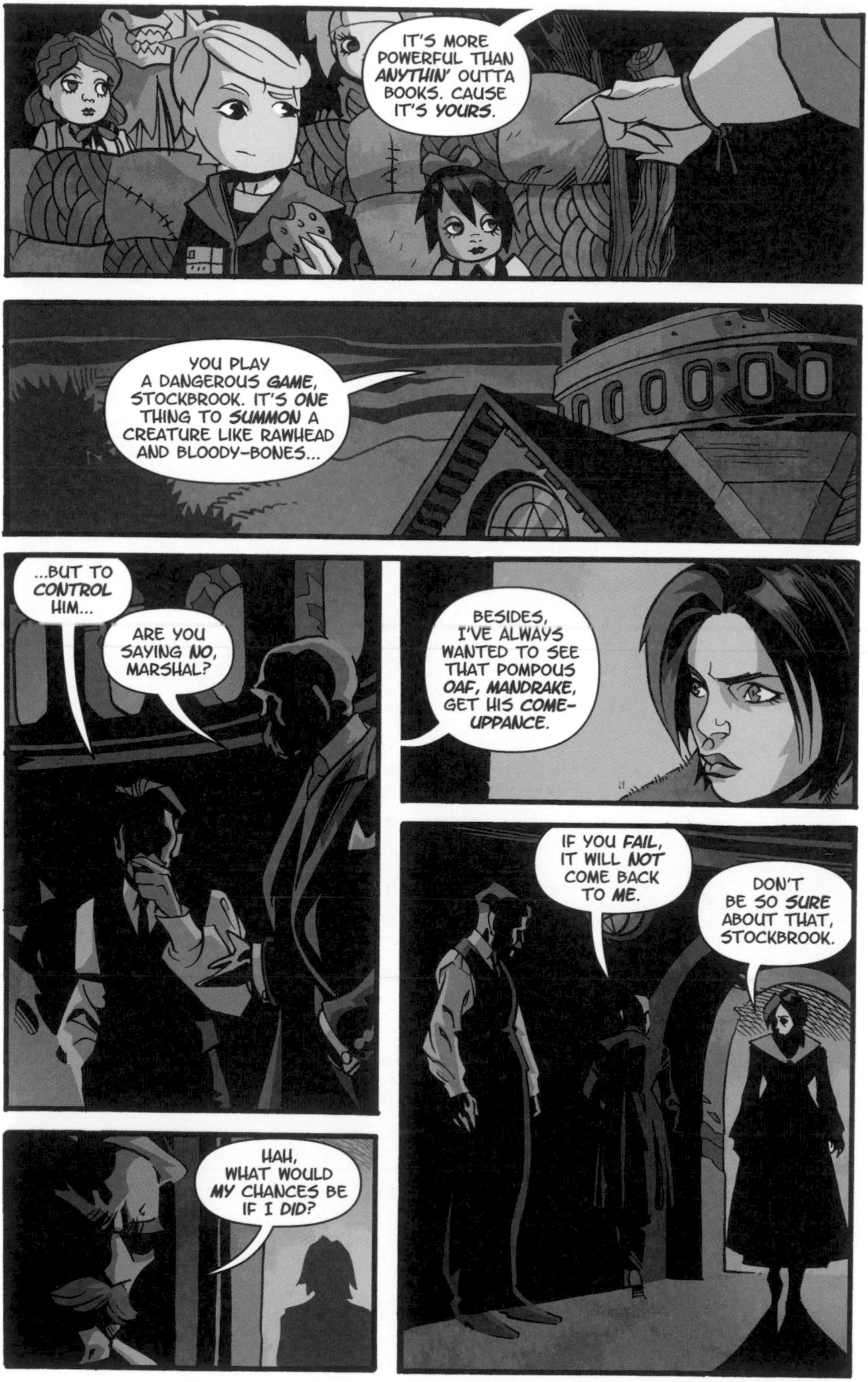
IT'S MORE POWERFUL THAN ANYTHIN' OUTTA BOOKS. CAUSE IT'S YOURS.
YOU PLAY A DANGEROUS GAME, STOCKBROOK. IT'S ONE THING TO SUMMON A CREATURE LIKE RAWHEAD AND BLOODY-BONES...
...BUT TO CONTROL HIM...
ARE YOU SAYING NO, MARSHAL?
HAH, WHAT WOULD MY CHANCES BE IF I DID?
BESIDES, I'VE ALWAYS WANTED TO SEE THAT POMPOUS OAF, MANDRAKE, GET HIS COME-UPPANCE.
IF YOU FAIL, IT WILL NOT COME BACK TO ME.
DON'T BE SO SURE ABOUT THAT, STOCKBROOK.

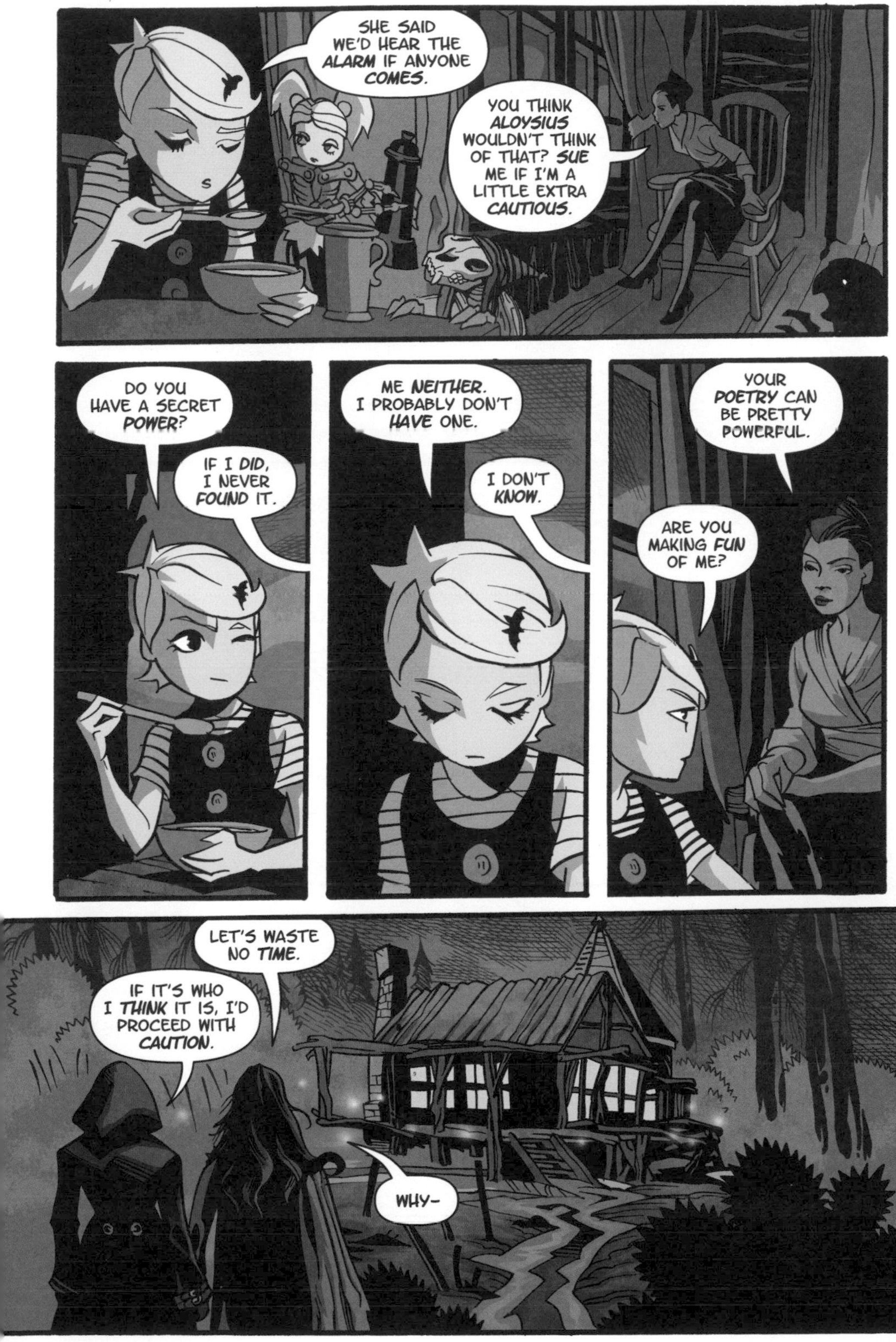
SHE SAID WE'D HEAR THE ALARM IF ANYONE COMES.
YOU THINK ALOYSIUS WOULDN'T THINK OF THAT? SUE ME IF I'M A LITTLE EXTRA CAUTIOUS.
DO YOU HAVE A SECRET POWER?
IF I DID, I NEVER FOUND IT.
ME NEITHER. I PROBABLY DON'T HAVE ONE.
I DON'T KNOW.
YOUR POETRY CAN BE PRETTY POWERFUL.
ARE YOU MAKING FUN OF ME?
LET'S WASTE NO TIME.
IF IT'S WHO I THINK IT IS, I'D PROCEED WITH CAUTION.
WHY-

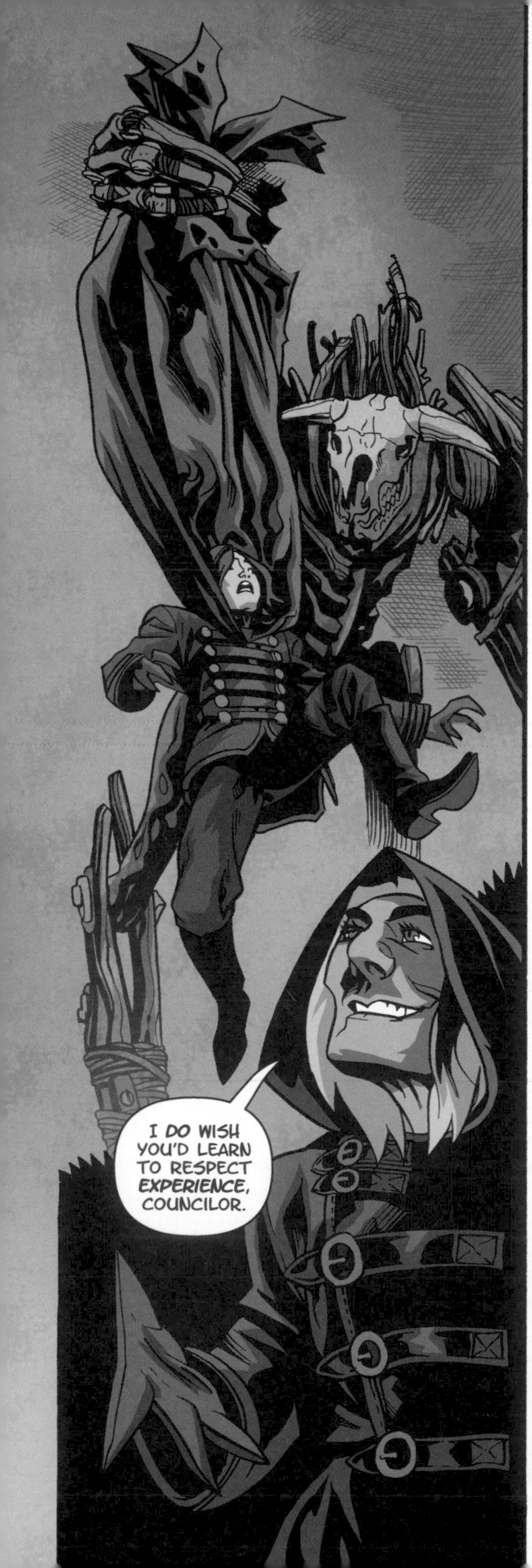
I DO WISH YOU'D LEARN TO RESPECT EXPERIENCE, COUNCILOR.

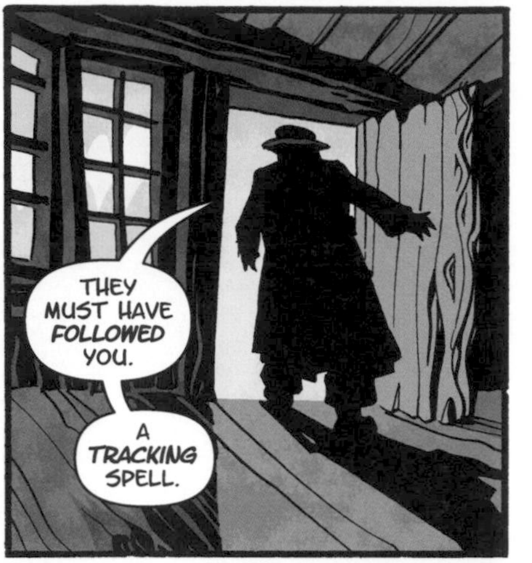
THEY MUST HAVE FOLLOWED YOU.
A TRACKING SPELL.

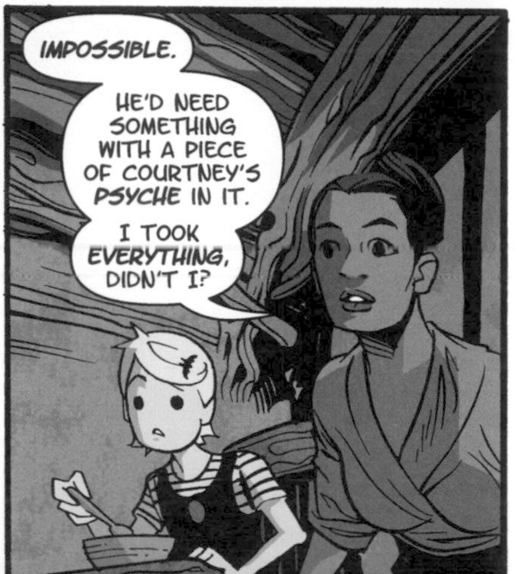
IMPOSSIBLE.
HE'D NEED SOMETHING WITH A PIECE OF COURTNEY'S PSYCHE IN IT.
I TOOK EVERYTHING, DIDN'T I?

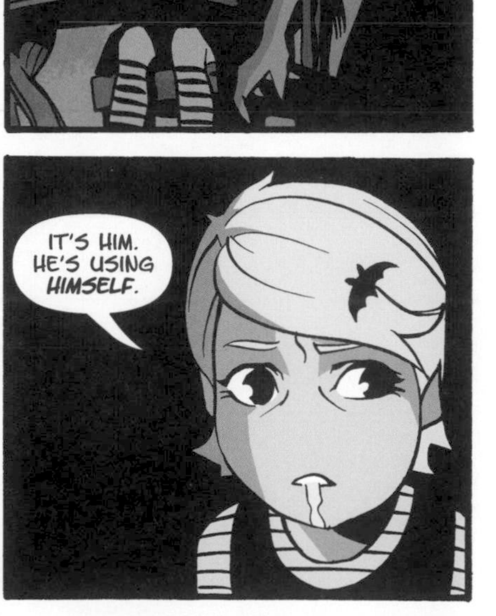
IT'S HIM. HE'S USING HIMSELF.

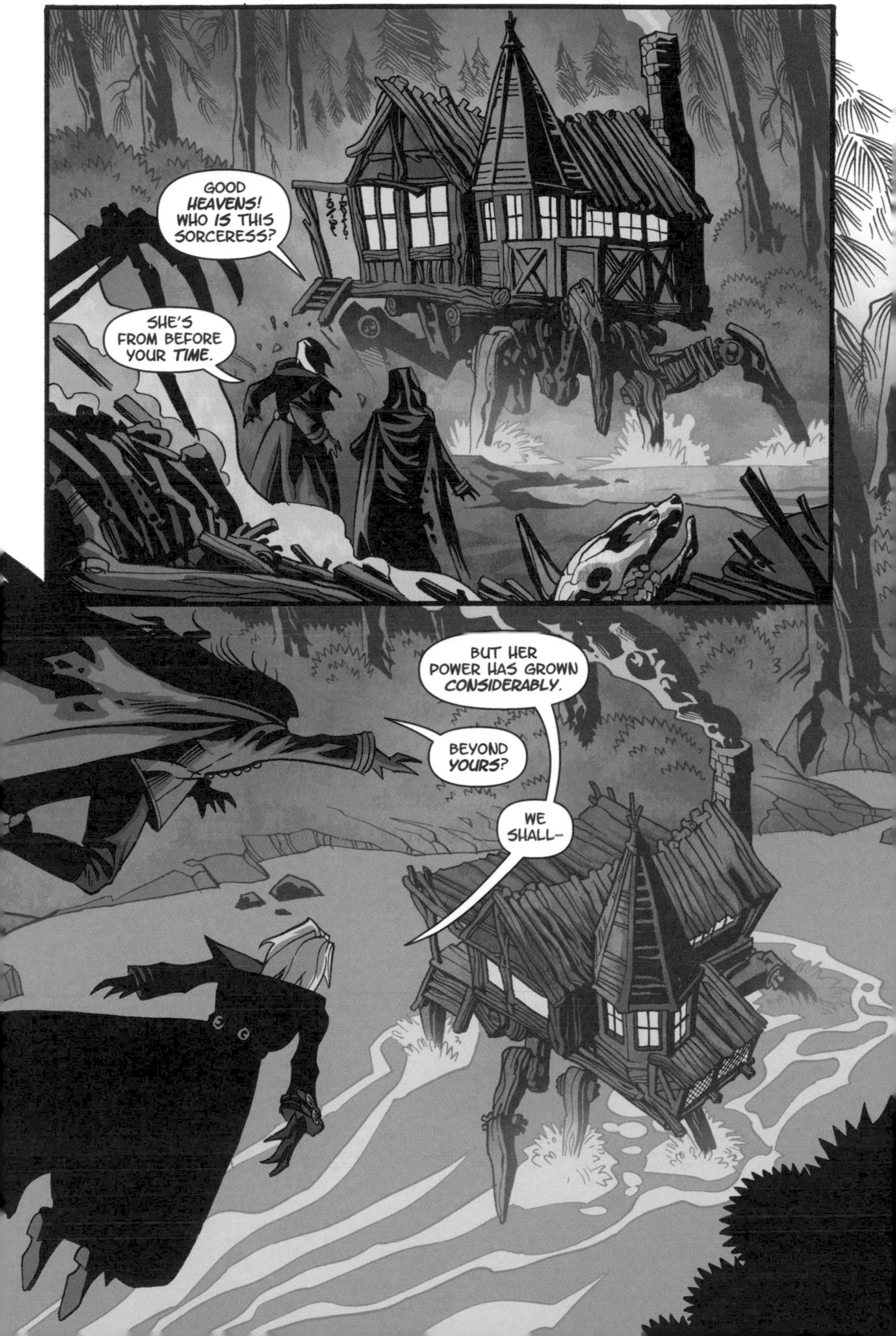
GOOD HEAVENS! WHO IS THIS SORCERESS?
SHE'S FROM BEFORE YOUR TIME.
BUT HER POWER HAS GROWN CONSIDERABLY.
BEYOND YOURS?
WE SHALL-

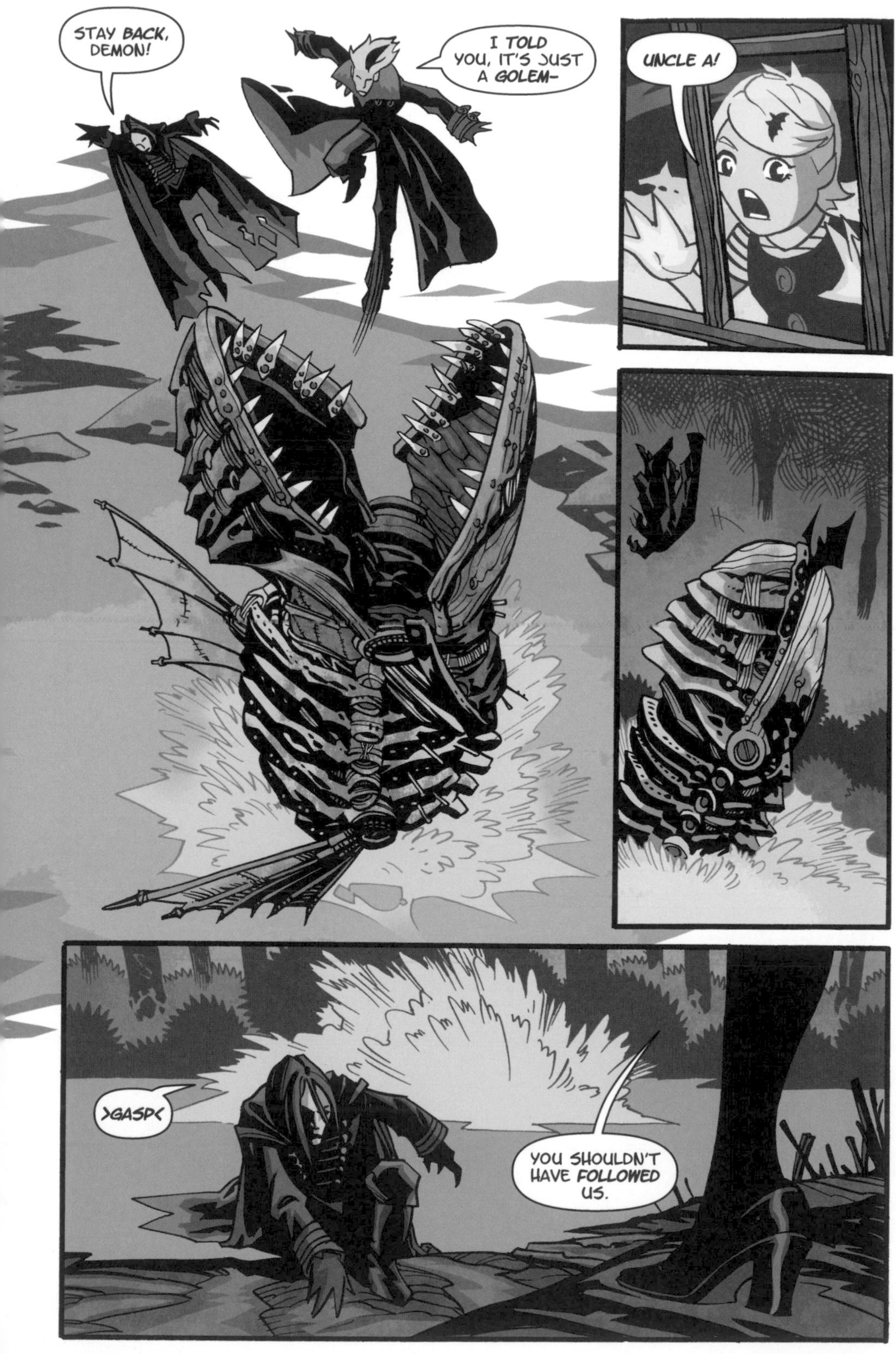
STAY BACK, DEMON!
I TOLD YOU, IT'S JUST A GOLEM-
UNCLE A!
>GASP<
YOU SHOULDN'T HAVE FOLLOWED US.

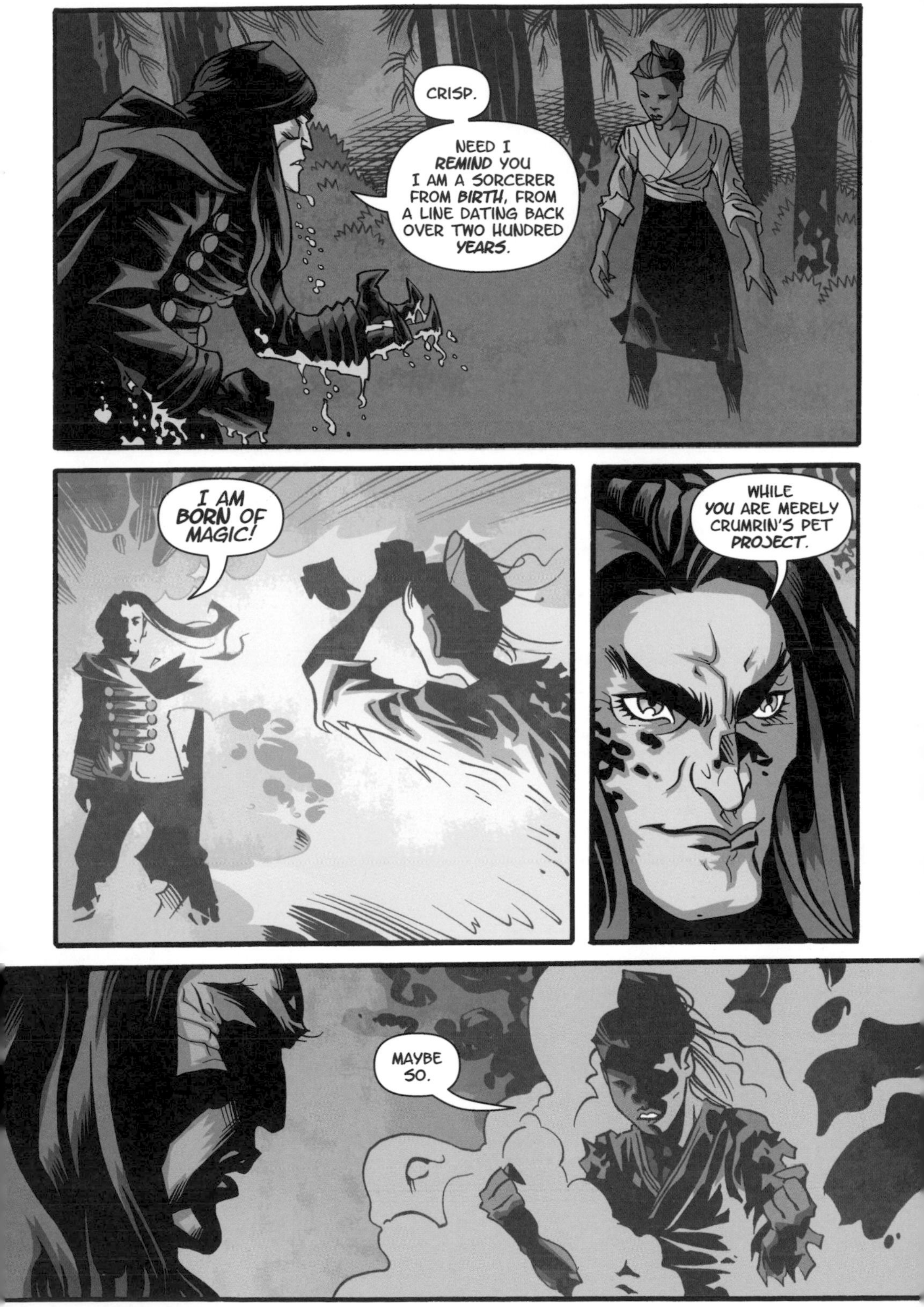
CRISP.
NEED I *REMIND* YOU I AM A SORCERER FROM *BIRTH*, FROM A LINE DATING BACK OVER TWO HUNDRED *YEARS*.
I AM *BORN* OF *MAGIC*!
WHILE YOU ARE MERELY CRUMRIN'S PET *PROJECT*.
MAYBE SO.

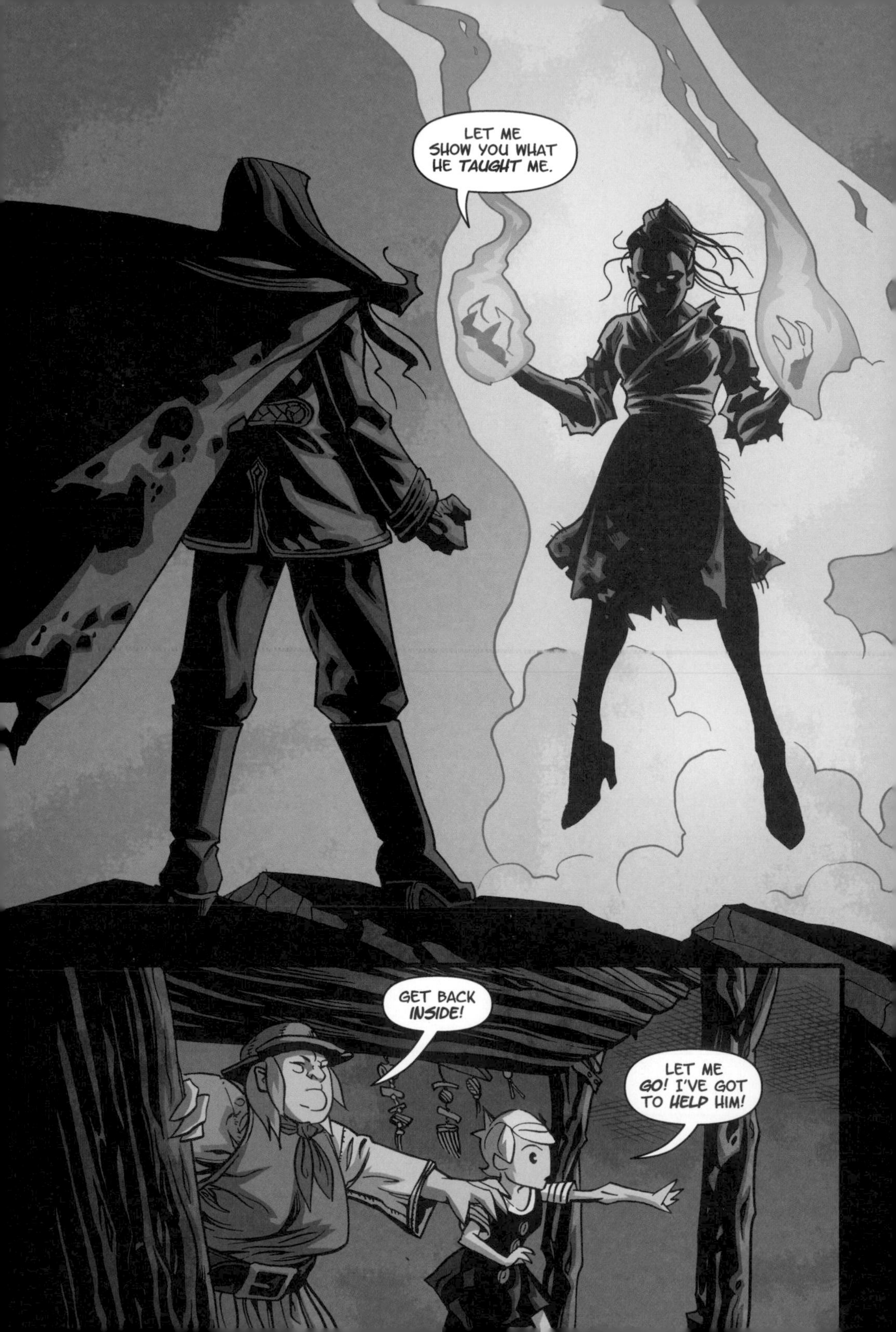
LET ME SHOW YOU WHAT HE TAUGHT ME.
GET BACK INSIDE!
LET ME GO! I'VE GOT TO HELP HIM!

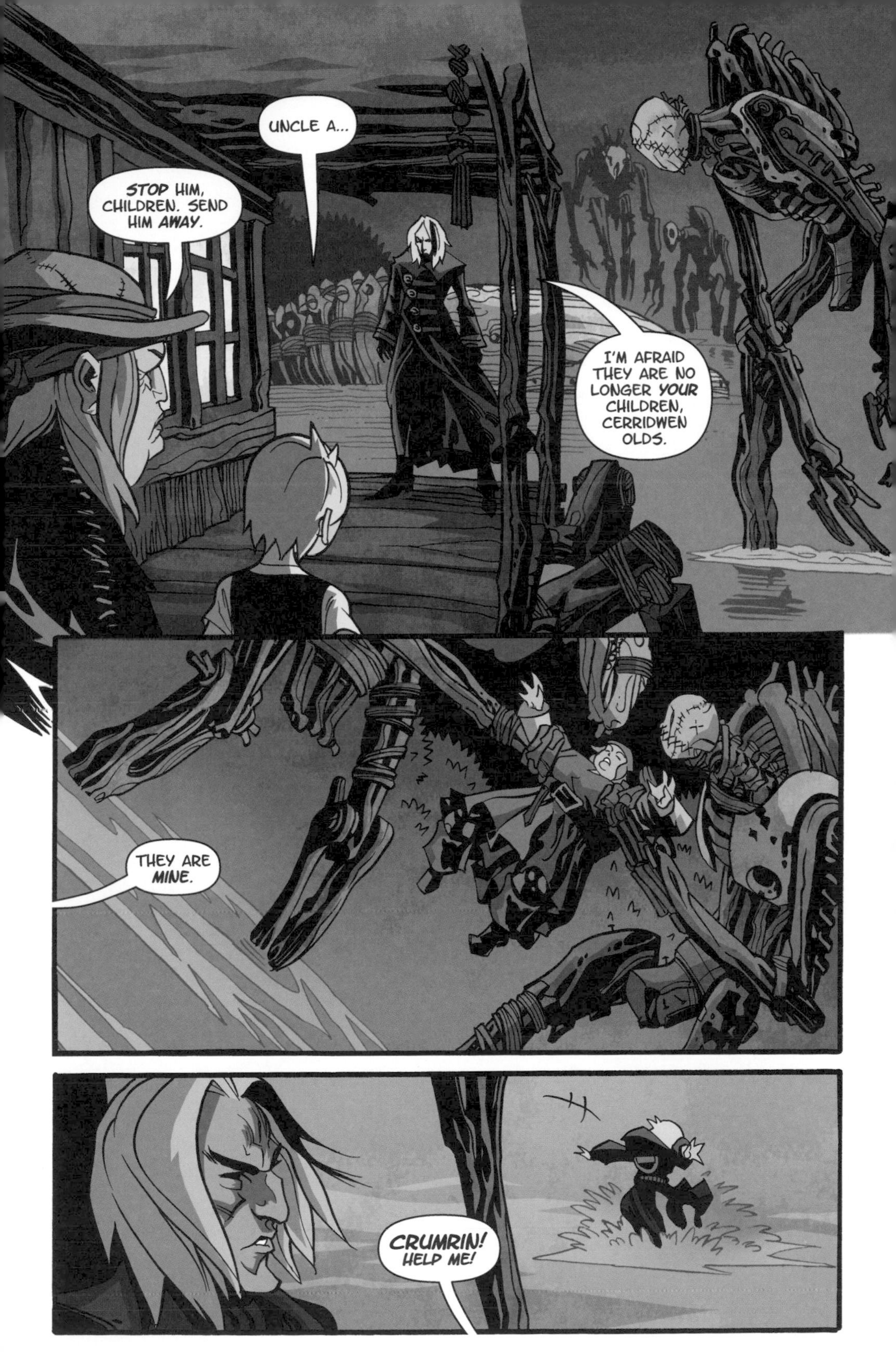

STOP HIM, CHILDREN. SEND HIM AWAY.
UNCLE A...
I'M AFRAID THEY ARE NO LONGER YOUR CHILDREN, CERRIDWEN OLDS.
THEY ARE MINE.
CRUMRIN! HELP ME!

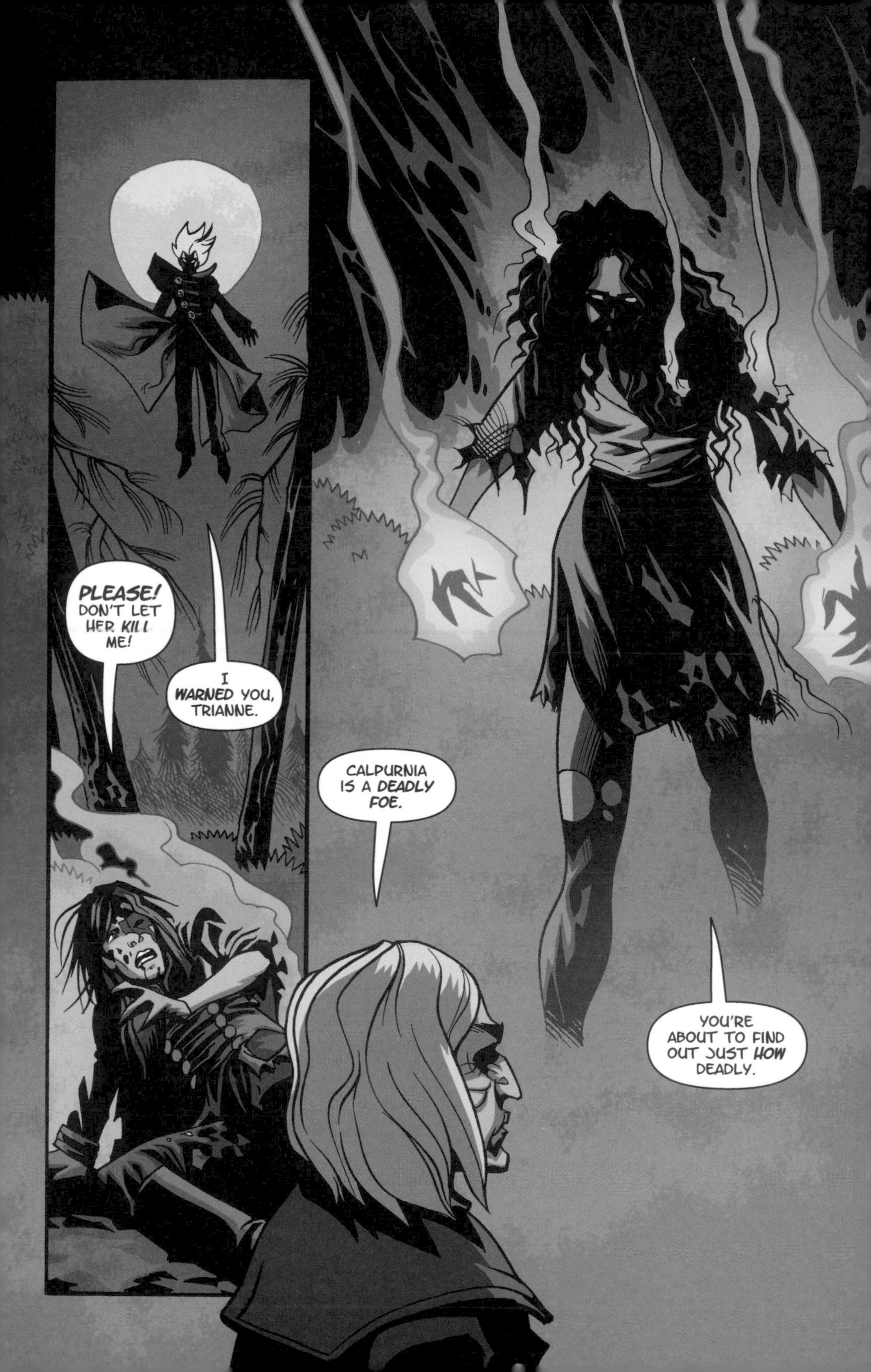
PLEASE! DON'T LET HER KILL ME!
I WARNED YOU, TRIANNE.
CALPURNIA IS A DEADLY FOE.
YOU'RE ABOUT TO FIND OUT JUST HOW DEADLY.

Chapter Three

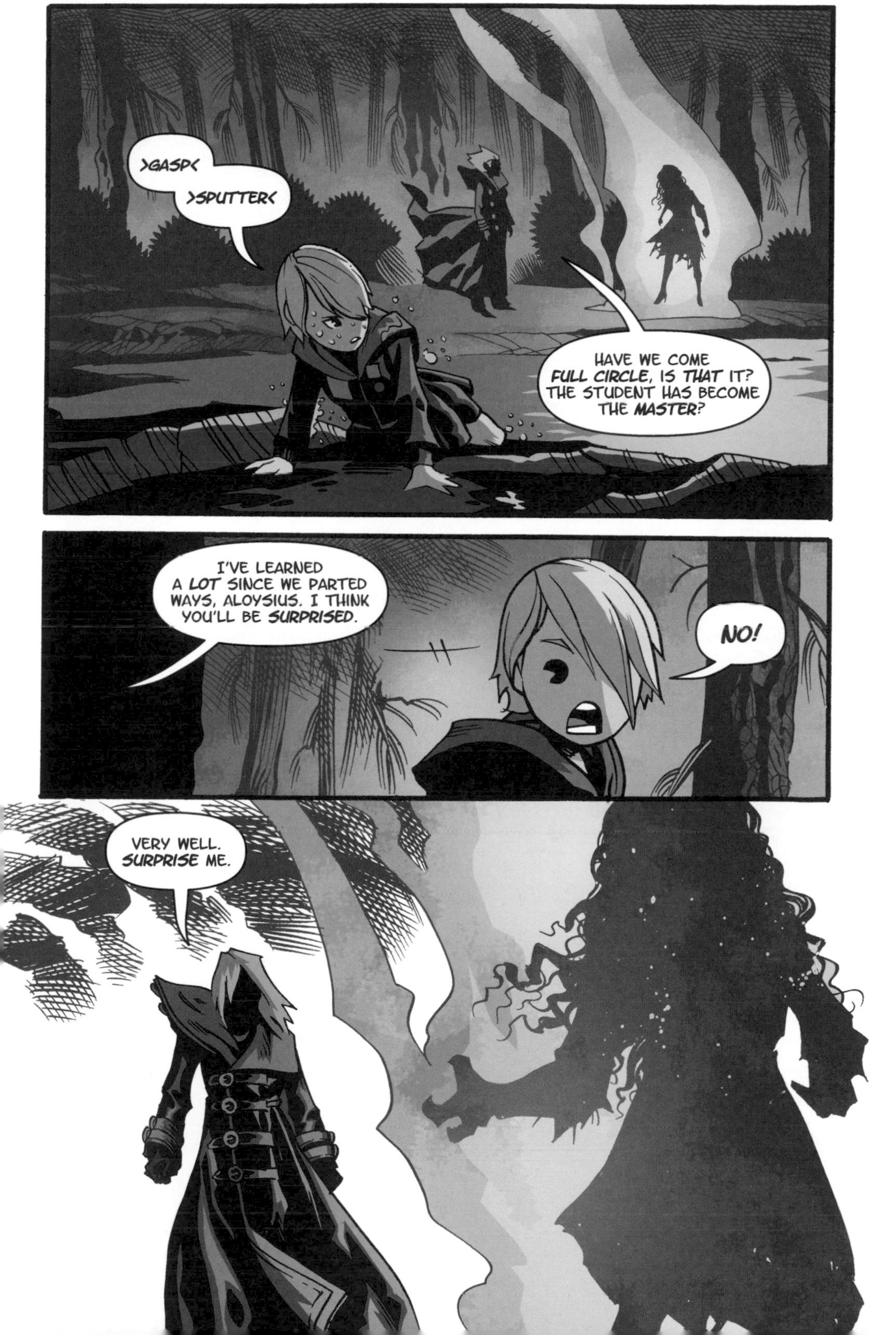
>GASP<
>SPUTTER<
HAVE WE COME FULL CIRCLE, IS THAT IT? THE STUDENT HAS BECOME THE MASTER?
I'VE LEARNED A LOT SINCE WE PARTED WAYS, ALOYSIUS. I THINK YOU'LL BE SURPRISED.
NO!
VERY WELL. SURPRISE ME.

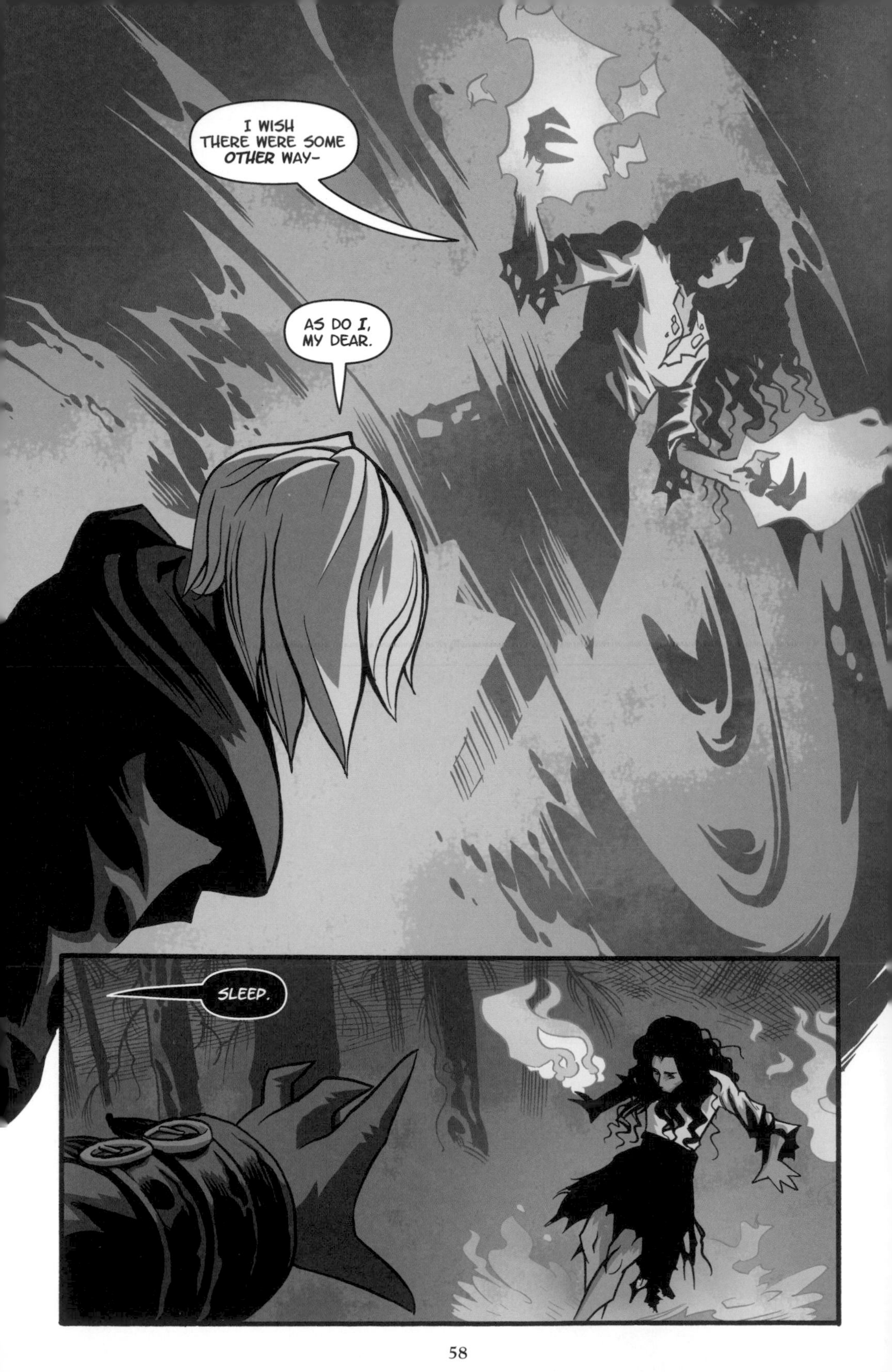
I WISH THERE WERE SOME OTHER WAY-
AS DO I, MY DEAR.
SLEEP.

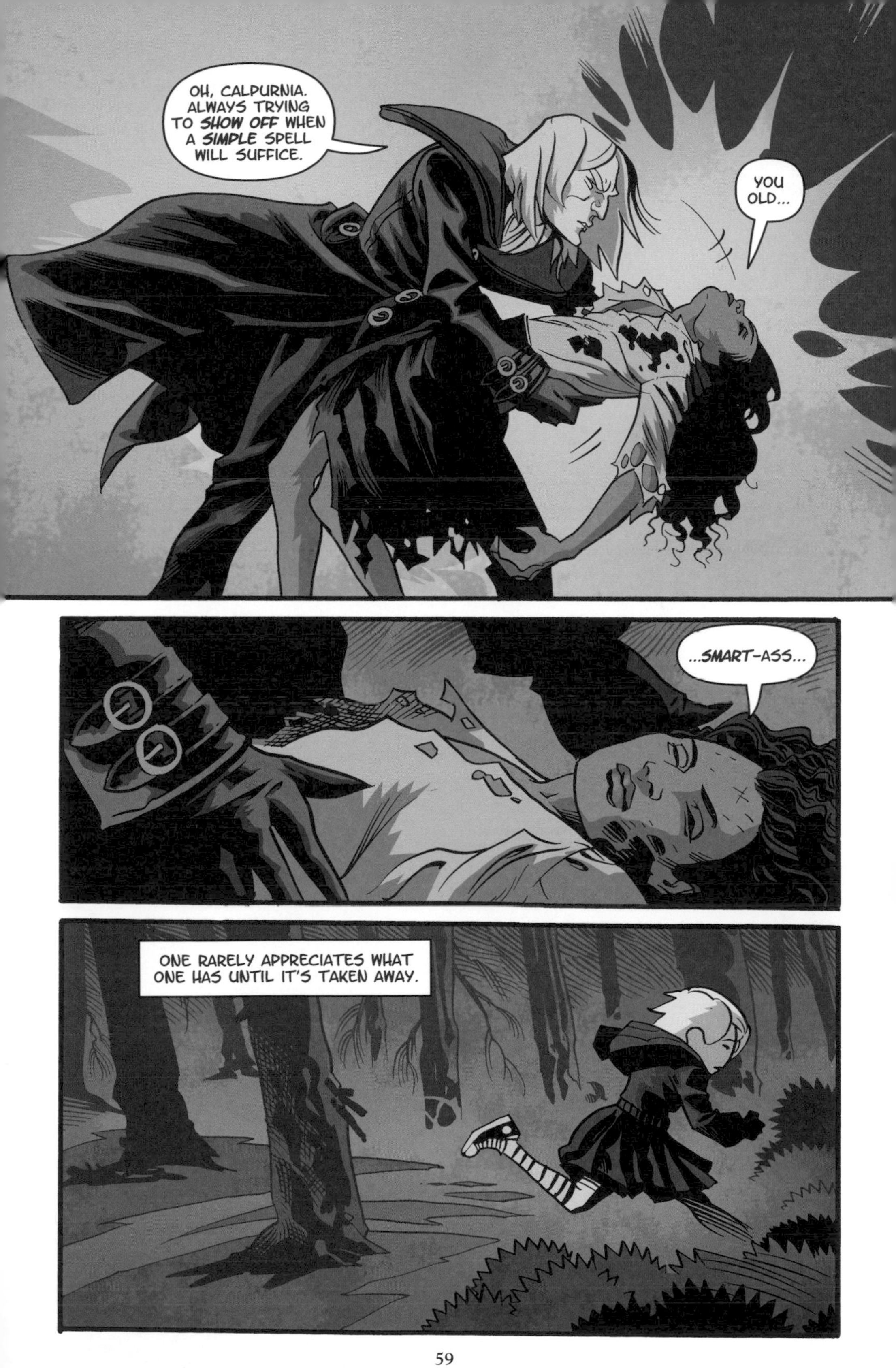
OH, CALPURNIA. ALWAYS TRYING TO SHOW OFF WHEN A SIMPLE SPELL WILL SUFFICE.
YOU OLD...
...SMART-ASS...
ONE RARELY APPRECIATES WHAT ONE HAS UNTIL IT'S TAKEN AWAY.

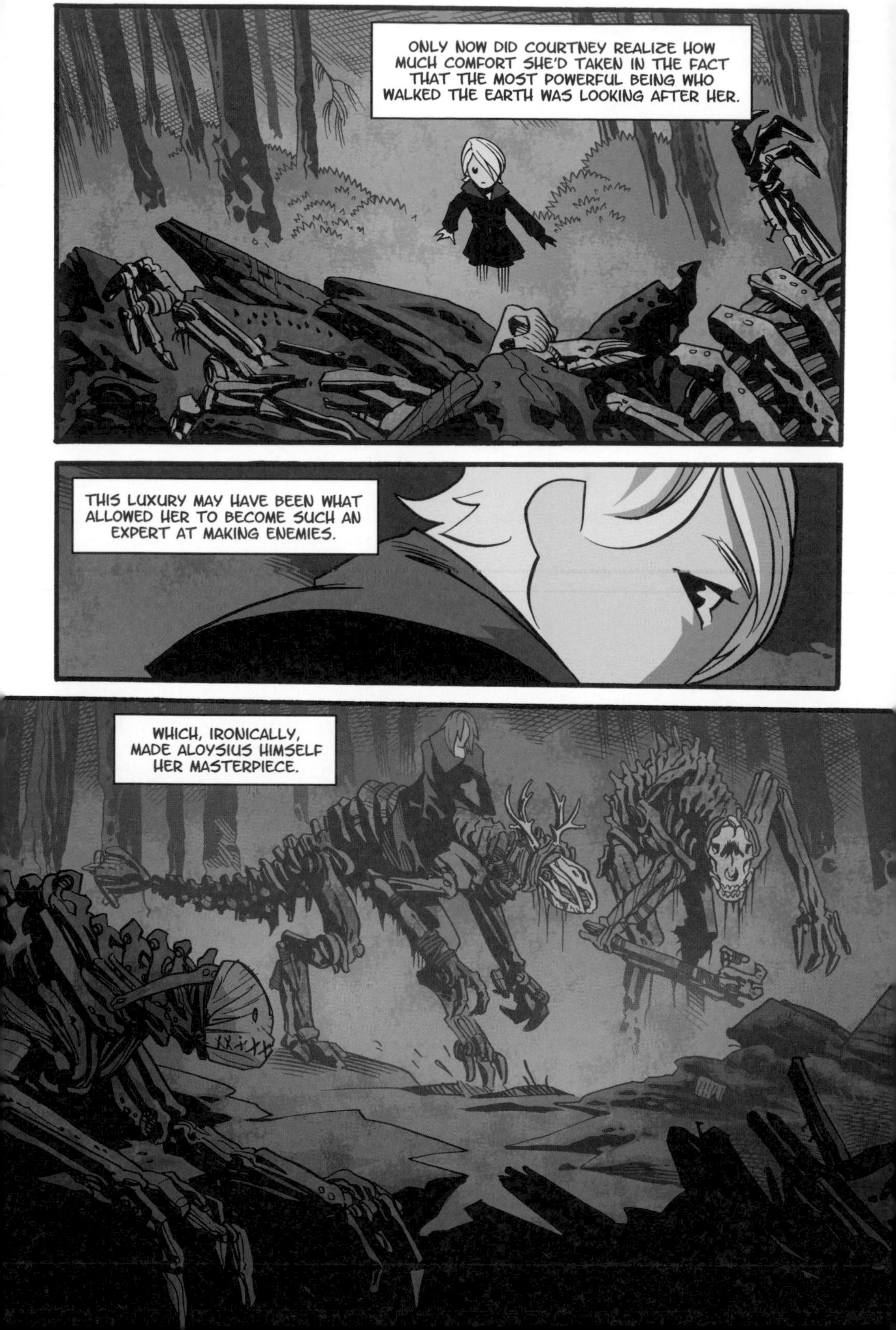
ONLY NOW DID COURTNEY REALIZE HOW MUCH COMFORT SHE'D TAKEN IN THE FACT THAT THE MOST POWERFUL BEING WHO WALKED THE EARTH WAS LOOKING AFTER HER.
THIS LUXURY MAY HAVE BEEN WHAT ALLOWED HER TO BECOME SUCH AN EXPERT AT MAKING ENEMIES.
WHICH, IRONICALLY, MADE ALOYSIUS HIMSELF HER MASTERPIECE.

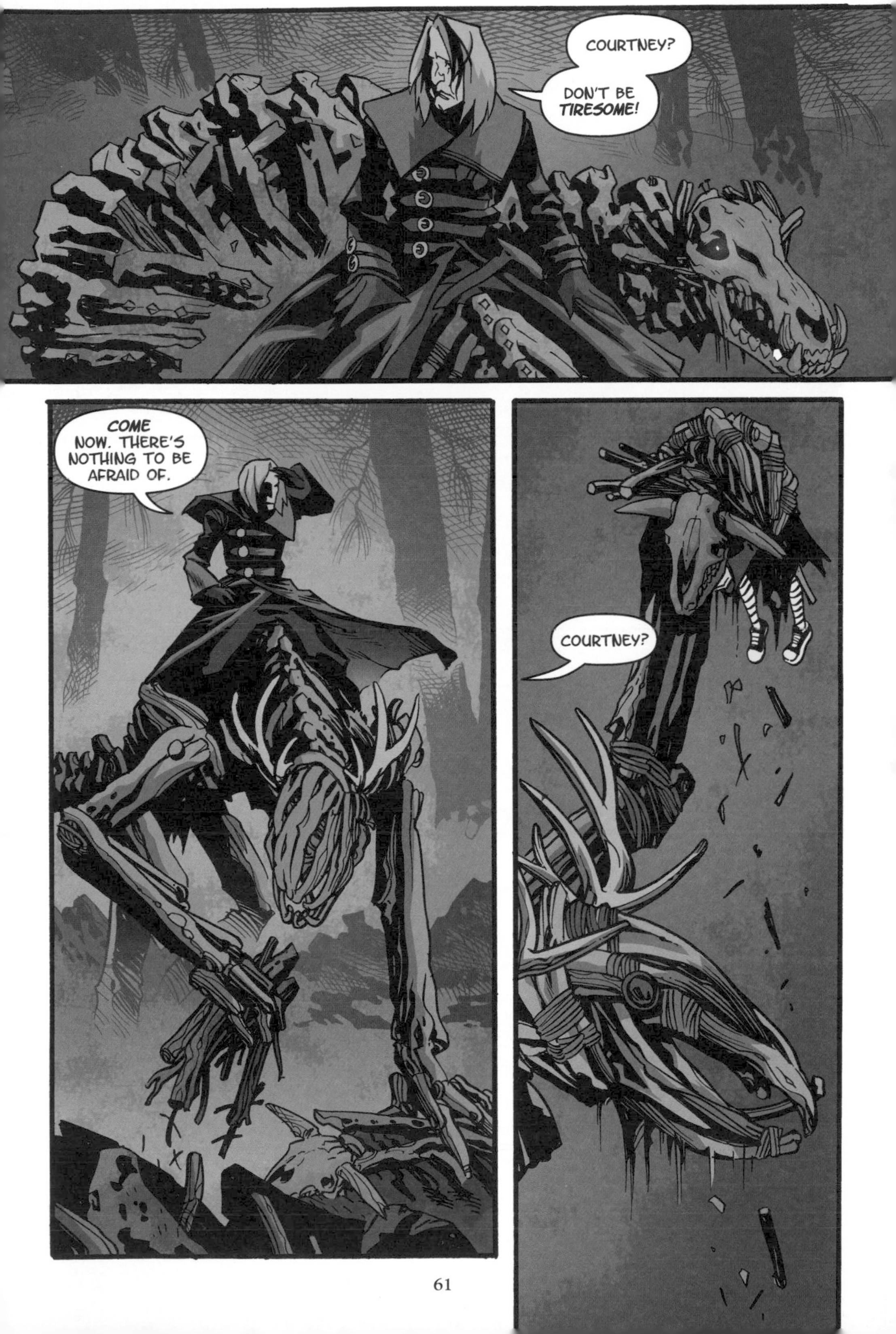
COURTNEY?
DON'T BE *TIRESOME!*
COME NOW. THERE'S NOTHING TO BE AFRAID OF.
COURTNEY?

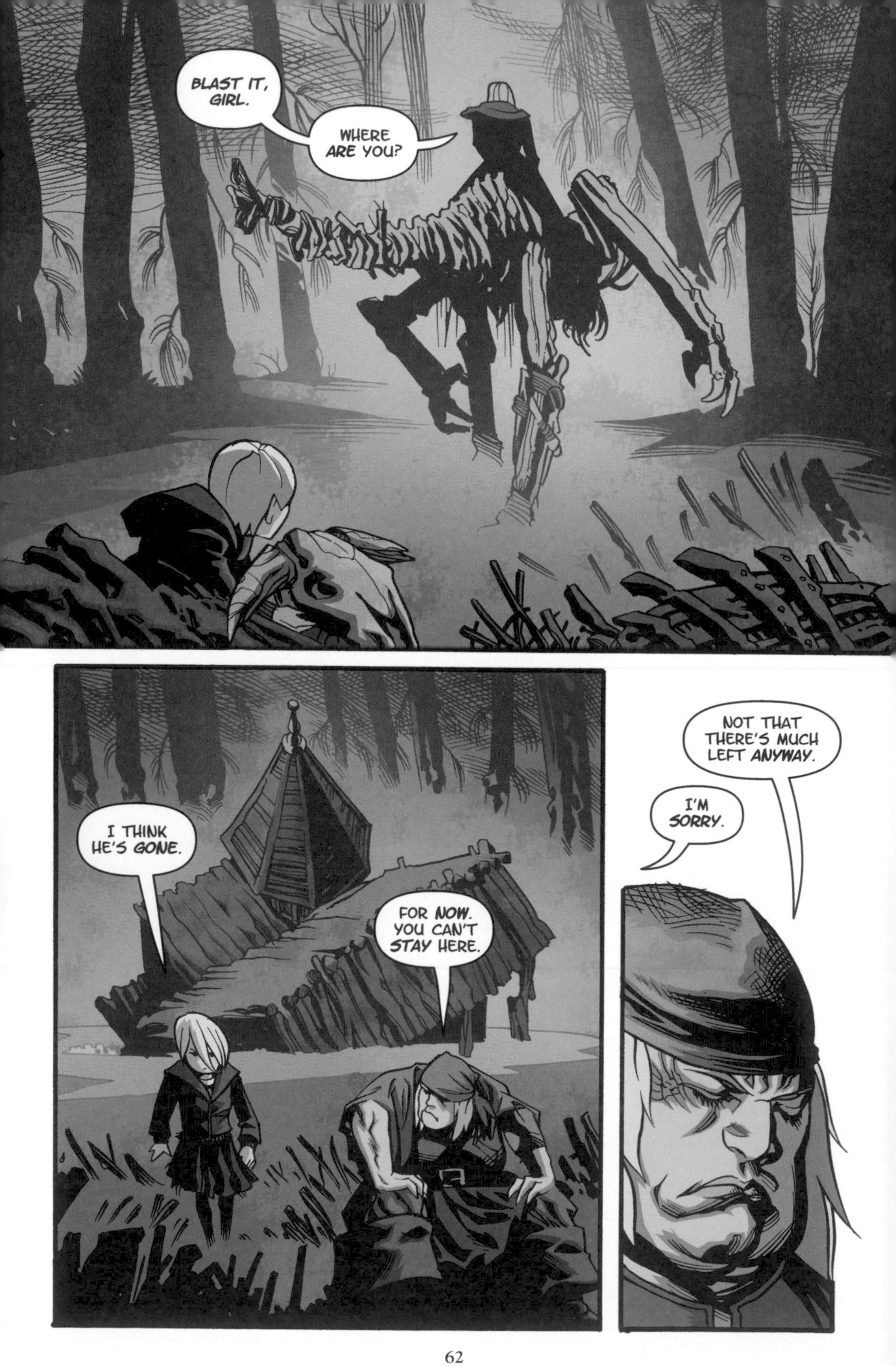
BLAST IT, GIRL.
WHERE ARE YOU?
I THINK HE'S GONE.
FOR NOW. YOU CAN'T STAY HERE.
NOT THAT THERE'S MUCH LEFT ANYWAY.
I'M SORRY.

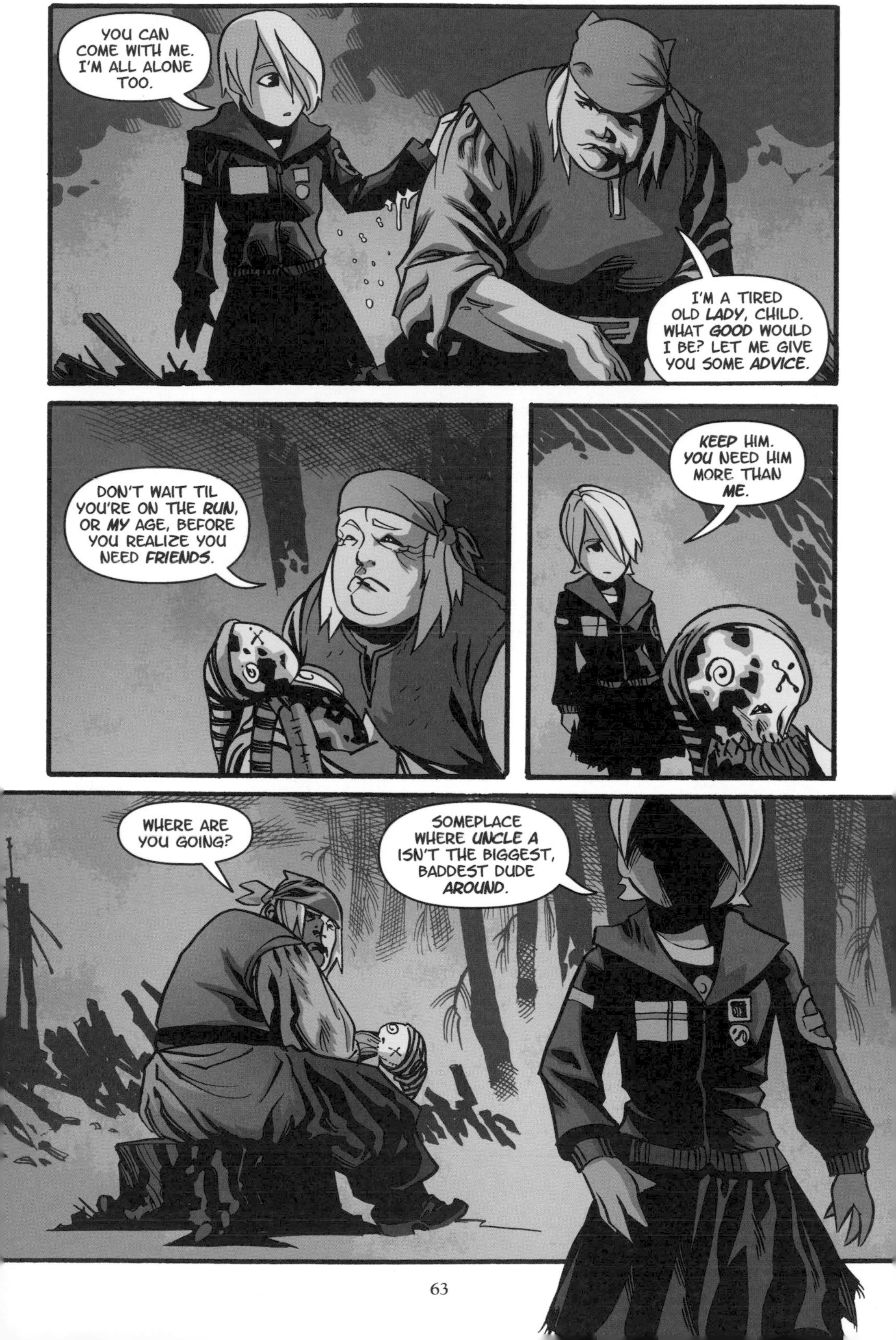
YOU CAN COME WITH ME. I'M ALL ALONE TOO.
I'M A TIRED OLD LADY, CHILD. WHAT GOOD WOULD I BE? LET ME GIVE YOU SOME ADVICE.
DON'T WAIT TIL YOU'RE ON THE RUN, OR MY AGE, BEFORE YOU REALIZE YOU NEED FRIENDS.
KEEP HIM. YOU NEED HIM MORE THAN ME.
WHERE ARE YOU GOING?
SOMEPLACE WHERE UNCLE A ISN'T THE BIGGEST, BADDEST DUDE AROUND.

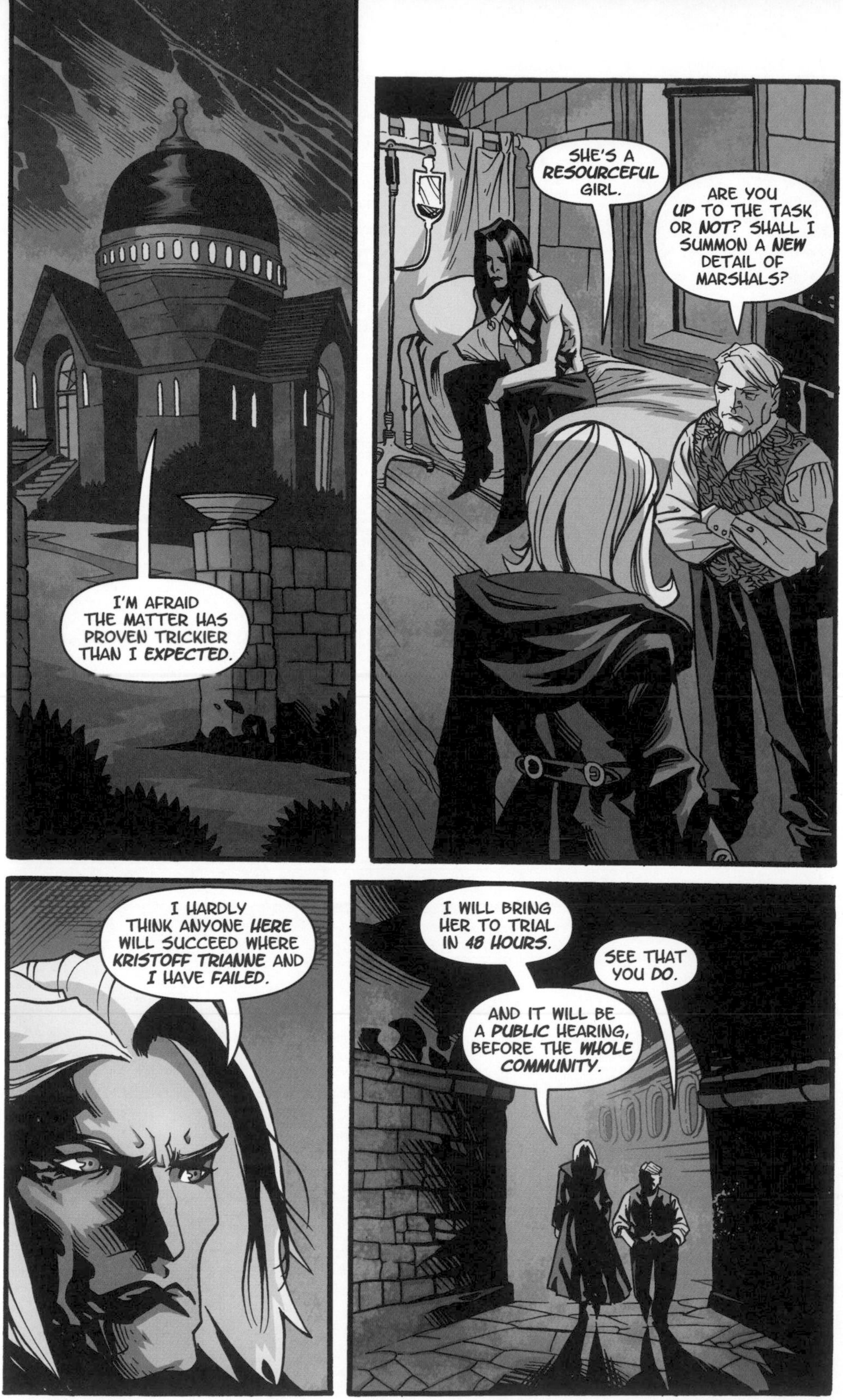
I'M AFRAID THE MATTER HAS PROVEN TRICKIER THAN I EXPECTED.
SHE'S A RESOURCEFUL GIRL.
ARE YOU UP TO THE TASK OR NOT? SHALL I SUMMON A NEW DETAIL OF MARSHALS?
I HARDLY THINK ANYONE HERE WILL SUCCEED WHERE KRISTOFF TRIANNE AND I HAVE FAILED.
I WILL BRING HER TO TRIAL IN 48 HOURS.
AND IT WILL BE A PUBLIC HEARING, BEFORE THE WHOLE COMMUNITY.
SEE THAT YOU DO.

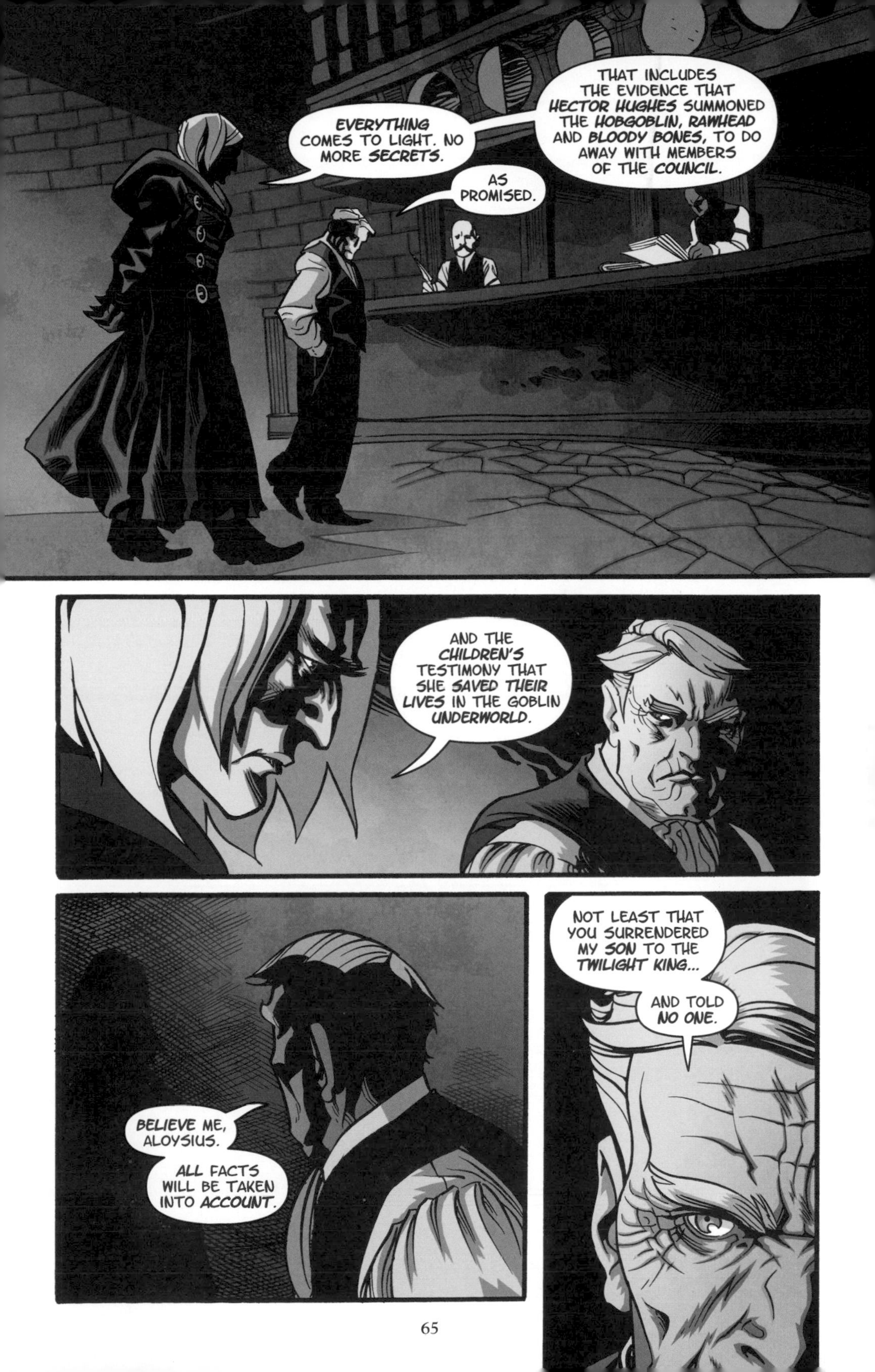
EVERYTHING COMES TO LIGHT. NO MORE SECRETS.
THAT INCLUDES THE EVIDENCE THAT HECTOR HUGHES SUMMONED THE HOBGOBLIN, RAWHEAD AND BLOODY BONES, TO DO AWAY WITH MEMBERS OF THE COUNCIL.
AS PROMISED.
AND THE CHILDREN'S TESTIMONY THAT SHE SAVED THEIR LIVES IN THE GOBLIN UNDERWORLD.
NOT LEAST THAT YOU SURRENDERED MY SON TO THE TWILIGHT KING...
AND TOLD NO ONE.
BELIEVE ME, ALOYSIUS.
ALL FACTS WILL BE TAKEN INTO ACCOUNT.

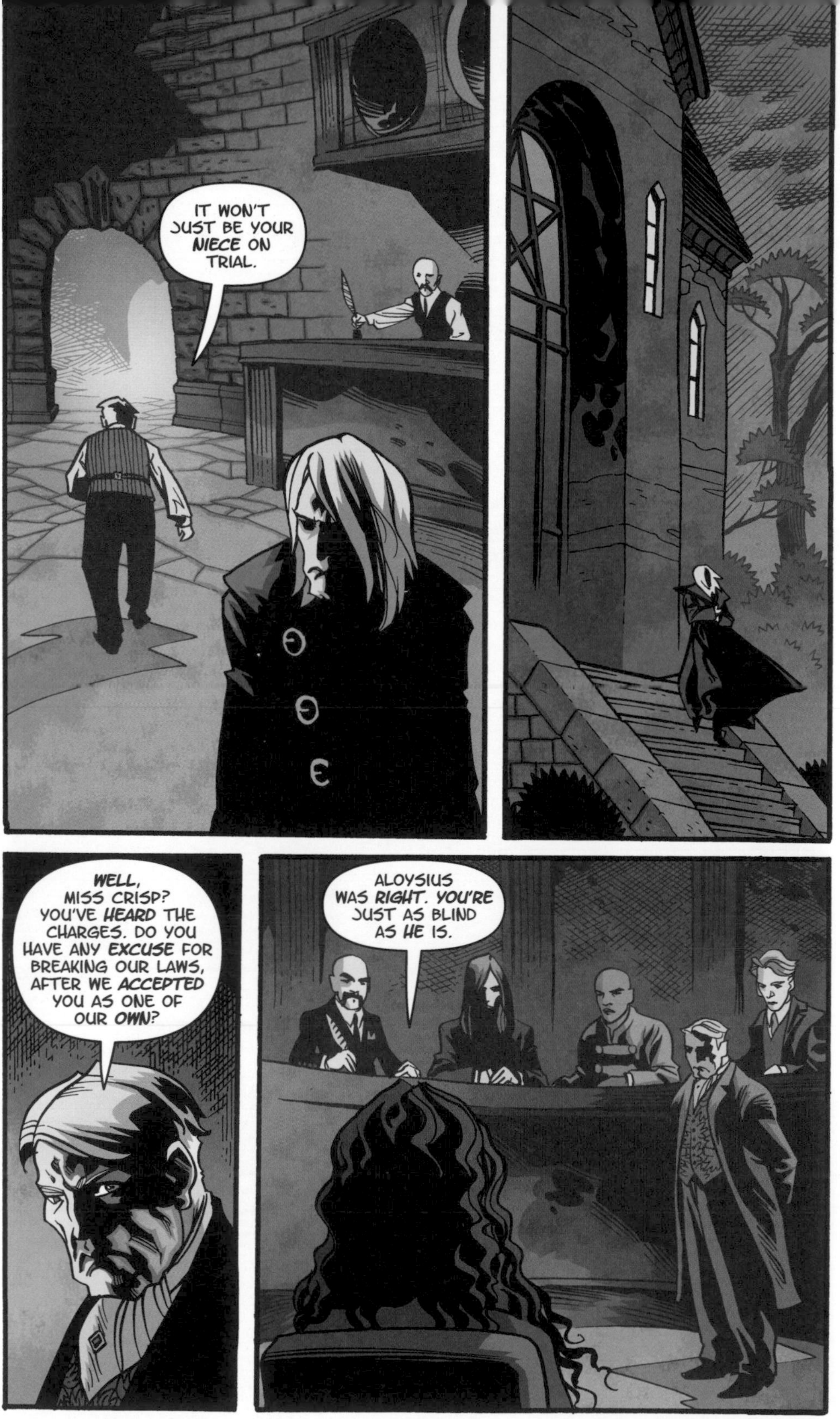
IT WON'T JUST BE YOUR NIECE ON TRIAL.
WELL, MISS CRISP? YOU'VE HEARD THE CHARGES. DO YOU HAVE ANY EXCUSE FOR BREAKING OUR LAWS, AFTER WE ACCEPTED YOU AS ONE OF OUR OWN?
ALOYSIUS WAS RIGHT. YOU'RE JUST AS BLIND AS HE IS.

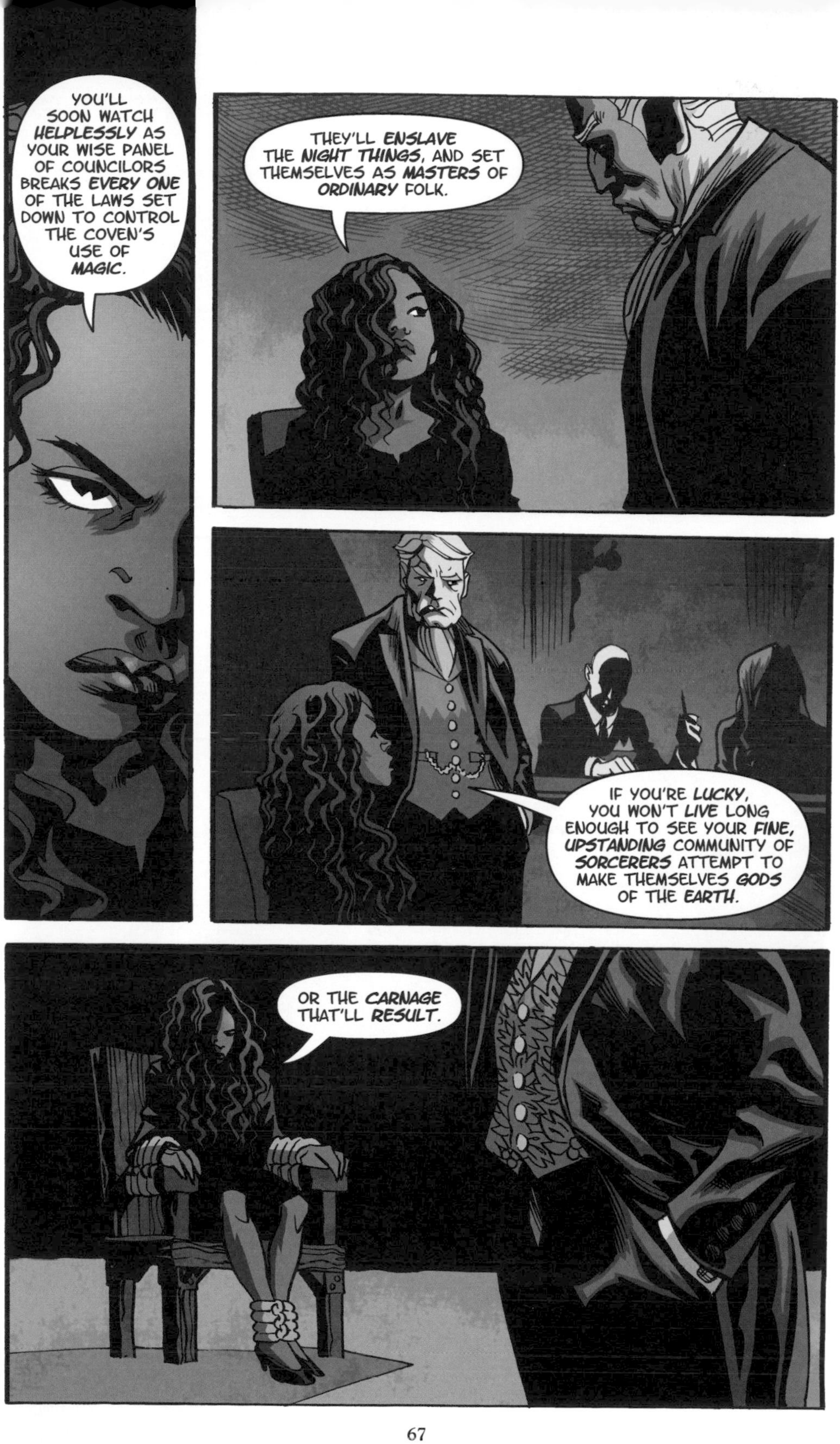
YOU'LL SOON WATCH HELPLESSLY AS YOUR WISE PANEL OF COUNCILORS BREAKS EVERY ONE OF THE LAWS SET DOWN TO CONTROL THE COVEN'S USE OF MAGIC.
THEY'LL ENSLAVE THE NIGHT THINGS, AND SET THEMSELVES AS MASTERS OF ORDINARY FOLK.
IF YOU'RE LUCKY, YOU WON'T LIVE LONG ENOUGH TO SEE YOUR FINE, UPSTANDING COMMUNITY OF SORCERERS ATTEMPT TO MAKE THEMSELVES GODS OF THE EARTH.
OR THE CARNAGE THAT'LL RESULT.

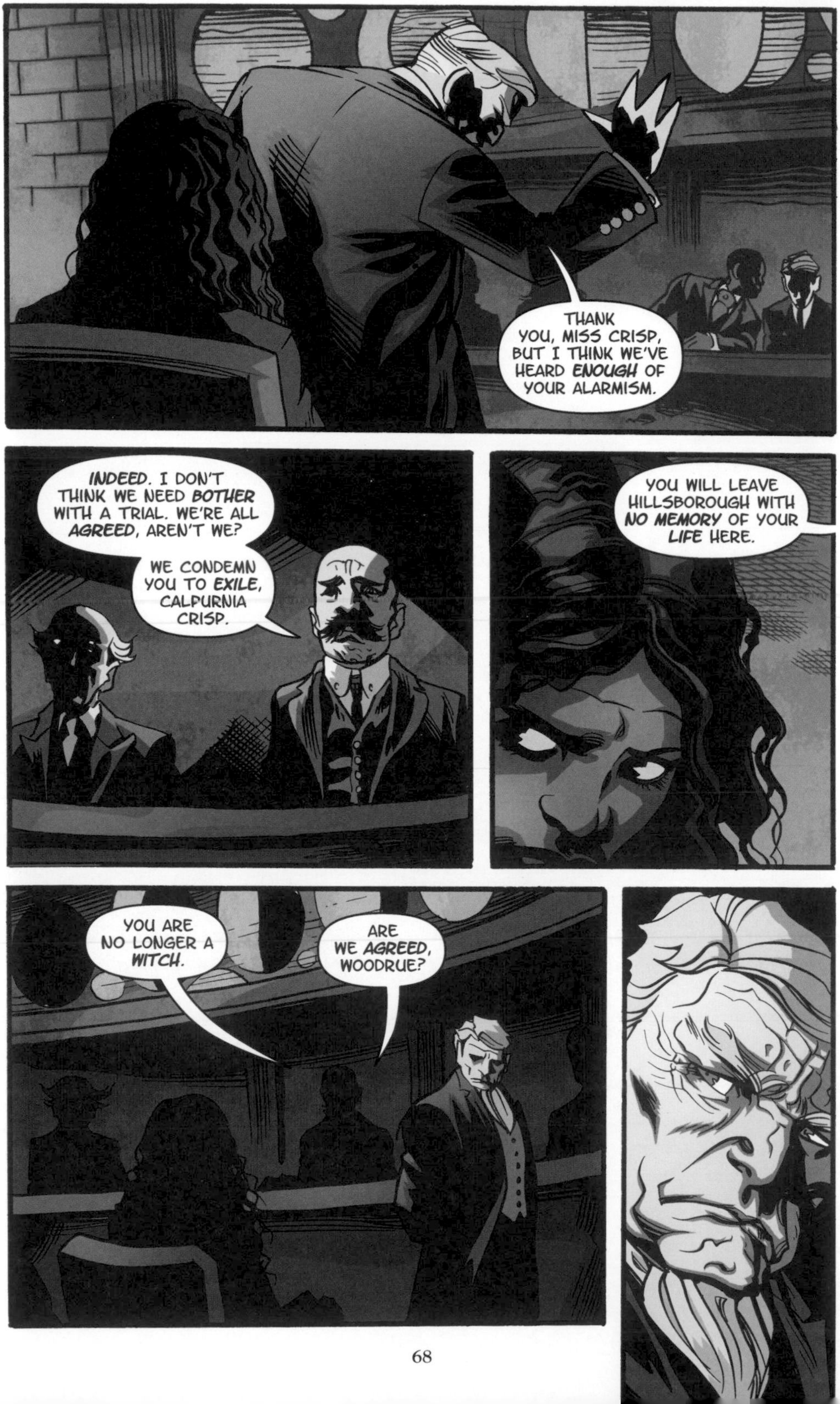
THANK YOU, MISS CRISP, BUT I THINK WE'VE HEARD ENOUGH OF YOUR ALARMISM.
INDEED. I DON'T THINK WE NEED BOTHER WITH A TRIAL. WE'RE ALL AGREED, AREN'T WE?
WE CONDEMN YOU TO EXILE, CALPURNIA CRISP.
YOU WILL LEAVE HILLSBOROUGH WITH NO MEMORY OF YOUR LIFE HERE.
YOU ARE NO LONGER A WITCH.
ARE WE AGREED, WOODRUE?

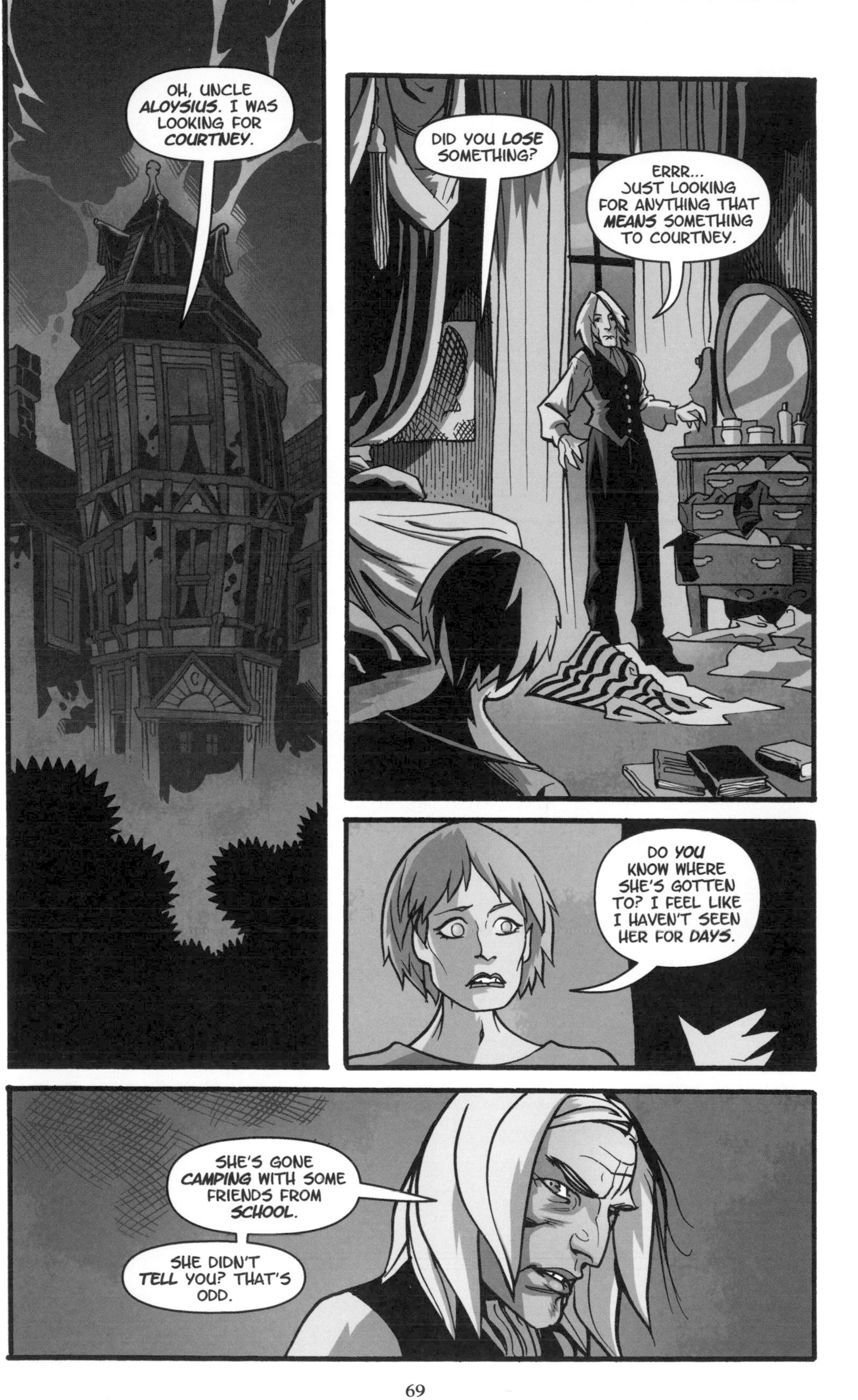

OH, UNCLE ALOYSIUS. I WAS LOOKING FOR COURTNEY.
DID YOU LOSE SOMETHING?
ERRR... JUST LOOKING FOR ANYTHING THAT MEANS SOMETHING TO COURTNEY.
DO YOU KNOW WHERE SHE'S GOTTEN TO? I FEEL LIKE I HAVEN'T SEEN HER FOR DAYS.
SHE'S GONE CAMPING WITH SOME FRIENDS FROM SCHOOL.
SHE DIDN'T TELL YOU? THAT'S ODD.

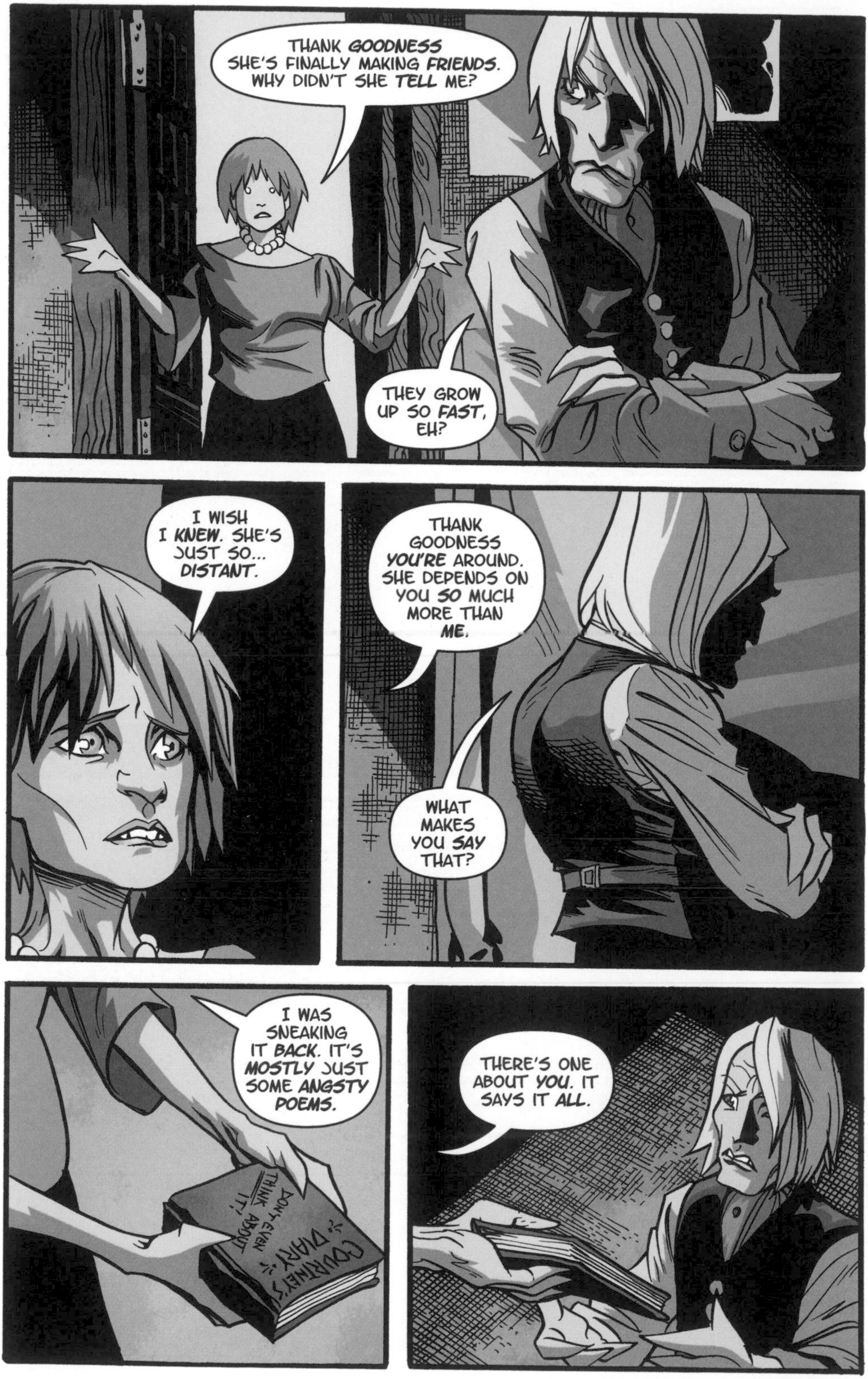
THANK GOODNESS SHE'S FINALLY MAKING FRIENDS. WHY DIDN'T SHE TELL ME?
THEY GROW UP SO FAST, EH?
I WISH I KNEW. SHE'S JUST SO... DISTANT.
THANK GOODNESS YOU'RE AROUND. SHE DEPENDS ON YOU SO MUCH MORE THAN ME.
WHAT MAKES YOU SAY THAT?
I WAS SNEAKING IT BACK. IT'S MOSTLY JUST SOME ANGSTY POEMS.
COURTNEY'S DIARY
DON'T EVEN THINK ABOUT IT!
THERE'S ONE ABOUT YOU. IT SAYS IT ALL.

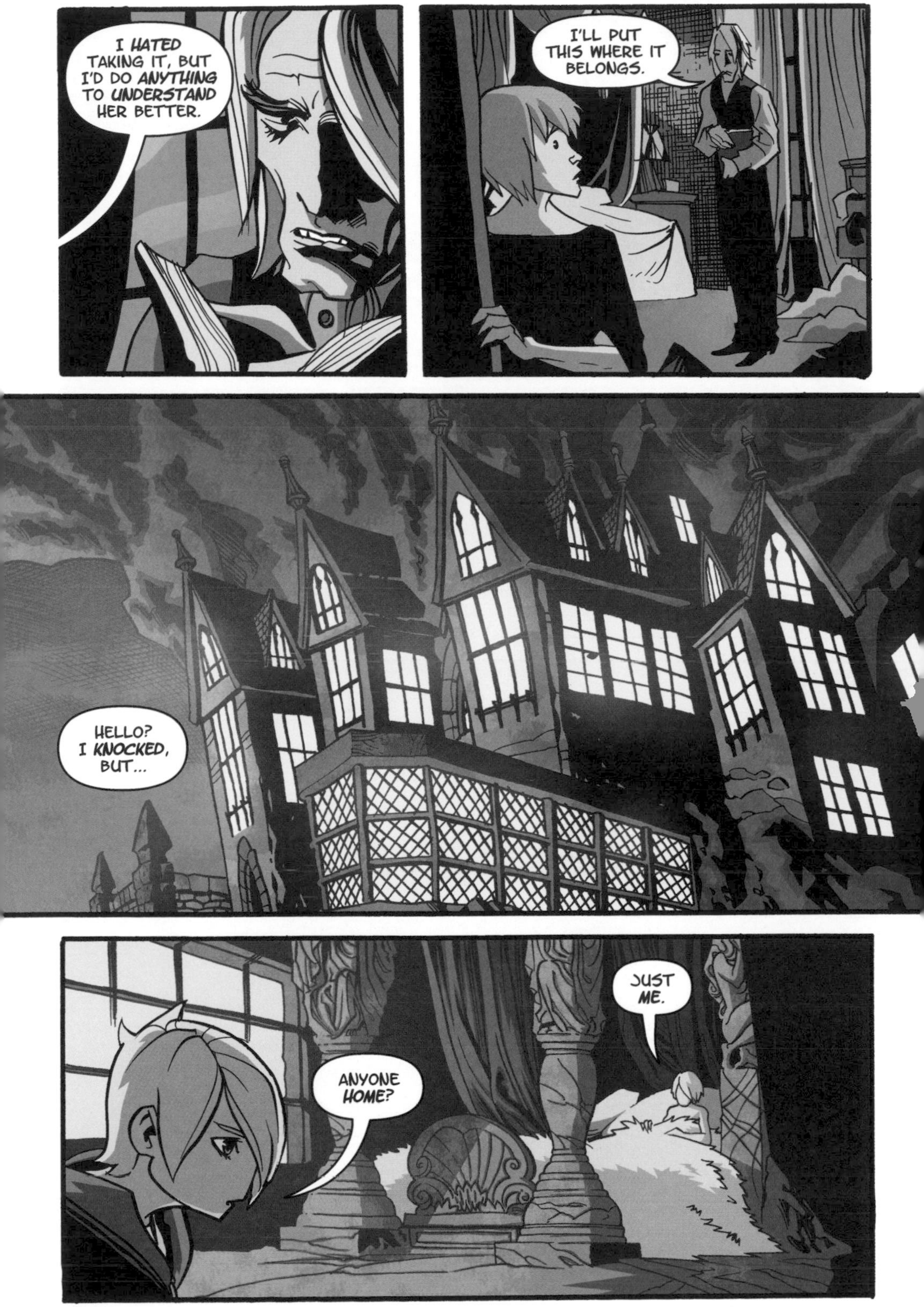
I HATED TAKING IT, BUT I'D DO ANYTHING TO UNDERSTAND HER BETTER.
I'LL PUT THIS WHERE IT BELONGS.
HELLO? I KNOCKED, BUT...
ANYONE HOME?
JUST ME.

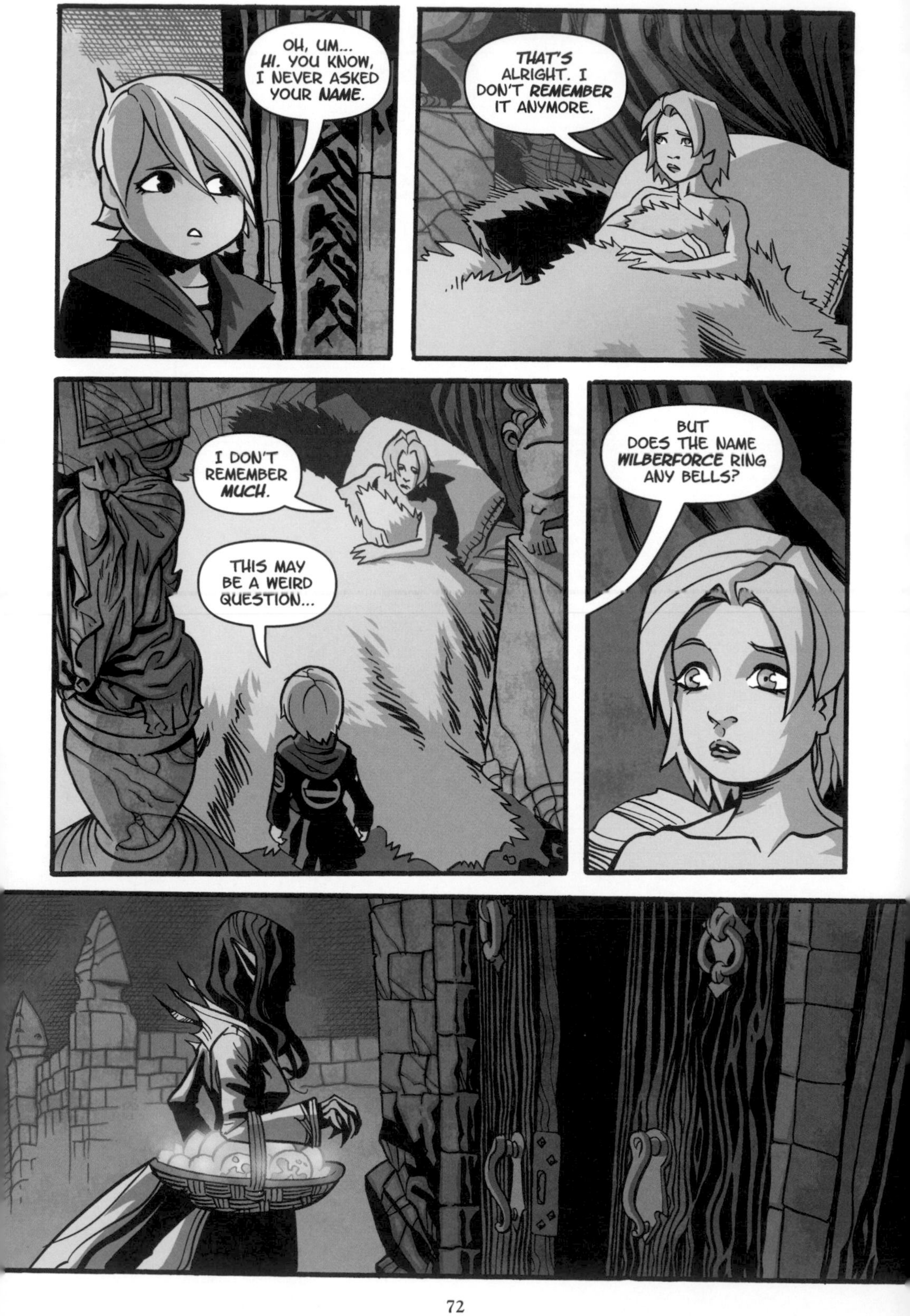
OH, UM... HI. YOU KNOW, I NEVER ASKED YOUR NAME.
THAT'S ALRIGHT. I DON'T REMEMBER IT ANYMORE.
I DON'T REMEMBER MUCH.
THIS MAY BE A WEIRD QUESTION...
BUT DOES THE NAME WILBERFORCE RING ANY BELLS?

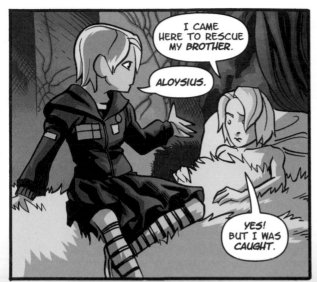

I CAME HERE TO RESCUE MY BROTHER.

ALOYSIUS.

YES! BUT I WAS CAUGHT.

IT'S ALL RIGHT *THERE*. HOW COULD I HAVE *FORGOTTEN*? THE DUCHESS GAVE US A *CHOICE*...

"...TO CONDEMN OURSELVES..."

LET HIM GO. I'LL STAY WITH YOU.

AND *YOU*, MORTAL? WHAT IS *YOUR* CHOICE?

"...OR EACH OTHER."

I CHOOSE...

...FOR *WILL* TO STAY.

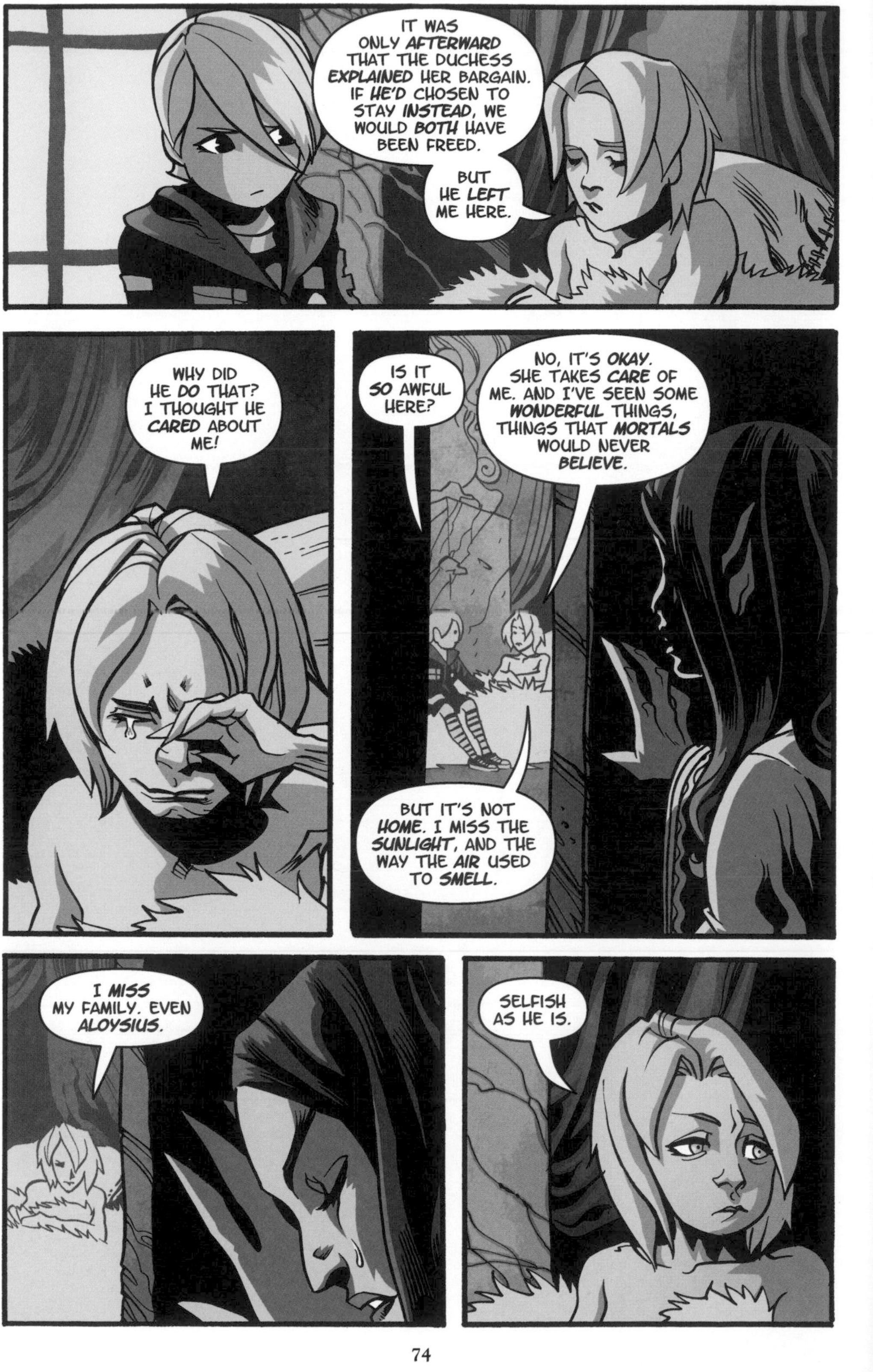
IT WAS ONLY AFTERWARD THAT THE DUCHESS EXPLAINED HER BARGAIN. IF HE'D CHOSEN TO STAY INSTEAD, WE WOULD BOTH HAVE BEEN FREED.
BUT HE LEFT ME HERE.
WHY DID HE DO THAT? I THOUGHT HE CARED ABOUT ME!
IS IT SO AWFUL HERE?
NO, IT'S OKAY. SHE TAKES CARE OF ME. AND I'VE SEEN SOME WONDERFUL THINGS, THINGS THAT MORTALS WOULD NEVER BELIEVE.
BUT IT'S NOT HOME. I MISS THE SUNLIGHT, AND THE WAY THE AIR USED TO SMELL.
I MISS MY FAMILY. EVEN ALOYSIUS.
SELFISH AS HE IS.

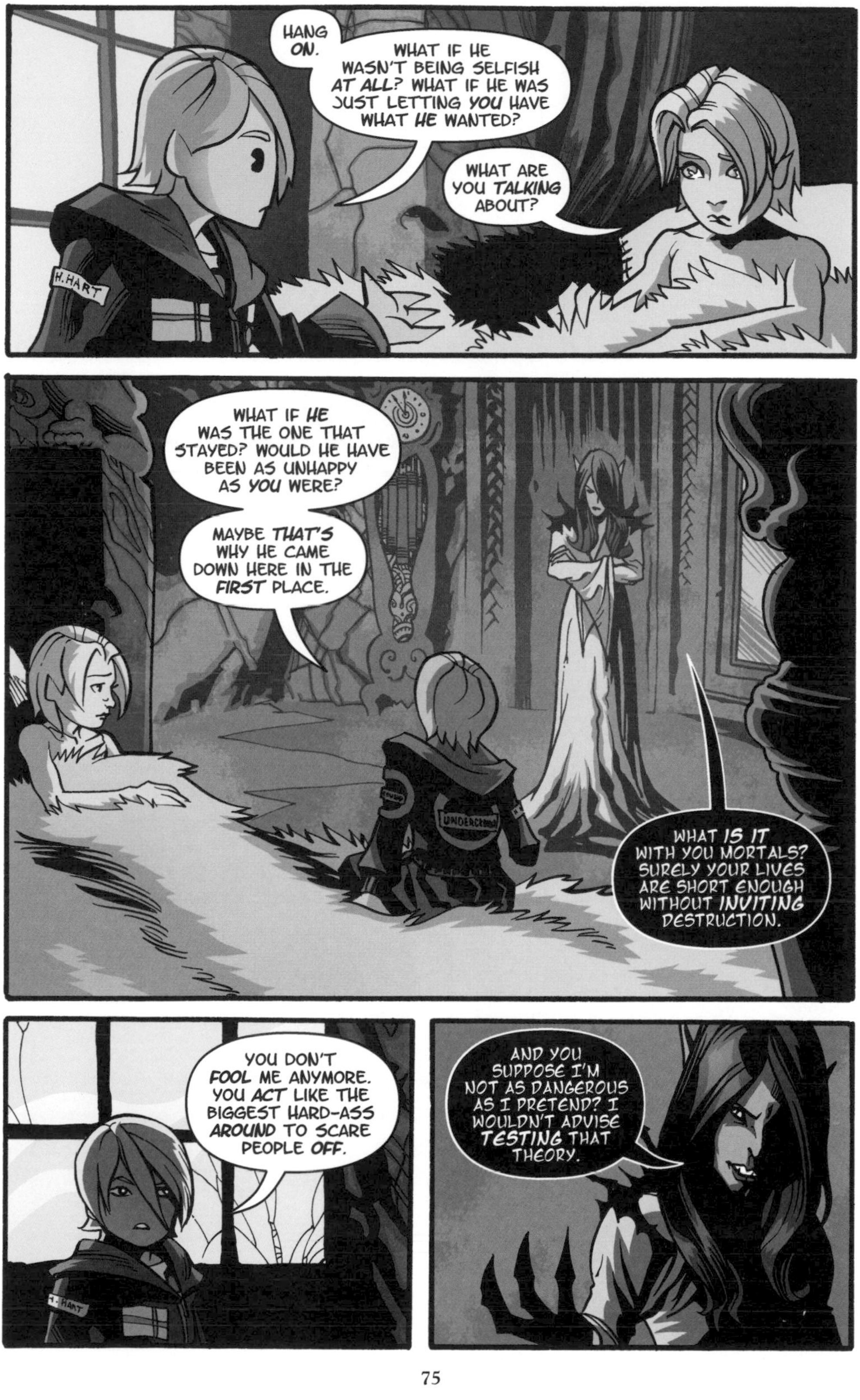
HANG ON.
WHAT IF HE WASN'T BEING SELFISH AT ALL? WHAT IF HE WAS JUST LETTING YOU HAVE WHAT HE WANTED?
WHAT ARE YOU TALKING ABOUT?
H.HART
WHAT IF HE WAS THE ONE THAT STAYED? WOULD HE HAVE BEEN AS UNHAPPY AS YOU WERE?
MAYBE THAT'S WHY HE CAME DOWN HERE IN THE FIRST PLACE.
WHAT IS IT WITH YOU MORTALS? SURELY YOUR LIVES ARE SHORT ENOUGH WITHOUT INVITING DESTRUCTION.
YOU DON'T FOOL ME ANYMORE. YOU ACT LIKE THE BIGGEST HARD-ASS AROUND TO SCARE PEOPLE OFF.
AND YOU SUPPOSE I'M NOT AS DANGEROUS AS I PRETEND? I WOULDN'T ADVISE TESTING THAT THEORY.

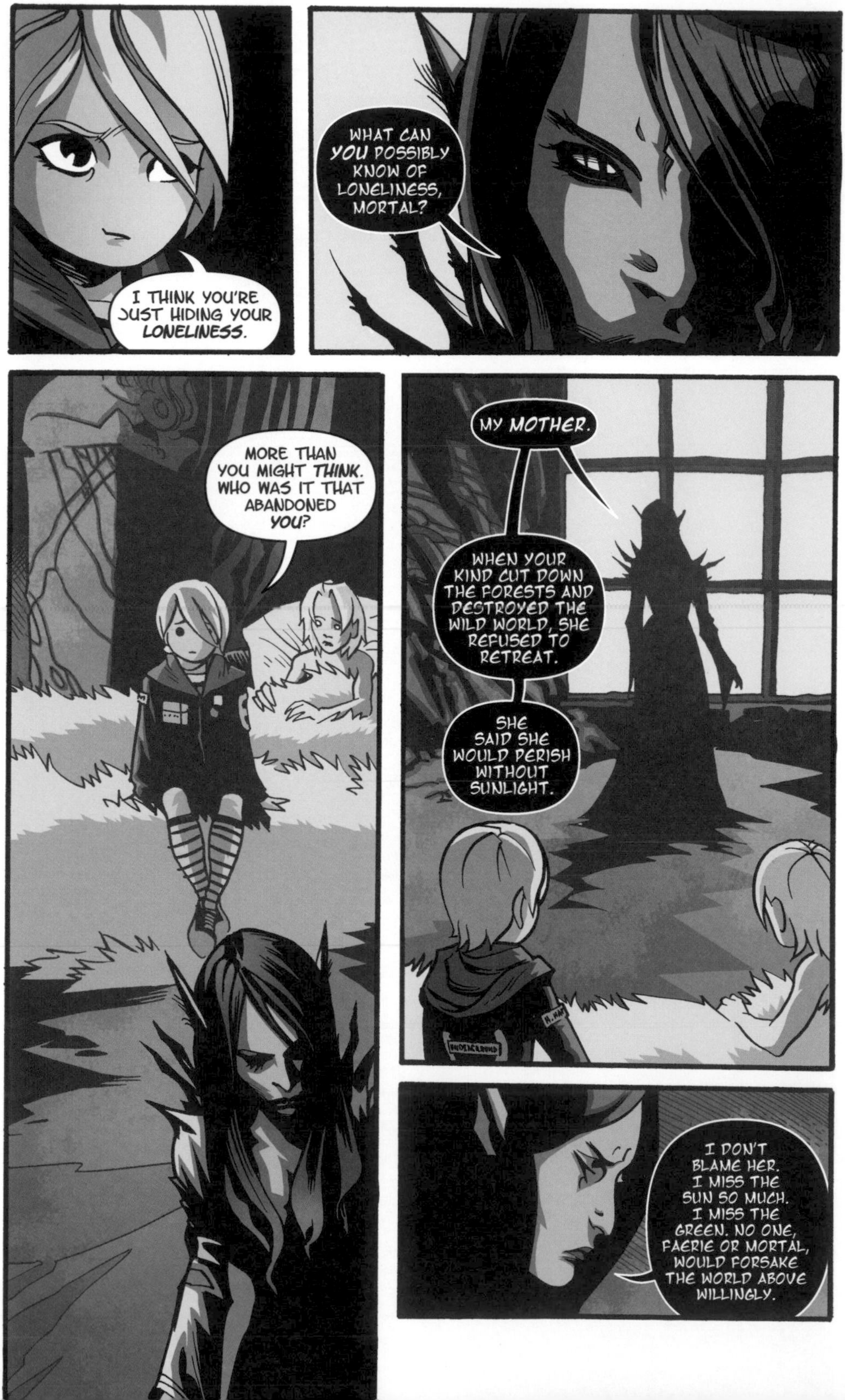
I THINK YOU'RE JUST HIDING YOUR LONELINESS.
WHAT CAN YOU POSSIBLY KNOW OF LONELINESS, MORTAL?
MORE THAN YOU MIGHT THINK. WHO WAS IT THAT ABANDONED YOU?
MY MOTHER.
WHEN YOUR KIND CUT DOWN THE FORESTS AND DESTROYED THE WILD WORLD, SHE REFUSED TO RETREAT.
SHE SAID SHE WOULD PERISH WITHOUT SUNLIGHT.
I DON'T BLAME HER. I MISS THE SUN SO MUCH. I MISS THE GREEN. NO ONE, FAERIE OR MORTAL, WOULD FORSAKE THE WORLD ABOVE WILLINGLY.

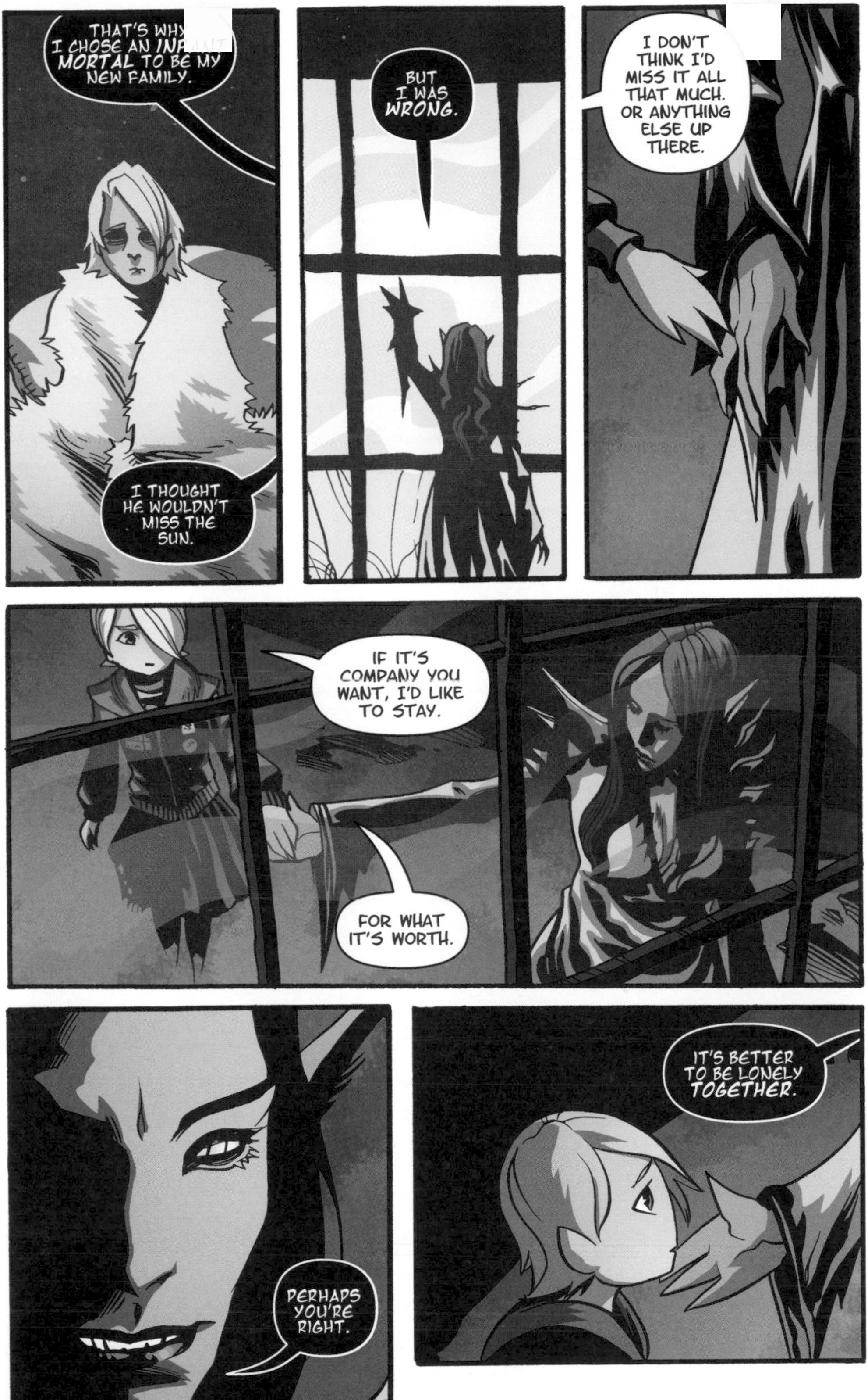
THAT'S WHY I CHOSE AN INFANT MORTAL TO BE MY NEW FAMILY.
I THOUGHT HE WOULDN'T MISS THE SUN.
BUT I WAS WRONG.
I DON'T THINK I'D MISS IT ALL THAT MUCH. OR ANYTHING ELSE UP THERE.
IF IT'S COMPANY YOU WANT, I'D LIKE TO STAY.
FOR WHAT IT'S WORTH.
PERHAPS YOU'RE RIGHT.
IT'S BETTER TO BE LONELY TOGETHER.

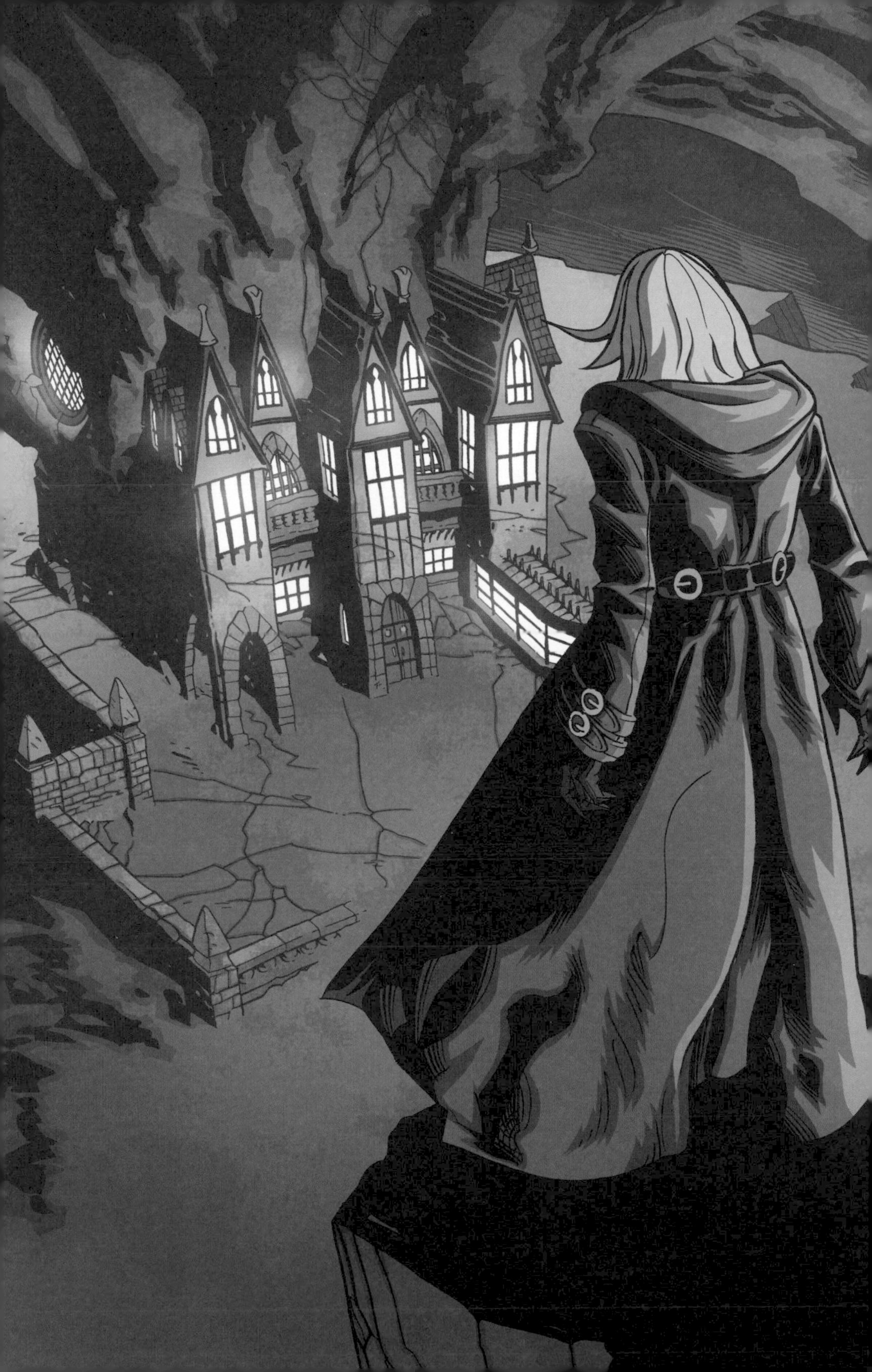

Chapter Four

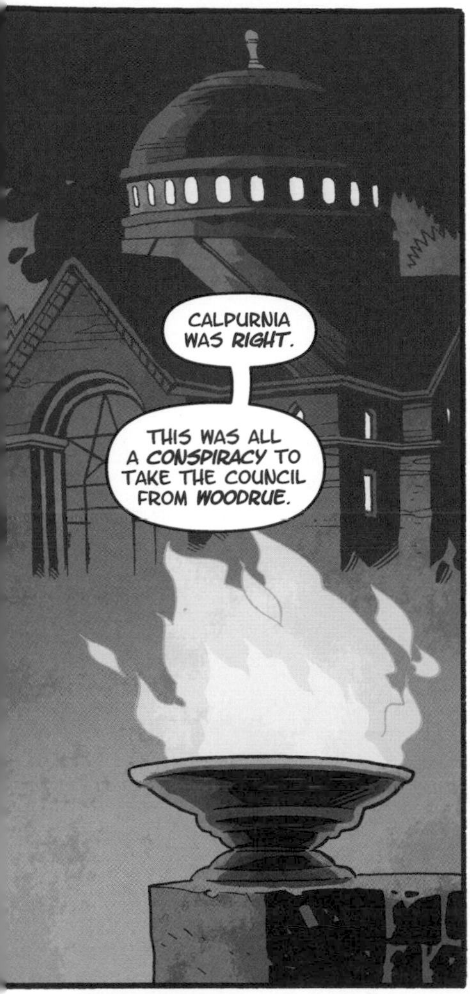
CALPURNIA WAS RIGHT.
THIS WAS ALL A CONSPIRACY TO TAKE THE COUNCIL FROM WOODRUE.

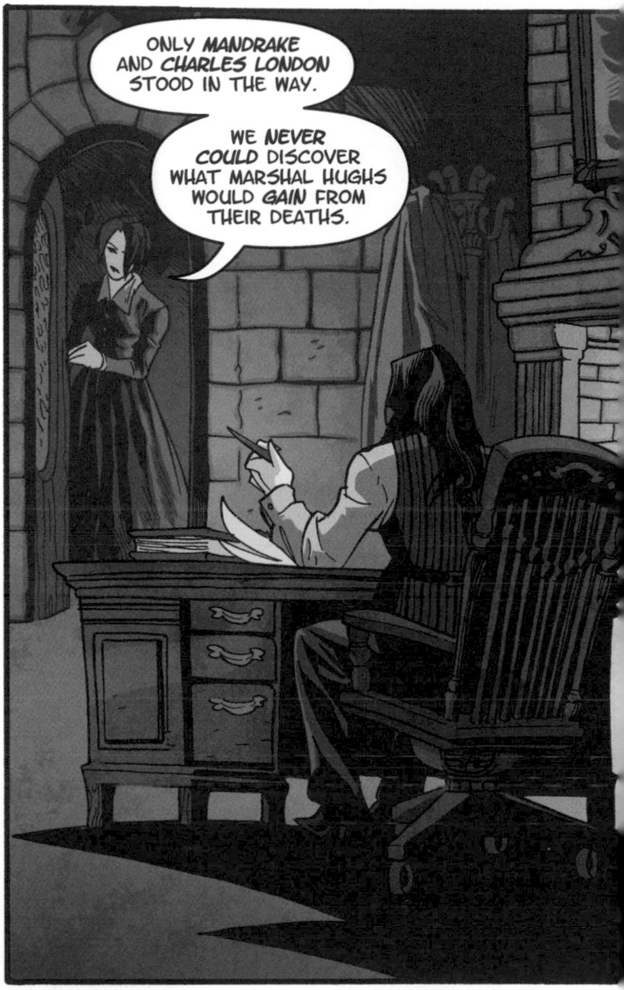
ONLY MANDRAKE AND CHARLES LONDON STOOD IN THE WAY.
WE NEVER COULD DISCOVER WHAT MARSHAL HUGHS WOULD GAIN FROM THEIR DEATHS.

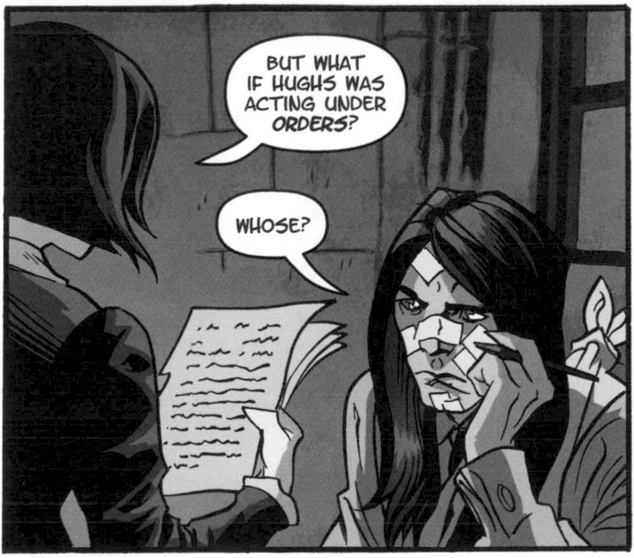
BUT WHAT IF HUGHS WAS ACTING UNDER ORDERS?
WHOSE?

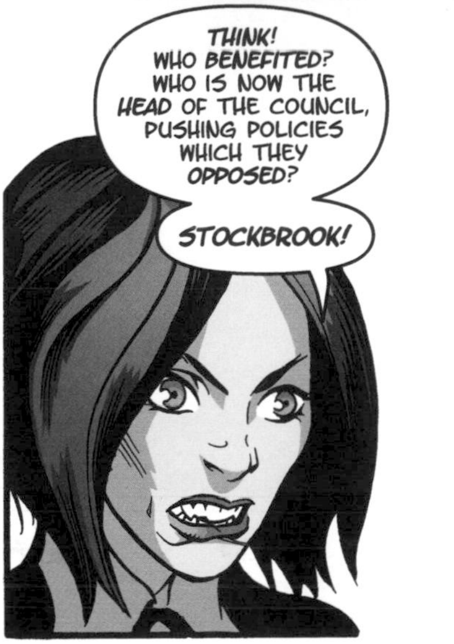
THINK! WHO BENEFITED? WHO IS NOW THE HEAD OF THE COUNCIL, PUSHING POLICIES WHICH THEY OPPOSED?
STOCKBROOK!

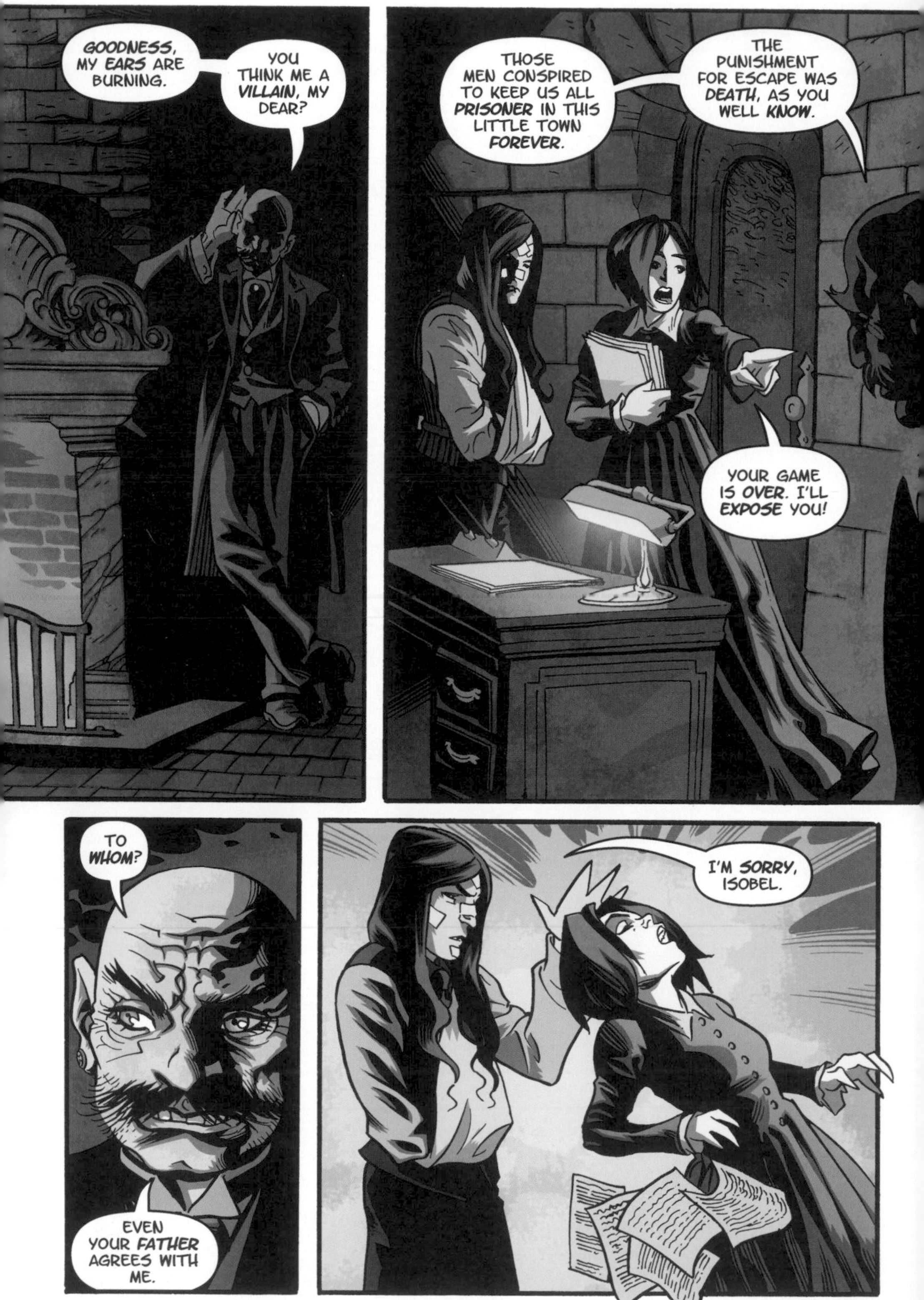
GOODNESS, MY EARS ARE BURNING.
YOU THINK ME A VILLAIN, MY DEAR?
THOSE MEN CONSPIRED TO KEEP US ALL PRISONER IN THIS LITTLE TOWN FOREVER.
THE PUNISHMENT FOR ESCAPE WAS DEATH, AS YOU WELL KNOW.
YOUR GAME IS OVER. I'LL EXPOSE YOU!
TO WHOM?
EVEN YOUR FATHER AGREES WITH ME.
I'M SORRY, ISOBEL.

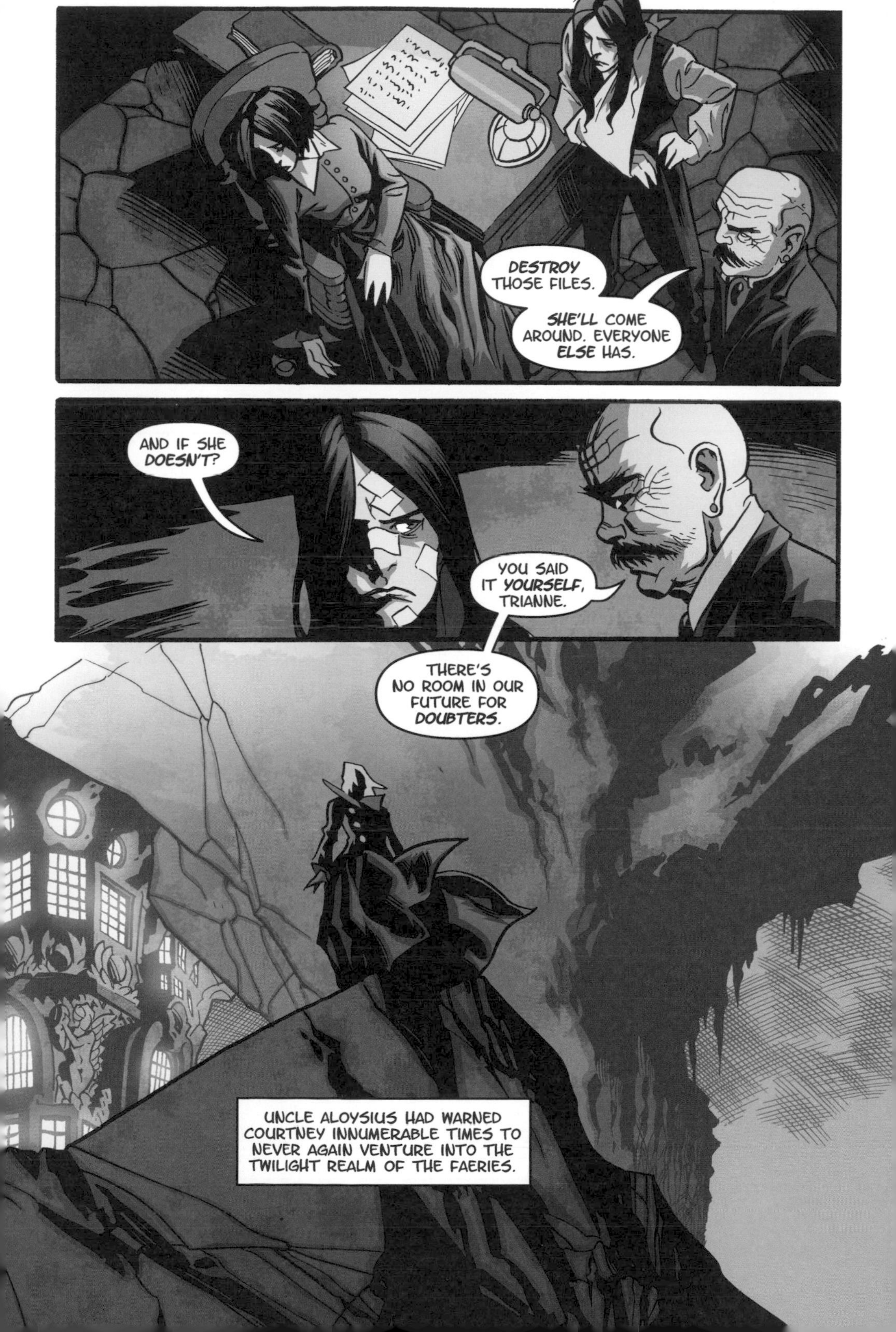
DESTROY THOSE FILES.
SHE'LL COME AROUND. EVERYONE ELSE HAS.
AND IF SHE DOESN'T?
YOU SAID IT YOURSELF, TRIANNE.
THERE'S NO ROOM IN OUR FUTURE FOR DOUBTERS.
UNCLE ALOYSIUS HAD WARNED COURTNEY INNUMERABLE TIMES TO NEVER AGAIN VENTURE INTO THE TWILIGHT REALM OF THE FAERIES.

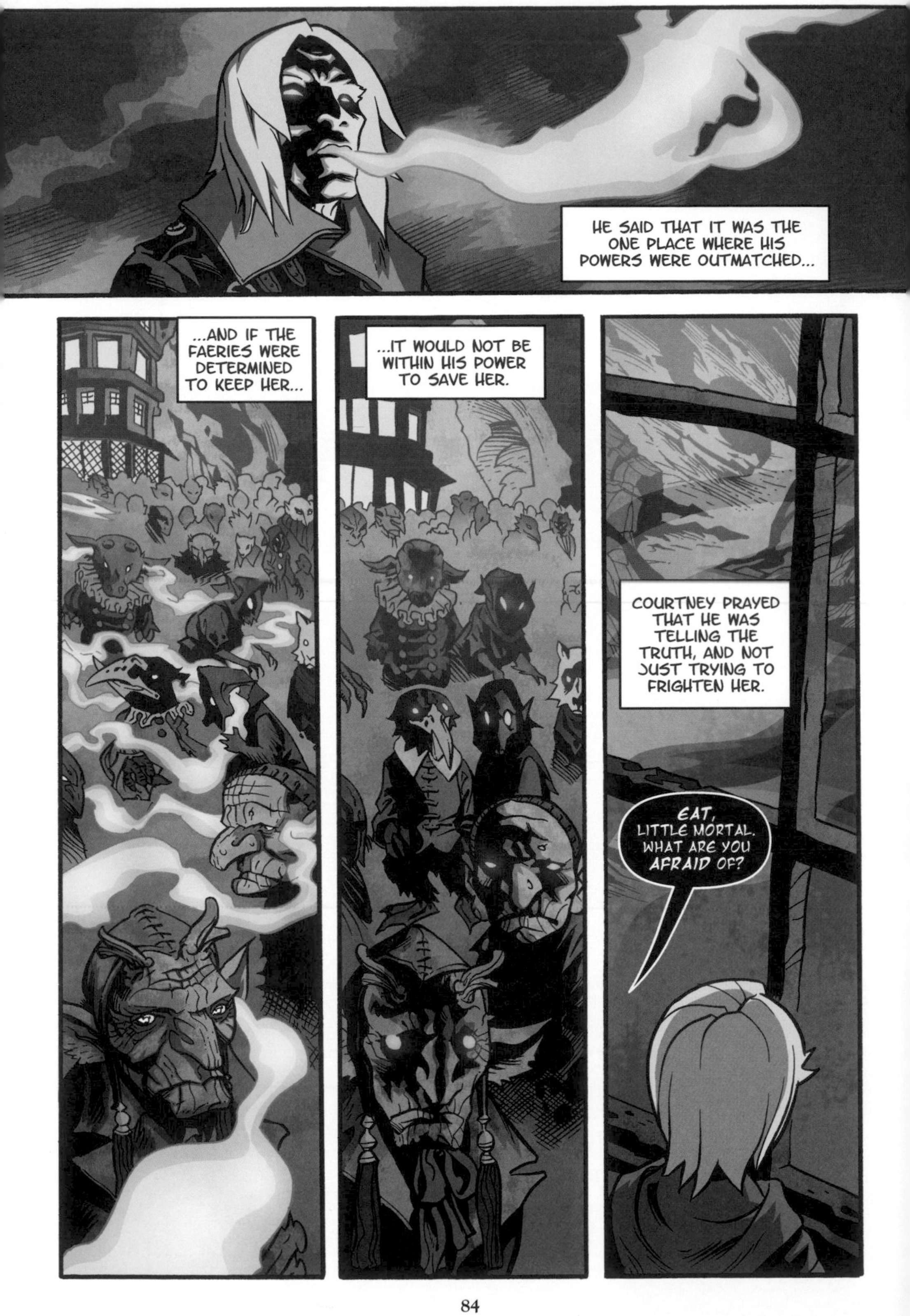
HE SAID THAT IT WAS THE ONE PLACE WHERE HIS POWERS WERE OUTMATCHED...
...AND IF THE FAERIES WERE DETERMINED TO KEEP HER...
...IT WOULD NOT BE WITHIN HIS POWER TO SAVE HER.
COURTNEY PRAYED THAT HE WAS TELLING THE TRUTH, AND NOT JUST TRYING TO FRIGHTEN HER.
EAT, LITTLE MORTAL. WHAT ARE YOU AFRAID OF?

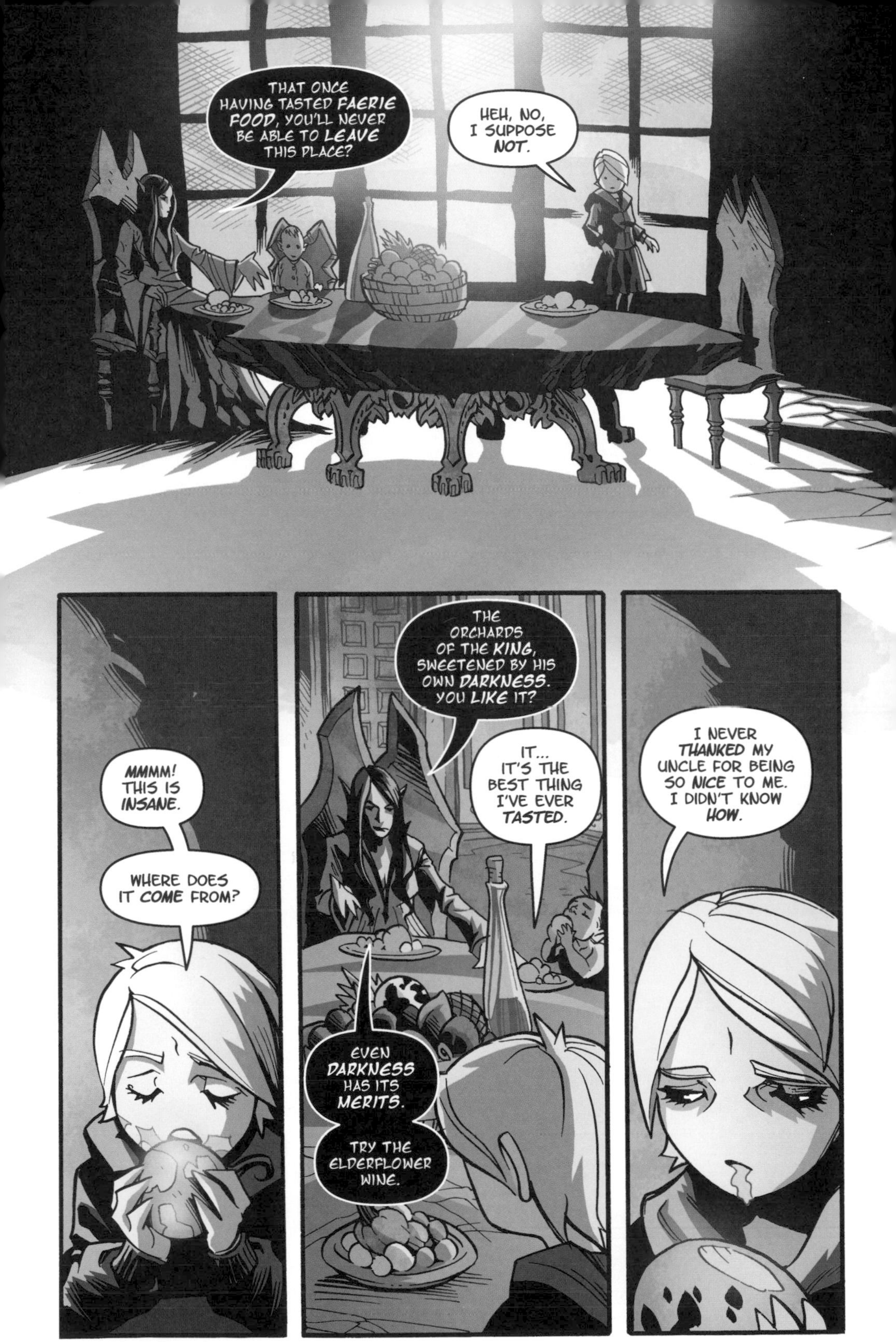
THAT ONCE HAVING TASTED FAERIE FOOD, YOU'LL NEVER BE ABLE TO LEAVE THIS PLACE?
HEH, NO, I SUPPOSE NOT.
MMMM! THIS IS INSANE.
WHERE DOES IT COME FROM?
THE ORCHARDS OF THE KING, SWEETENED BY HIS OWN DARKNESS. YOU LIKE IT?
IT... IT'S THE BEST THING I'VE EVER TASTED.
EVEN DARKNESS HAS ITS MERITS.
TRY THE ELDERFLOWER WINE.
I NEVER THANKED MY UNCLE FOR BEING SO NICE TO ME. I DIDN'T KNOW HOW.

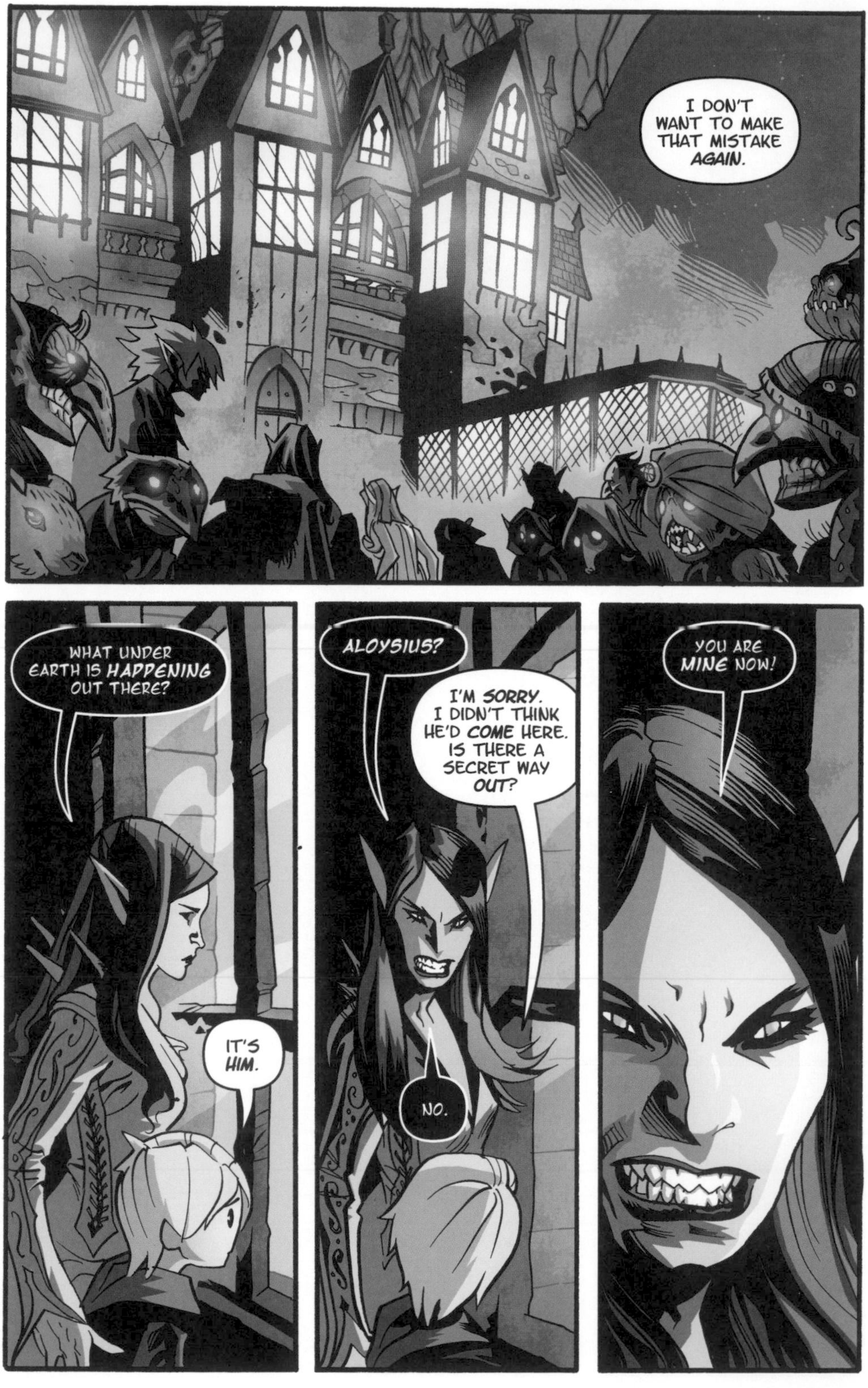
I DON'T WANT TO MAKE THAT MISTAKE AGAIN.
WHAT UNDER EARTH IS HAPPENING OUT THERE?
IT'S HIM.
ALOYSIUS?
I'M SORRY. I DIDN'T THINK HE'D COME HERE. IS THERE A SECRET WAY OUT?
NO.
YOU ARE MINE NOW!

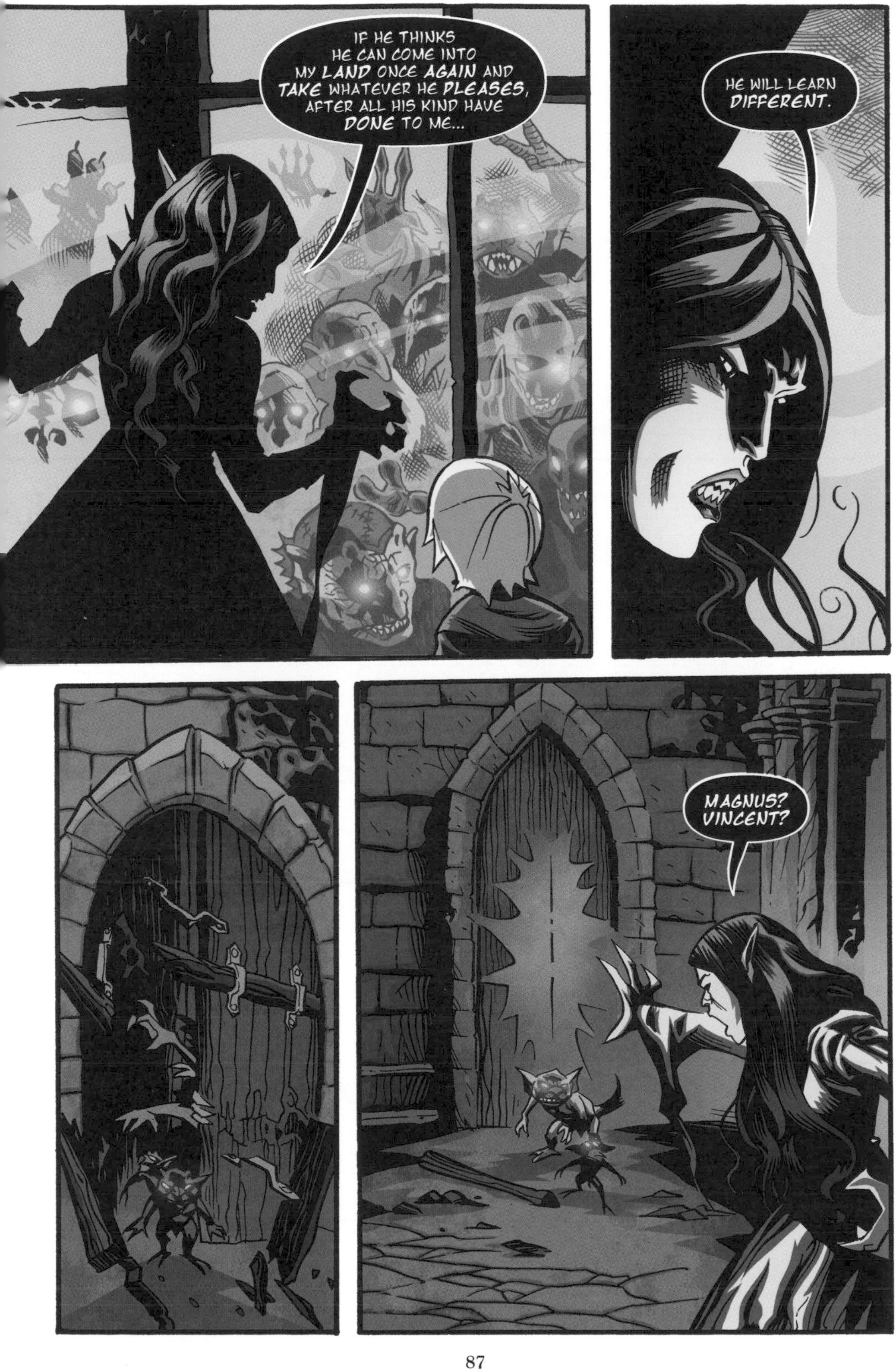
IF HE THINKS HE CAN COME INTO MY LAND ONCE AGAIN AND TAKE WHATEVER HE PLEASES, AFTER ALL HIS KIND HAVE DONE TO ME...
HE WILL LEARN DIFFERENT.
MAGNUS? VINCENT?

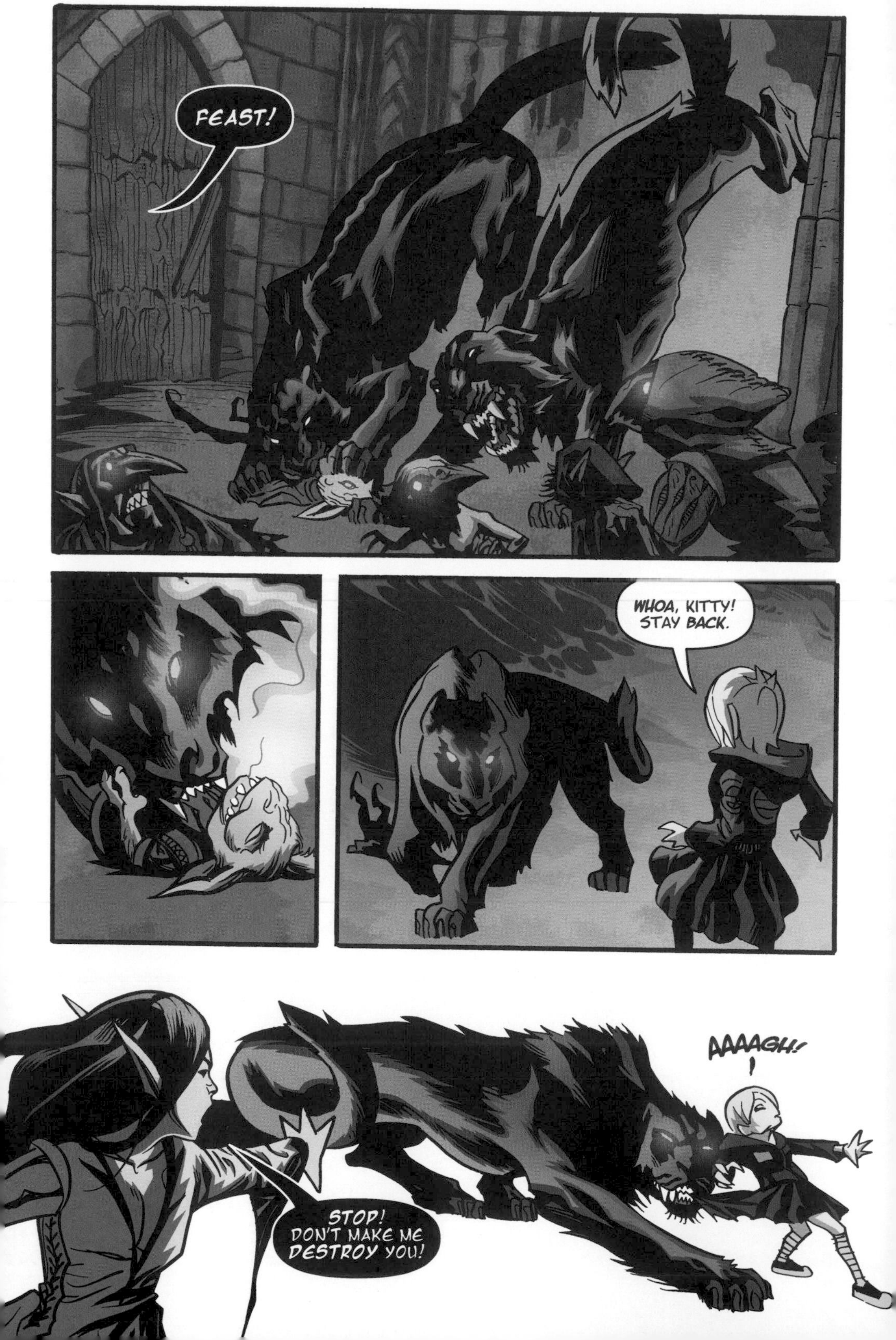
FEAST!
WHOA, KITTY! STAY BACK.
AAAAGH!
STOP! DON'T MAKE ME DESTROY YOU!

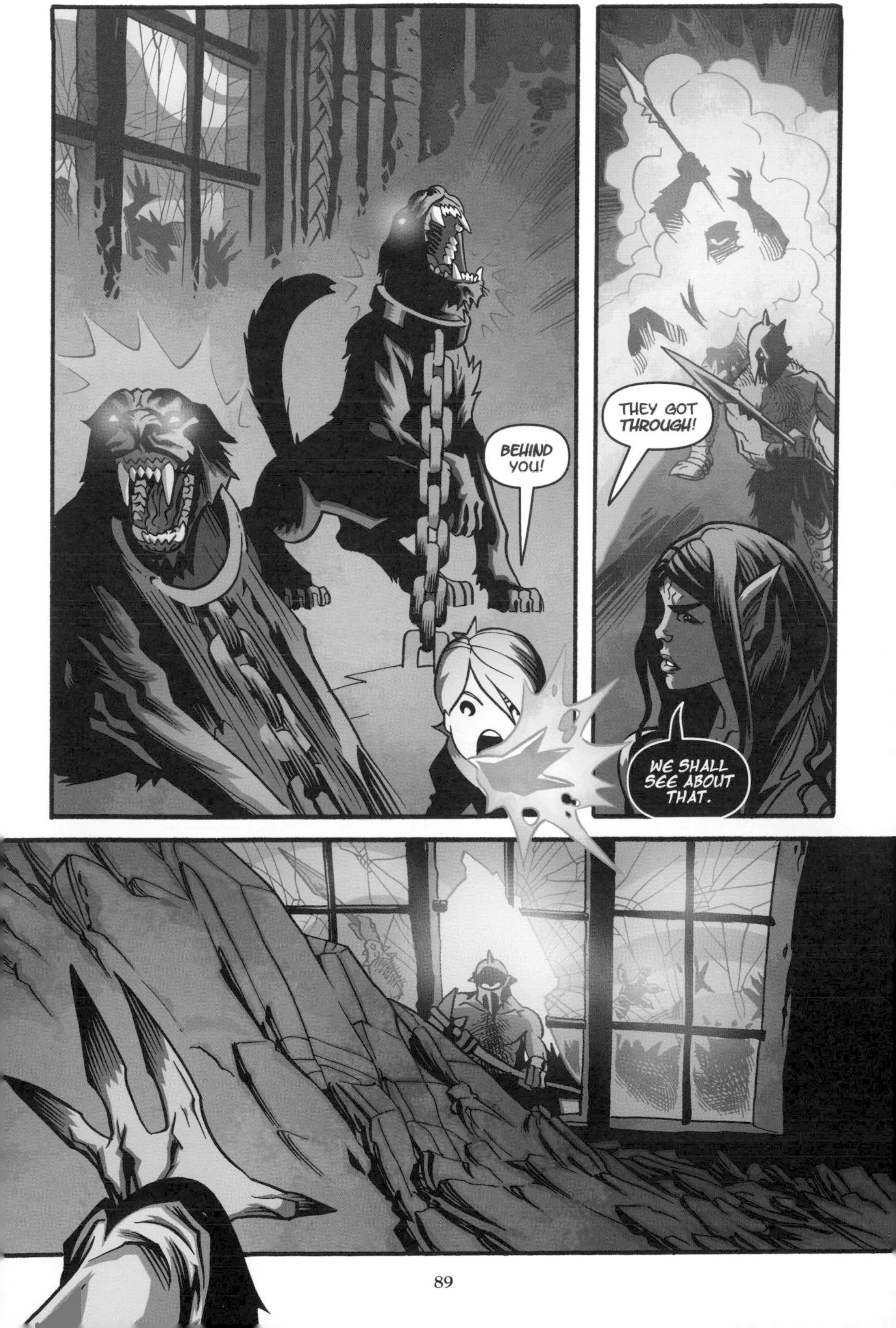
BEHIND YOU!
THEY GOT THROUGH!
WE SHALL SEE ABOUT THAT.

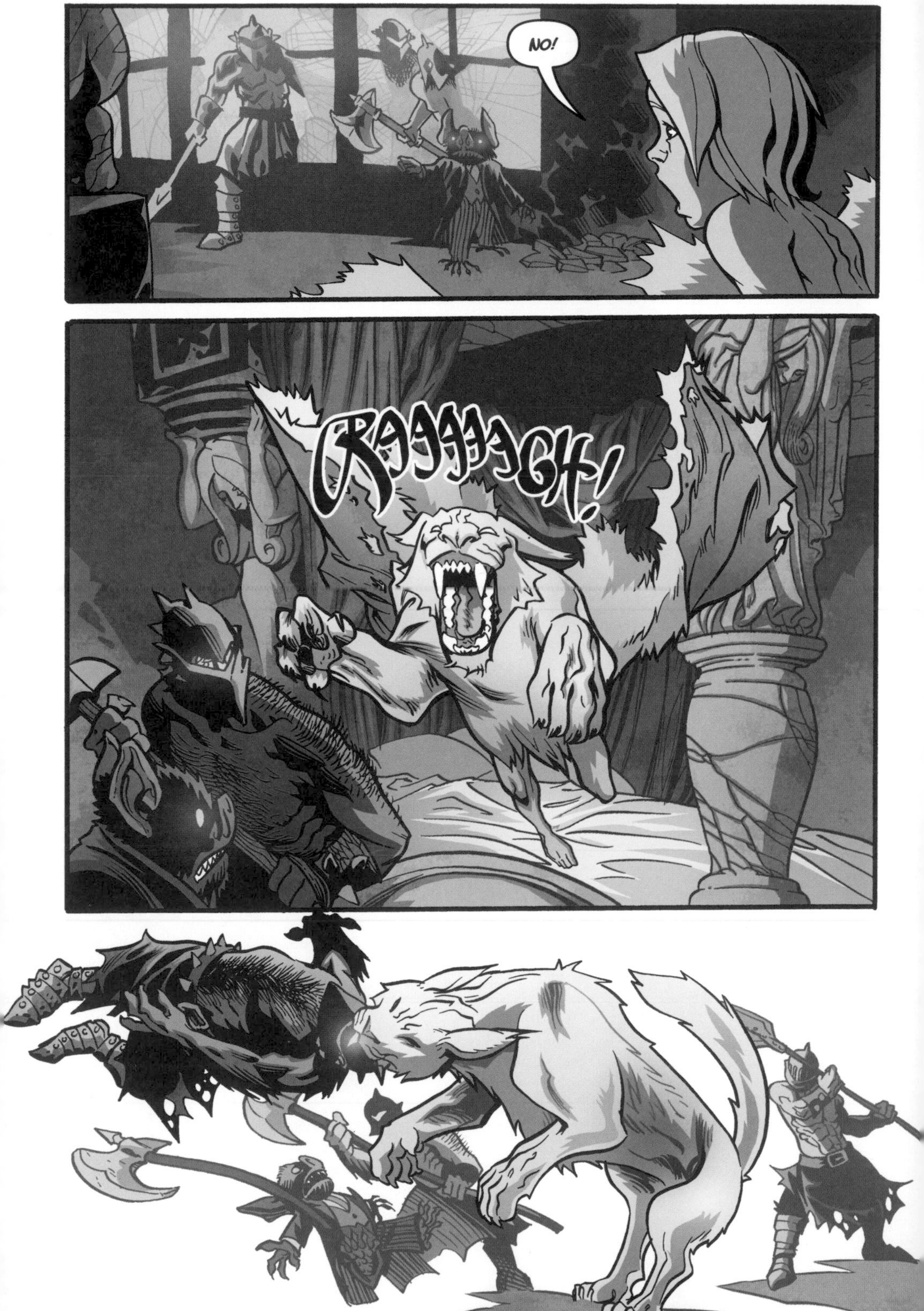
NO!
CRAAAAAGH!

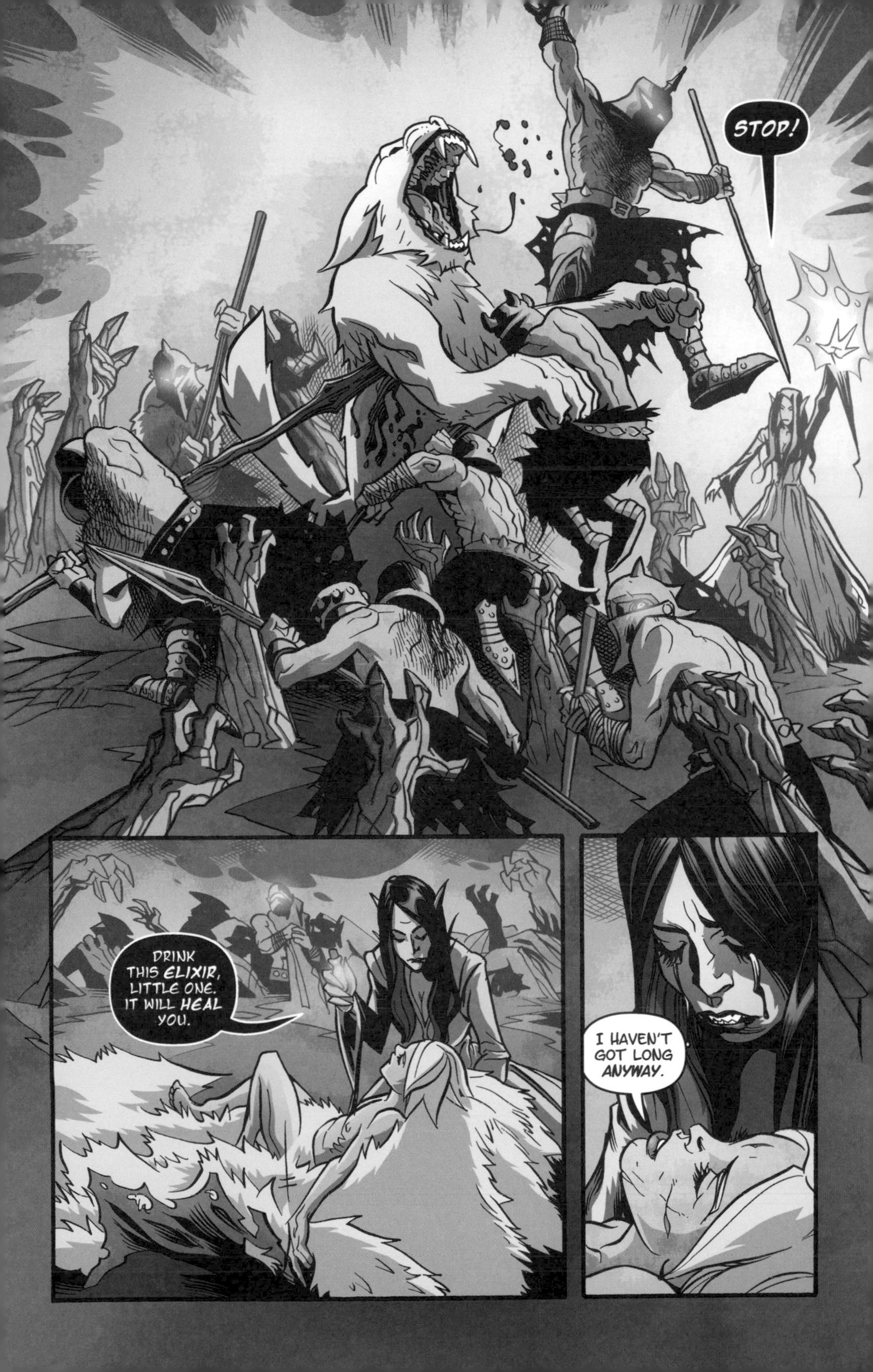
STOP!
DRINK THIS ELIXIR, LITTLE ONE. IT WILL HEAL YOU.
I HAVEN'T GOT LONG ANYWAY.

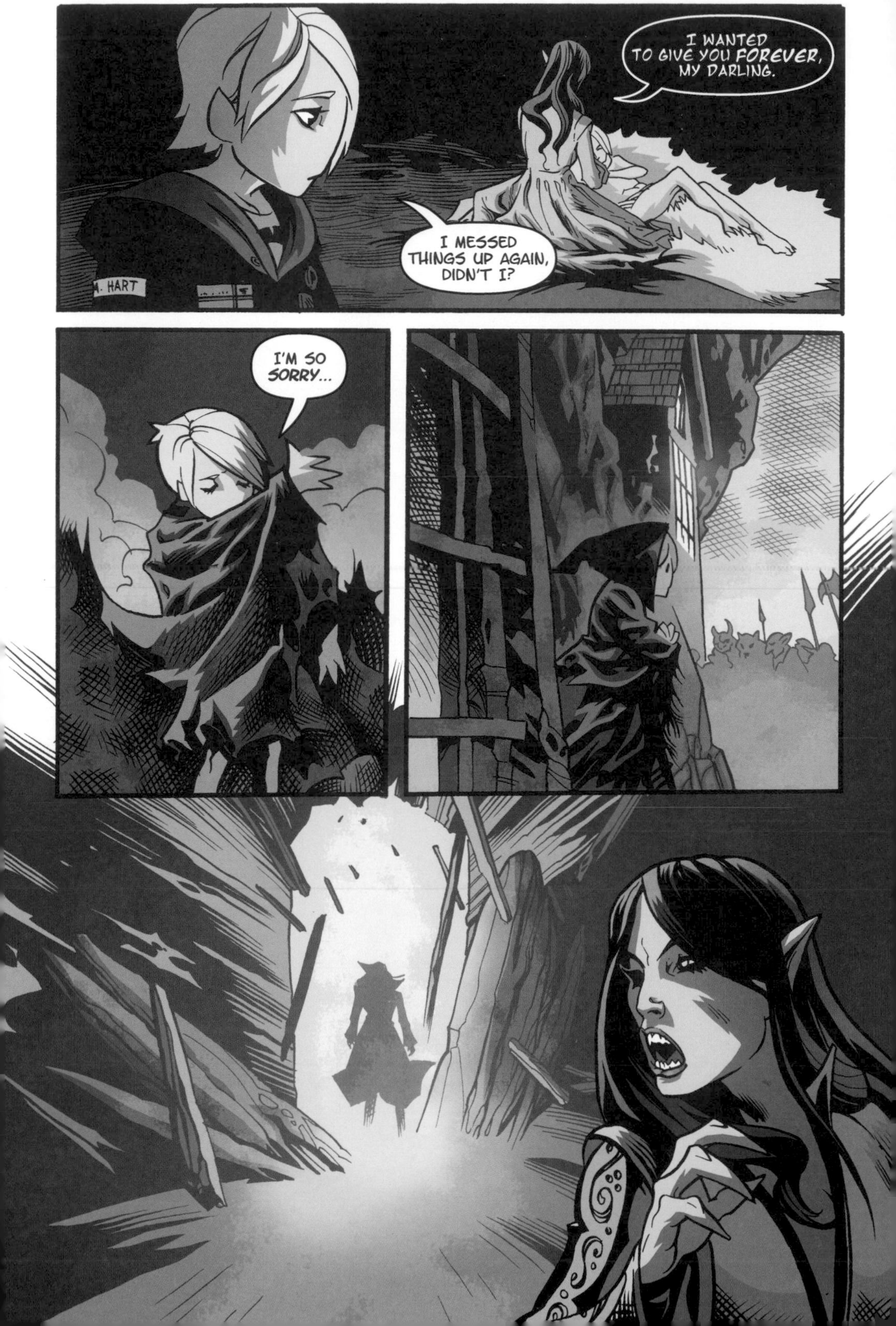
I WANTED TO GIVE YOU FOREVER, MY DARLING.
I MESSED THINGS UP AGAIN, DIDN'T I?
M. HART
I'M SO SORRY...

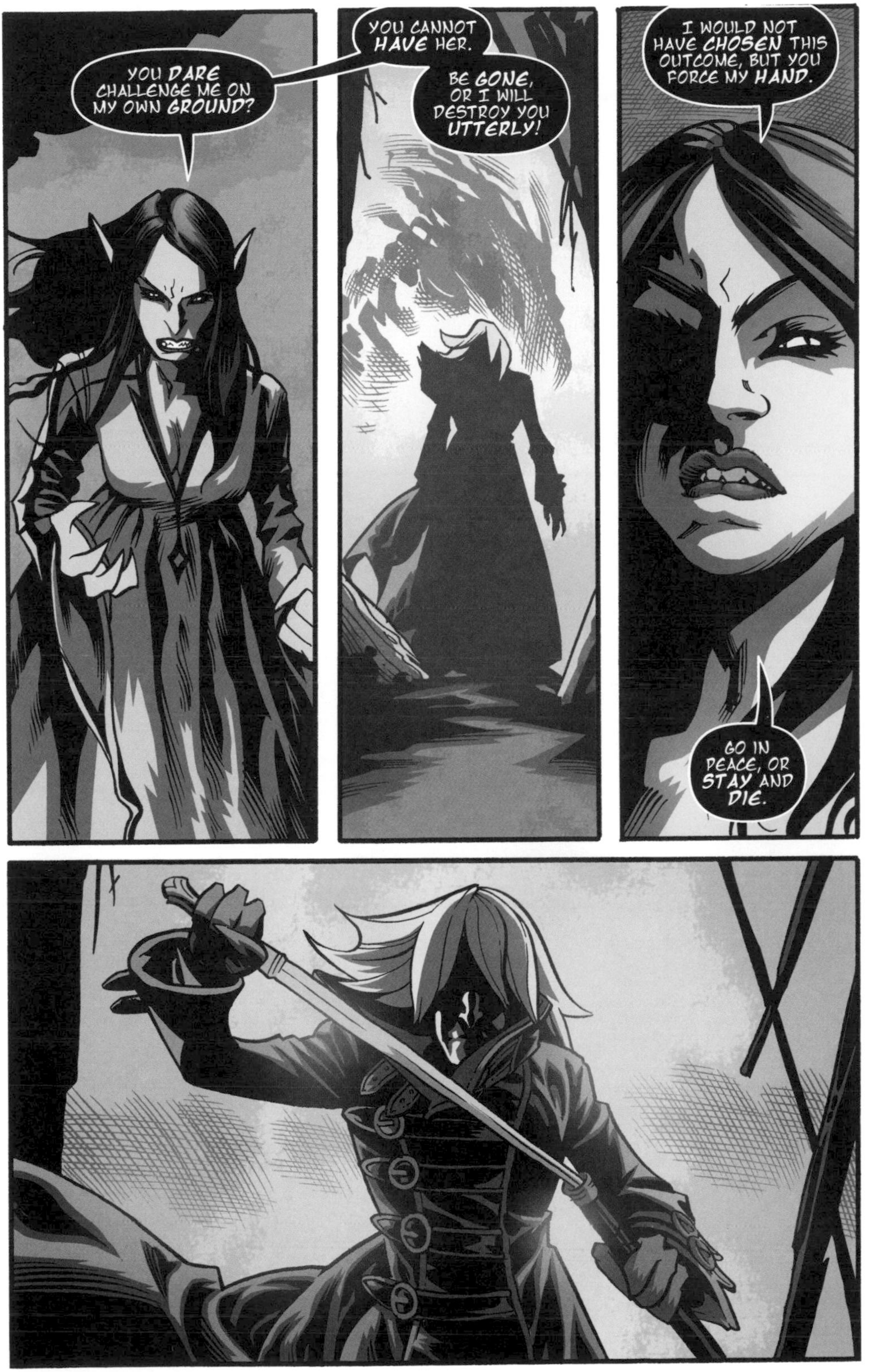
YOU DARE CHALLENGE ME ON MY OWN GROUND?
YOU CANNOT HAVE HER.
BE GONE, OR I WILL DESTROY YOU UTTERLY!
I WOULD NOT HAVE CHOSEN THIS OUTCOME, BUT YOU FORCE MY HAND.
GO IN PEACE, OR STAY AND DIE.

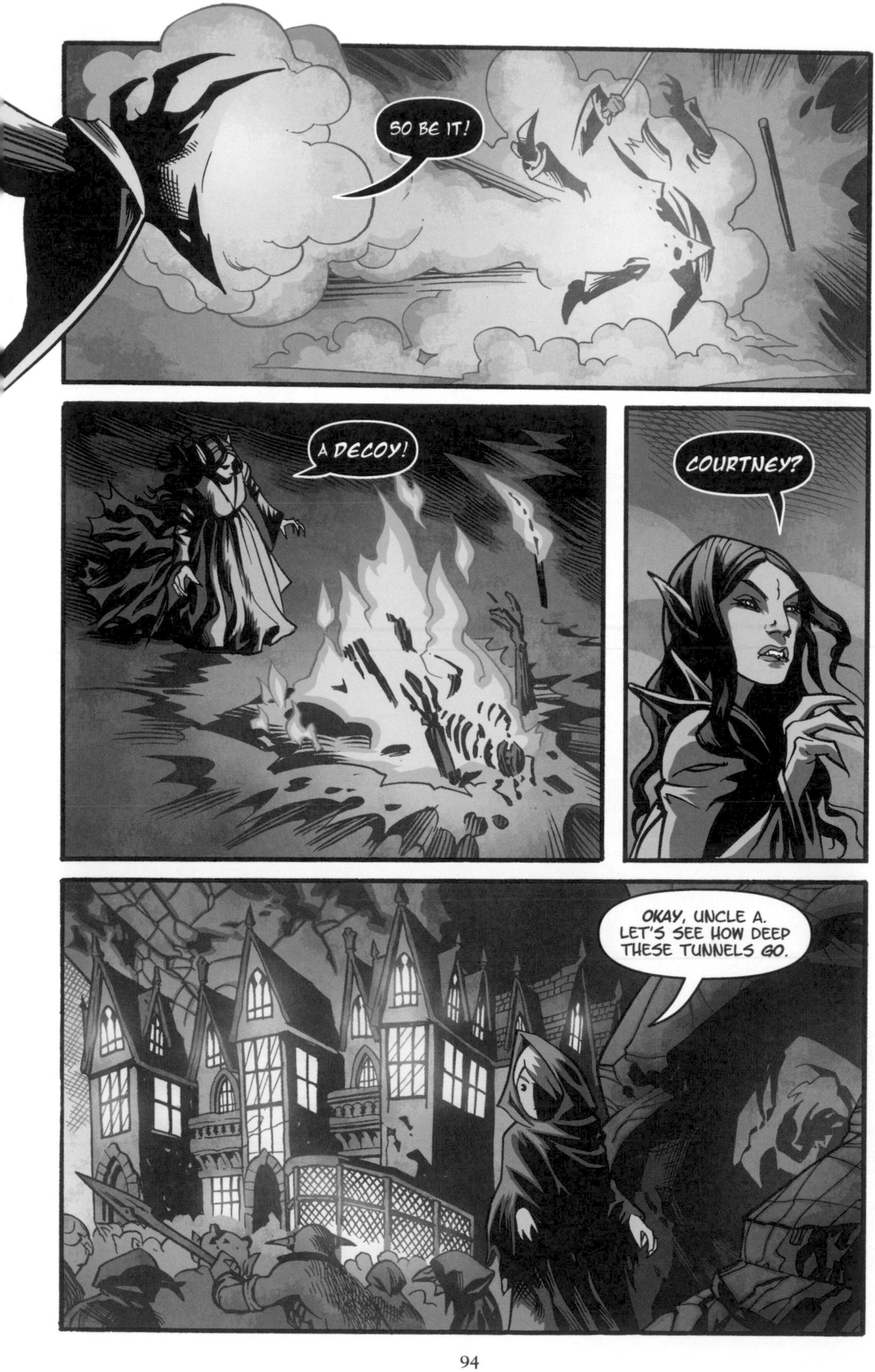
SO BE IT!
A DECOY!
COURTNEY?
OKAY, UNCLE A. LET'S SEE HOW DEEP THESE TUNNELS GO.

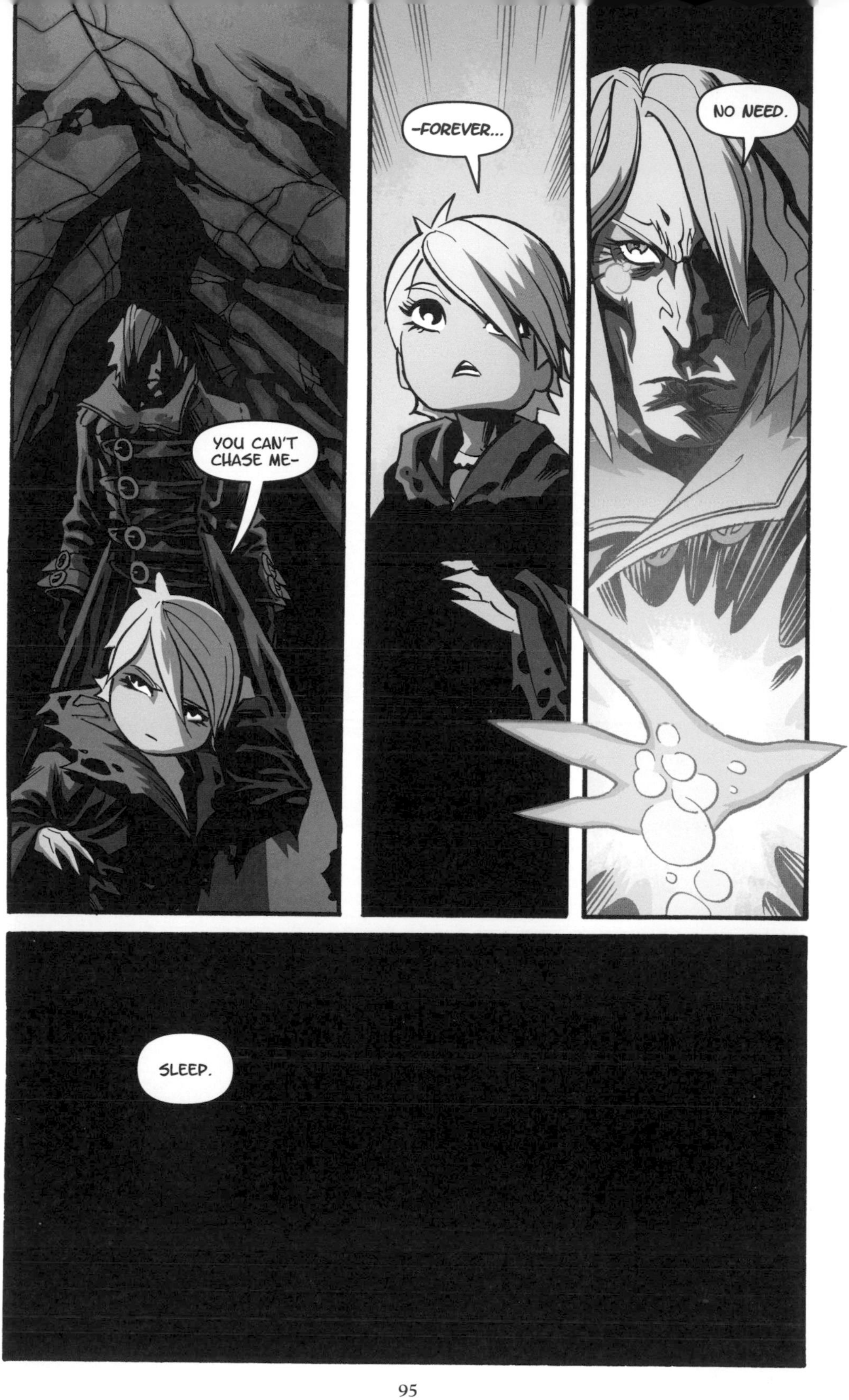
YOU CAN'T CHASE ME-
-FOREVER...
NO NEED.
SLEEP.

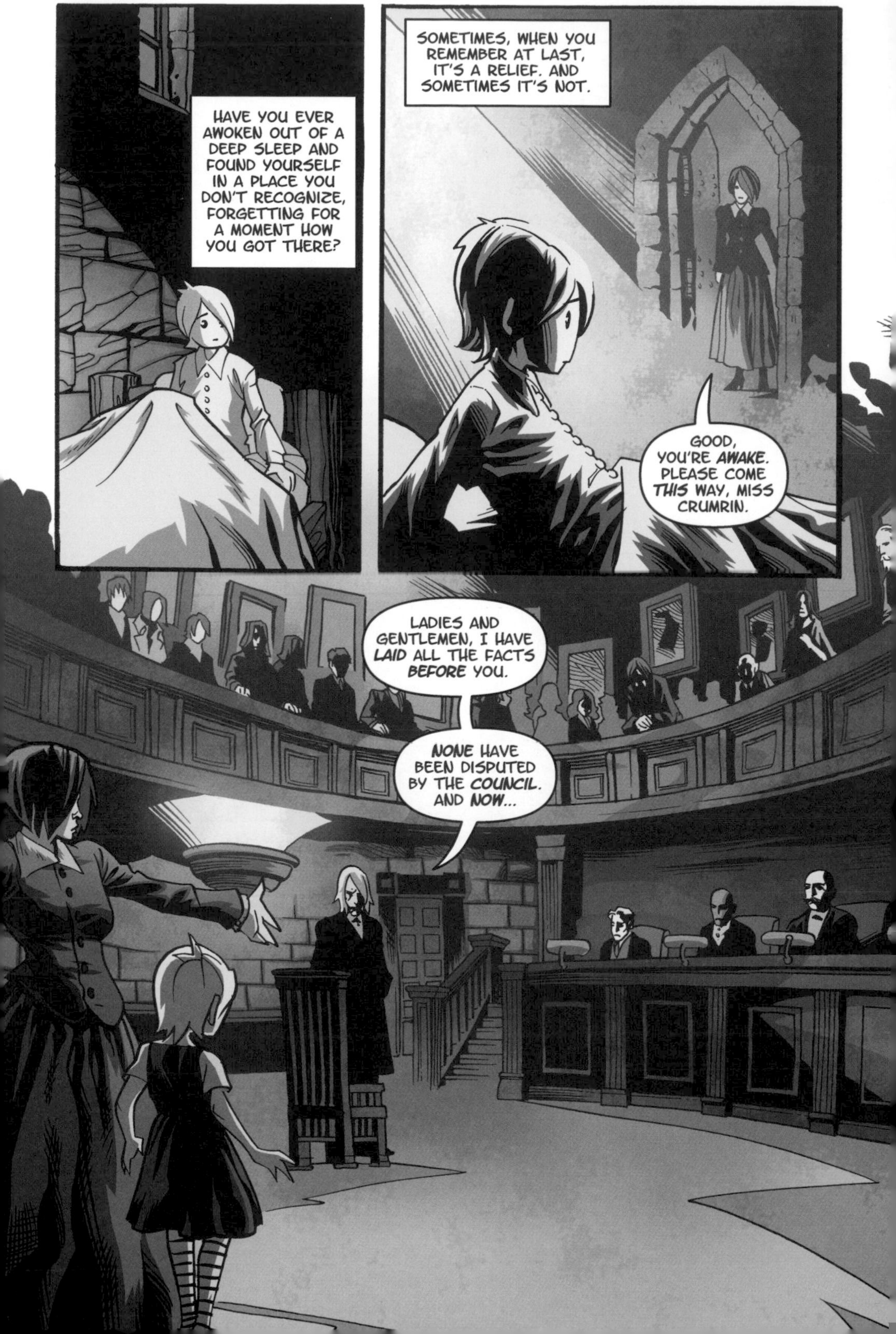
HAVE YOU EVER AWOKEN OUT OF A DEEP SLEEP AND FOUND YOURSELF IN A PLACE YOU DON'T RECOGNIZE, FORGETTING FOR A MOMENT HOW YOU GOT THERE?
SOMETIMES, WHEN YOU REMEMBER AT LAST, IT'S A RELIEF. AND SOMETIMES IT'S NOT.
GOOD, YOU'RE AWAKE. PLEASE COME THIS WAY, MISS CRUMRIN.
LADIES AND GENTLEMEN, I HAVE LAID ALL THE FACTS BEFORE YOU.
NONE HAVE BEEN DISPUTED BY THE COUNCIL. AND NOW...

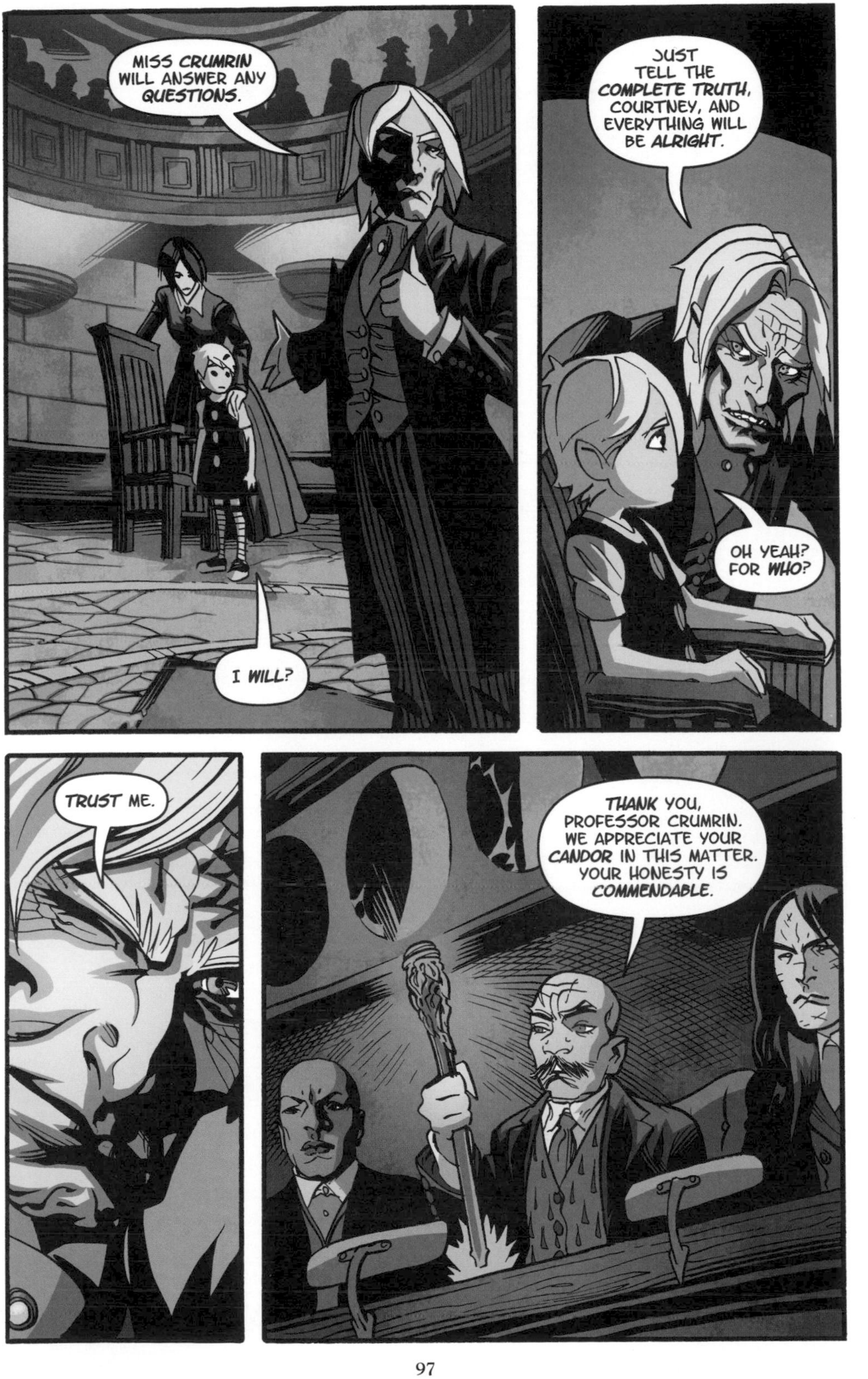

MISS CRUMRIN WILL ANSWER ANY QUESTIONS.
I WILL?
JUST TELL THE COMPLETE TRUTH, COURTNEY, AND EVERYTHING WILL BE ALRIGHT.
OH YEAH? FOR WHO?
TRUST ME.
THANK YOU, PROFESSOR CRUMRIN. WE APPRECIATE YOUR CANDOR IN THIS MATTER. YOUR HONESTY IS COMMENDABLE.

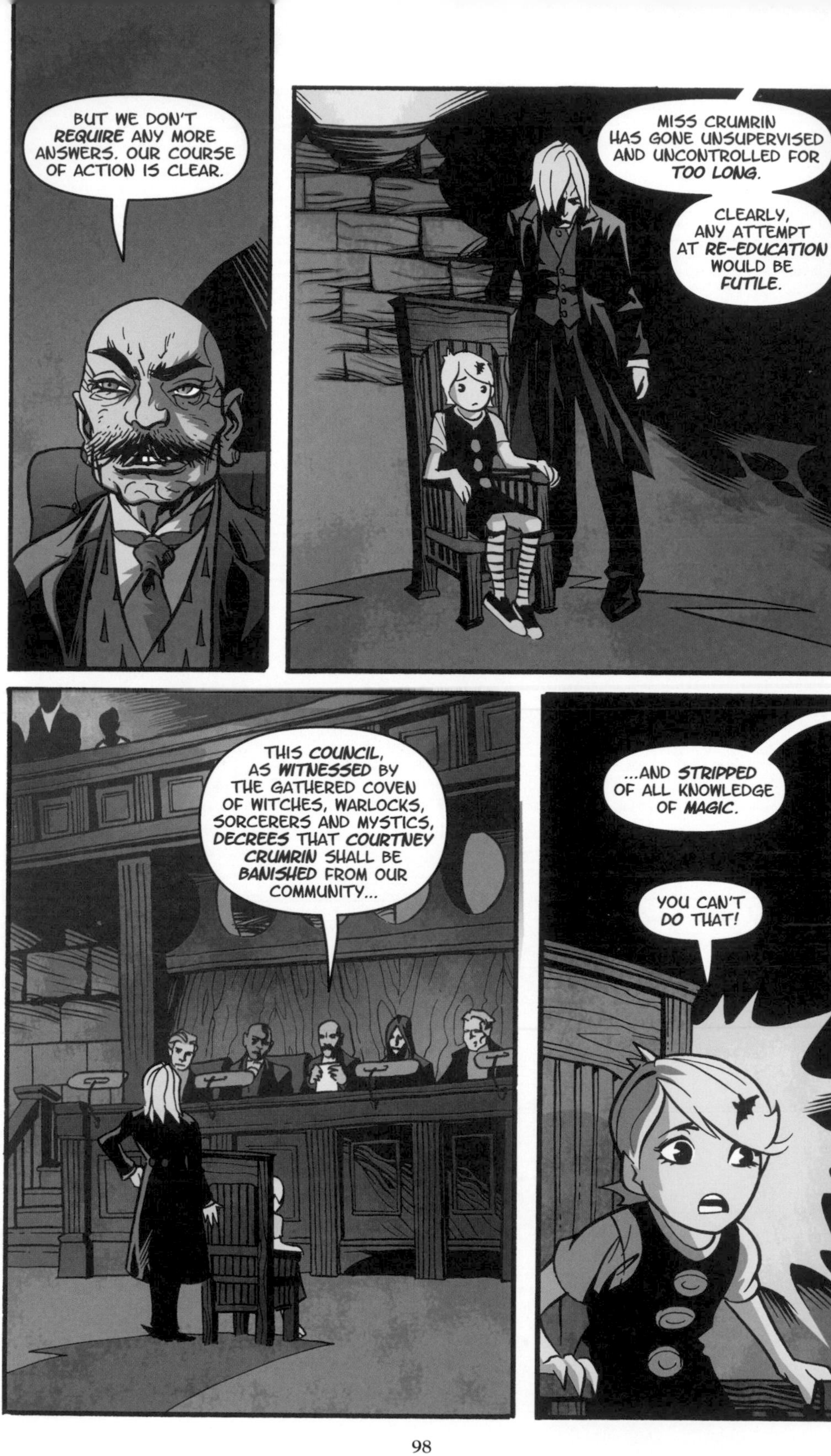
BUT WE DON'T REQUIRE ANY MORE ANSWERS. OUR COURSE OF ACTION IS CLEAR.
MISS CRUMRIN HAS GONE UNSUPERVISED AND UNCONTROLLED FOR TOO LONG.
CLEARLY, ANY ATTEMPT AT RE-EDUCATION WOULD BE FUTILE.
THIS COUNCIL, AS WITNESSED BY THE GATHERED COVEN OF WITCHES, WARLOCKS, SORCERERS AND MYSTICS, DECREES THAT COURTNEY CRUMRIN SHALL BE BANISHED FROM OUR COMMUNITY...
...AND STRIPPED OF ALL KNOWLEDGE OF MAGIC.
YOU CAN'T DO THAT!

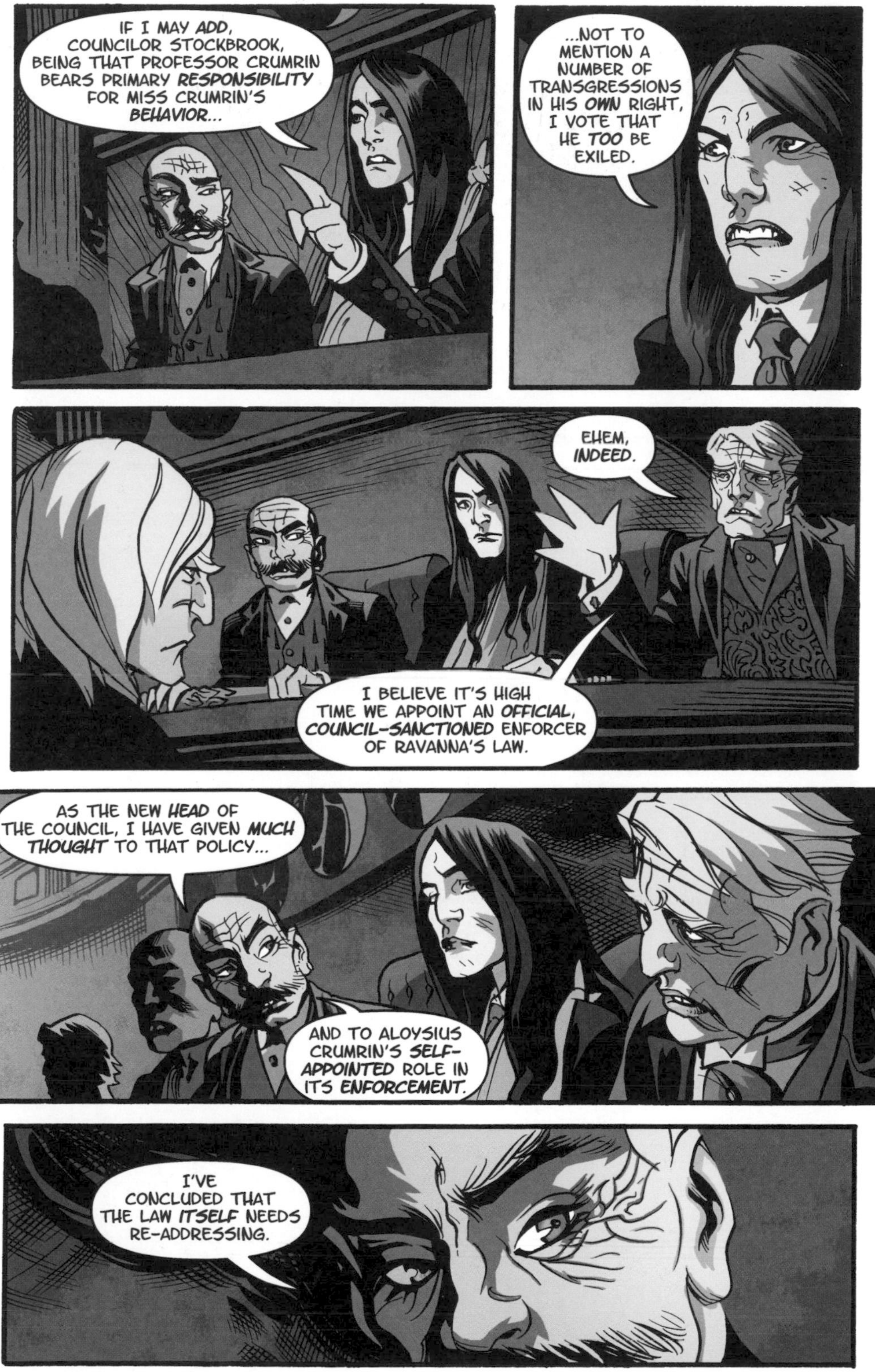
IF I MAY ADD, COUNCILOR STOCKBROOK, BEING THAT PROFESSOR CRUMRIN BEARS PRIMARY RESPONSIBILITY FOR MISS CRUMRIN'S BEHAVIOR...
...NOT TO MENTION A NUMBER OF TRANSGRESSIONS IN HIS OWN RIGHT, I VOTE THAT HE TOO BE EXILED.
EHEM, INDEED.
I BELIEVE IT'S HIGH TIME WE APPOINT AN OFFICIAL, COUNCIL-SANCTIONED ENFORCER OF RAVANNA'S LAW.
AS THE NEW HEAD OF THE COUNCIL, I HAVE GIVEN MUCH THOUGHT TO THAT POLICY...
AND TO ALOYSIUS CRUMRIN'S SELF-APPOINTED ROLE IN ITS ENFORCEMENT.
I'VE CONCLUDED THAT THE LAW ITSELF NEEDS RE-ADDRESSING.

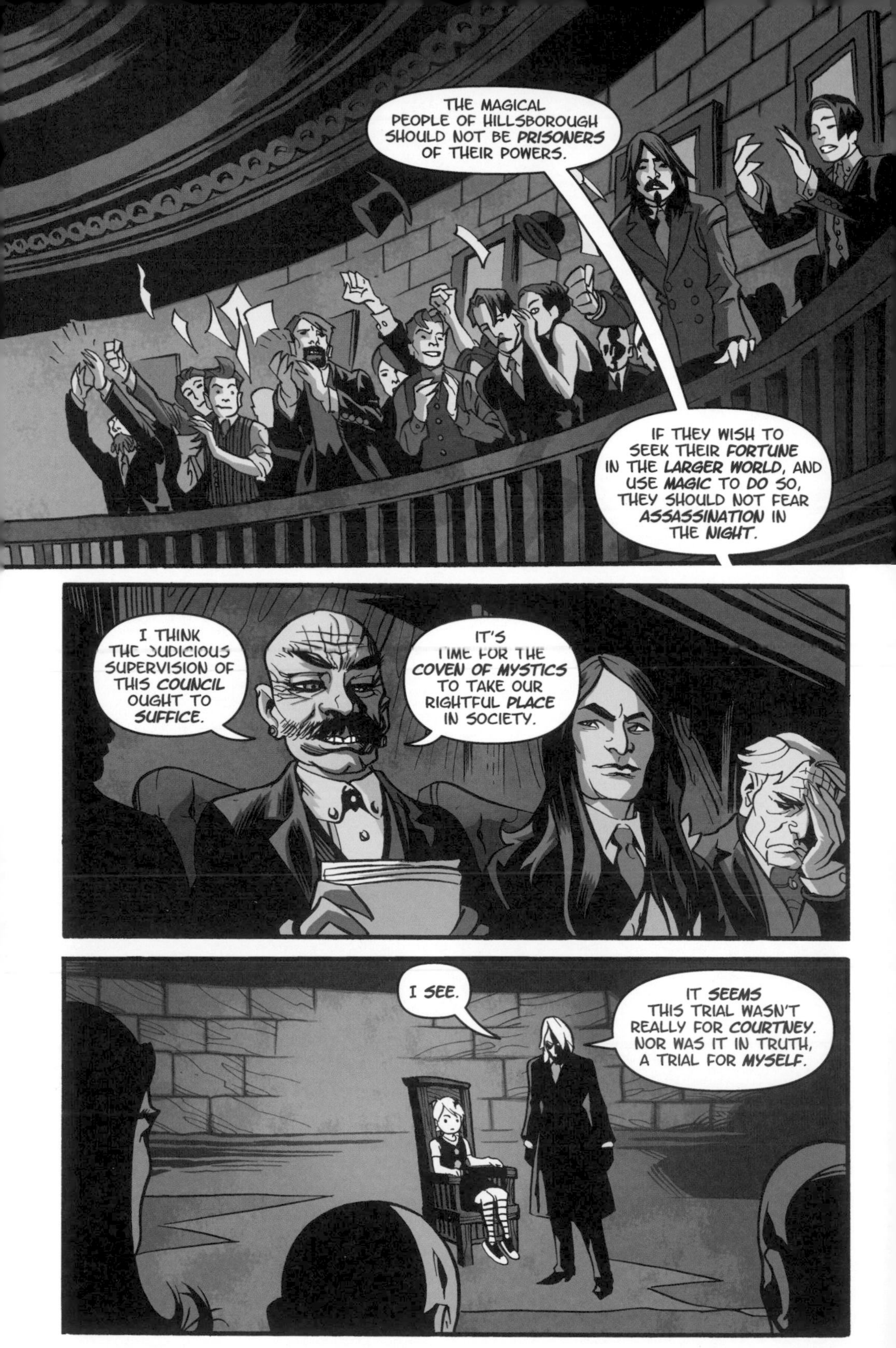
THE MAGICAL PEOPLE OF HILLSBOROUGH SHOULD NOT BE PRISONERS OF THEIR POWERS.
IF THEY WISH TO SEEK THEIR FORTUNE IN THE LARGER WORLD, AND USE MAGIC TO DO SO, THEY SHOULD NOT FEAR ASSASSINATION IN THE NIGHT.
I THINK THE JUDICIOUS SUPERVISION OF THIS COUNCIL OUGHT TO SUFFICE.
IT'S TIME FOR THE COVEN OF MYSTICS TO TAKE OUR RIGHTFUL PLACE IN SOCIETY.
I SEE.
IT SEEMS THIS TRIAL WASN'T REALLY FOR COURTNEY. NOR WAS IT IN TRUTH, A TRIAL FOR MYSELF.

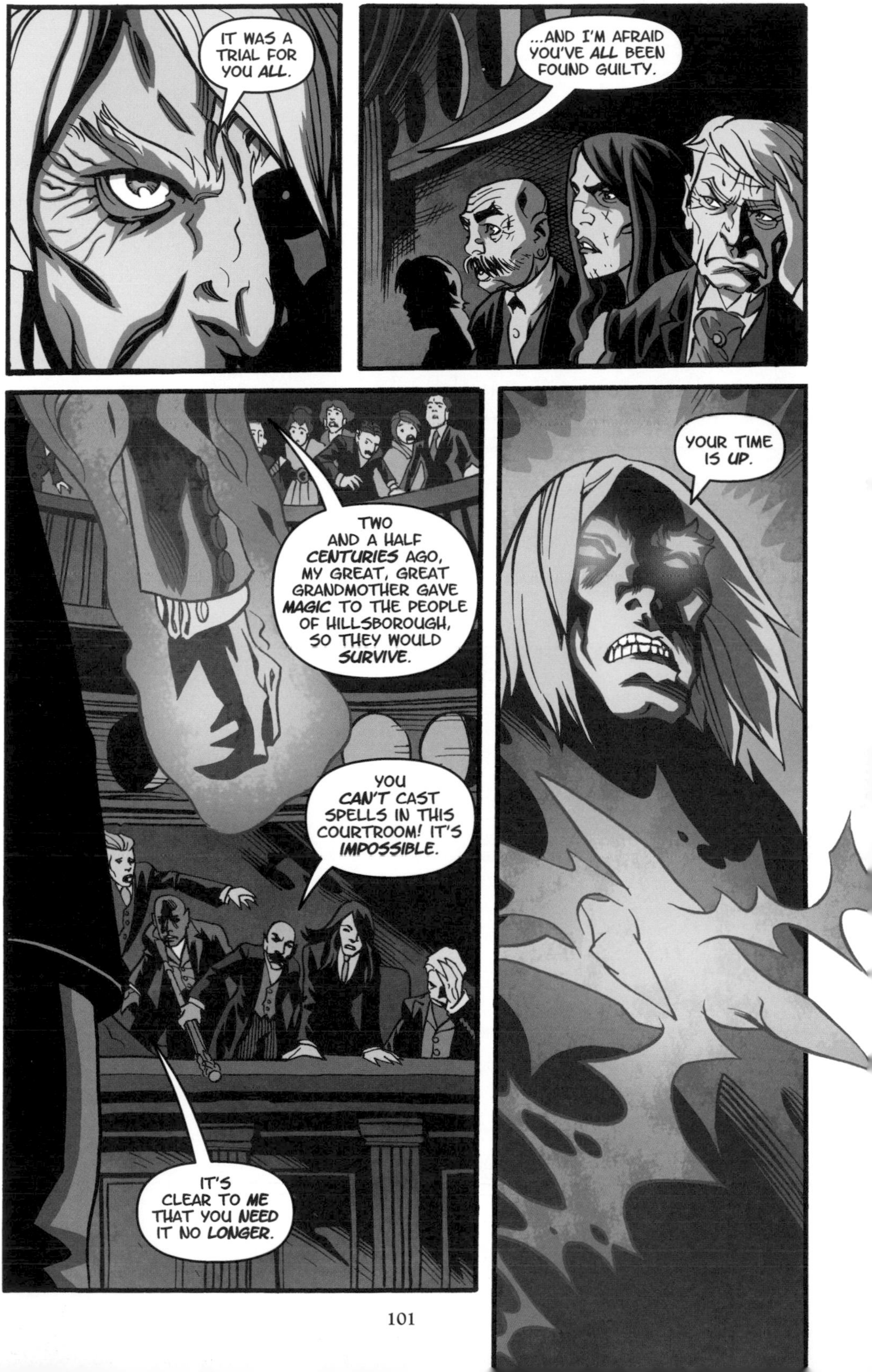
IT WAS A TRIAL FOR YOU ALL.
...AND I'M AFRAID YOU'VE ALL BEEN FOUND GUILTY.
TWO AND A HALF CENTURIES AGO, MY GREAT, GREAT GRANDMOTHER GAVE MAGIC TO THE PEOPLE OF HILLSBOROUGH, SO THEY WOULD SURVIVE.
YOU CAN'T CAST SPELLS IN THIS COURTROOM! IT'S IMPOSSIBLE.
IT'S CLEAR TO ME THAT YOU NEED IT NO LONGER.
YOUR TIME IS UP.

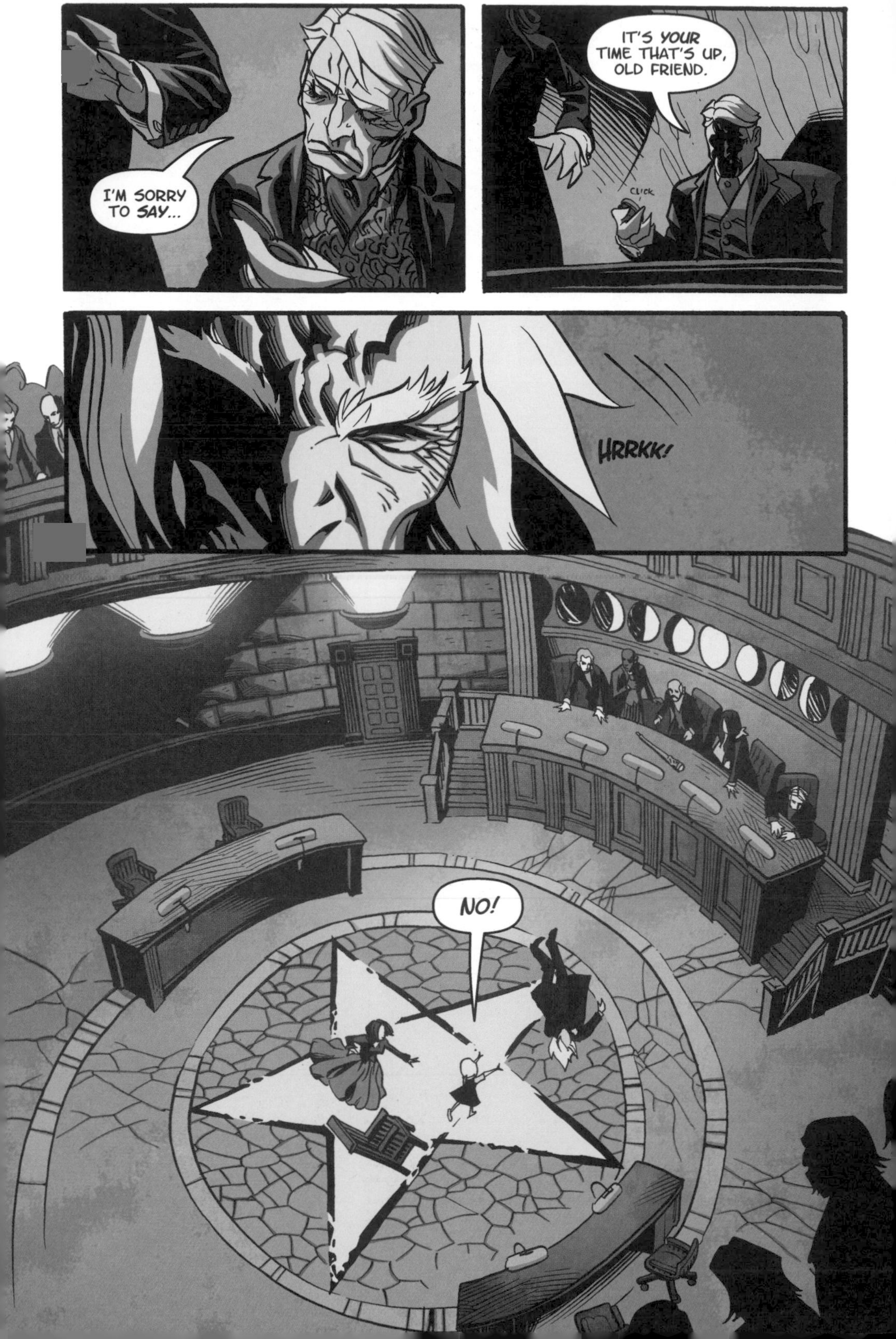
I'M SORRY TO SAY...
IT'S YOUR TIME THAT'S UP, OLD FRIEND.
CLICK
HRRKK!
NO!

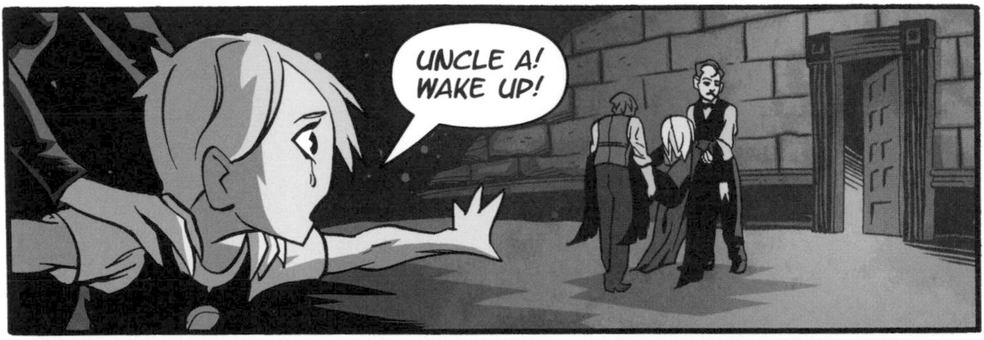
UNCLE A! WAKE UP!

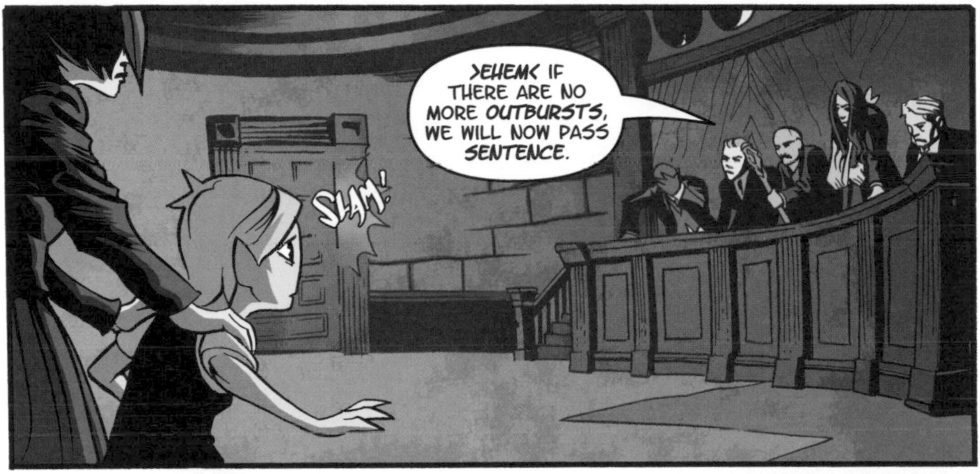
>EHEM< IF THERE ARE NO MORE *OUTBURSTS*, WE WILL NOW PASS *SENTENCE*.
SLAM!

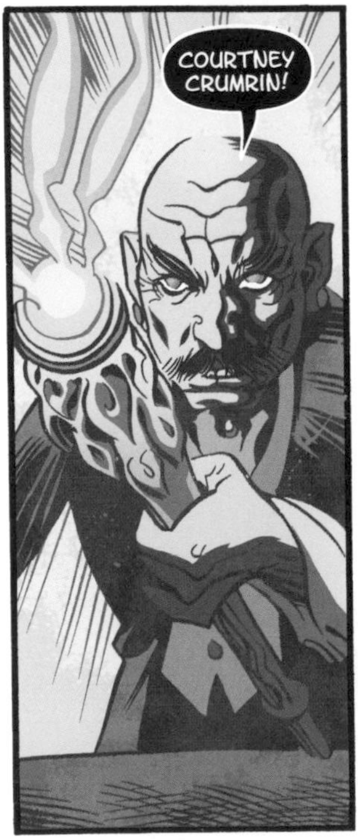
COURTNEY CRUMRIN!

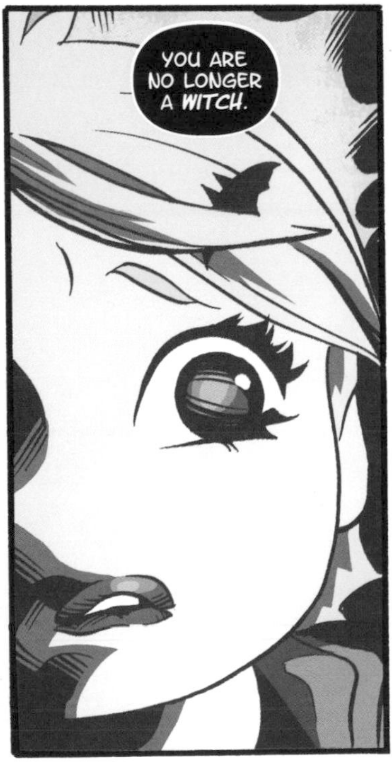
YOU ARE NO LONGER A *WITCH*.

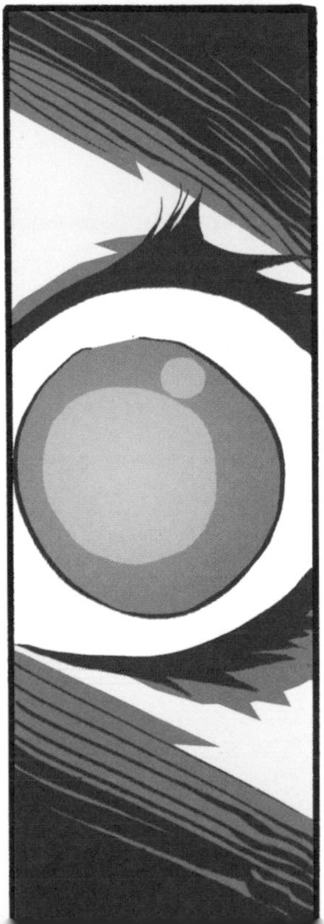

Chapter Five

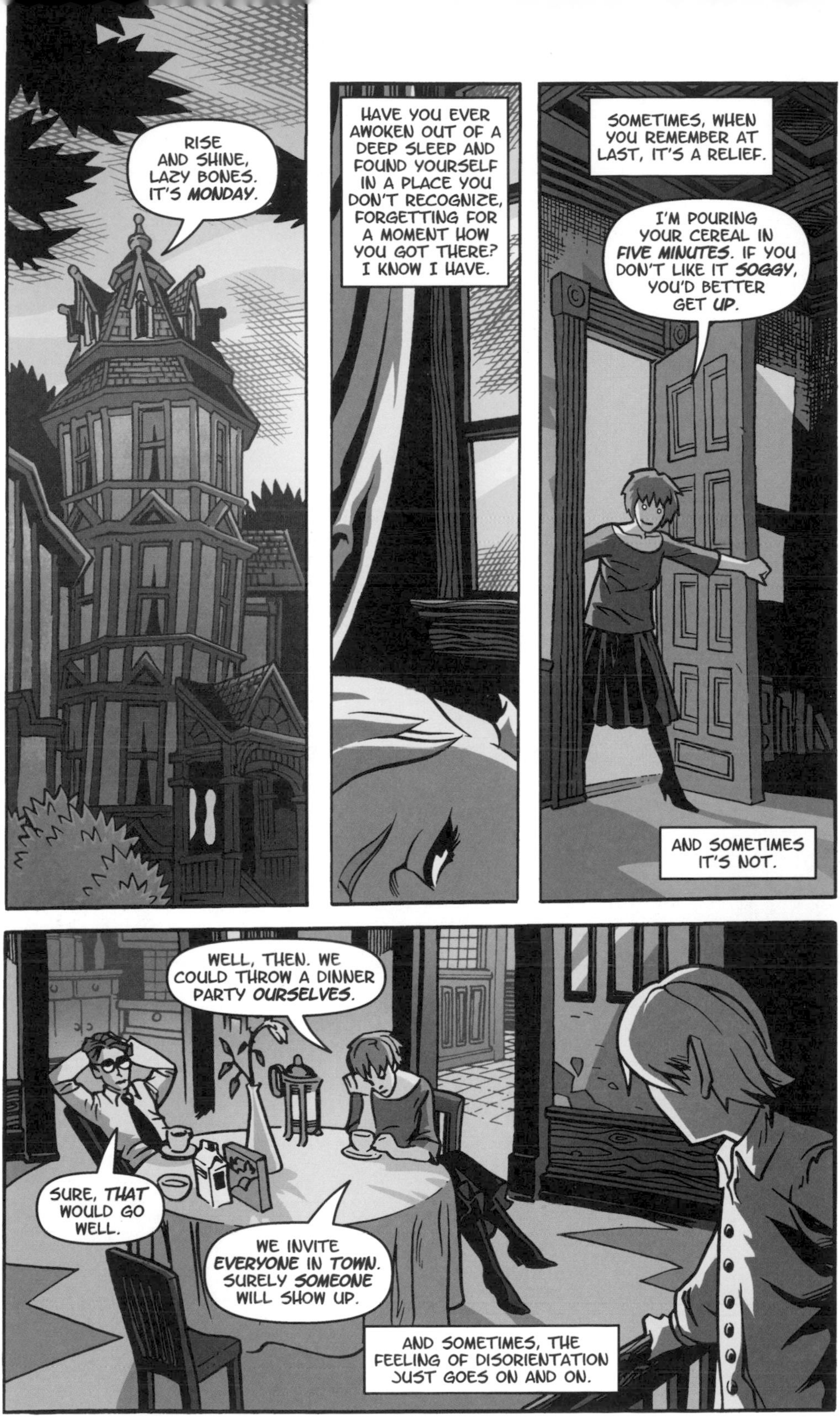
RISE AND SHINE, LAZY BONES. IT'S MONDAY.
HAVE YOU EVER AWOKEN OUT OF A DEEP SLEEP AND FOUND YOURSELF IN A PLACE YOU DON'T RECOGNIZE, FORGETTING FOR A MOMENT HOW YOU GOT THERE? I KNOW I HAVE.
SOMETIMES, WHEN YOU REMEMBER AT LAST, IT'S A RELIEF.
I'M POURING YOUR CEREAL IN FIVE MINUTES. IF YOU DON'T LIKE IT SOGGY, YOU'D BETTER GET UP.
AND SOMETIMES IT'S NOT.
WELL, THEN. WE COULD THROW A DINNER PARTY OURSELVES.
SURE, THAT WOULD GO WELL.
WE INVITE EVERYONE IN TOWN. SURELY SOMEONE WILL SHOW UP.
AND SOMETIMES, THE FEELING OF DISORIENTATION JUST GOES ON AND ON.

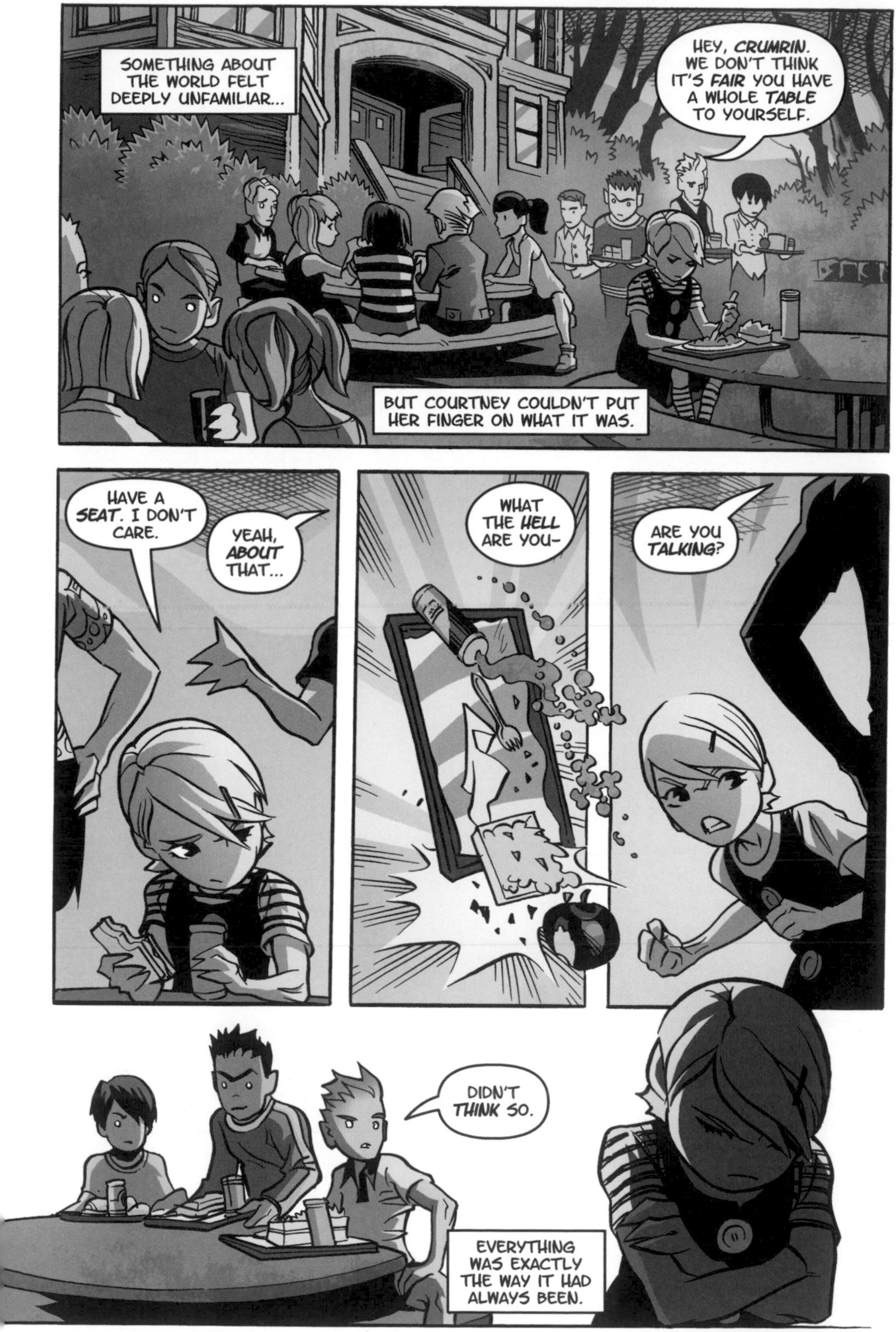
SOMETHING ABOUT THE WORLD FELT DEEPLY UNFAMILIAR...
HEY, CRUMRIN. WE DON'T THINK IT'S FAIR YOU HAVE A WHOLE TABLE TO YOURSELF.
BUT COURTNEY COULDN'T PUT HER FINGER ON WHAT IT WAS.
HAVE A SEAT. I DON'T CARE.
YEAH, ABOUT THAT...
WHAT THE HELL ARE YOU-
ARE YOU TALKING?
DIDN'T THINK SO.
EVERYTHING WAS EXACTLY THE WAY IT HAD ALWAYS BEEN.

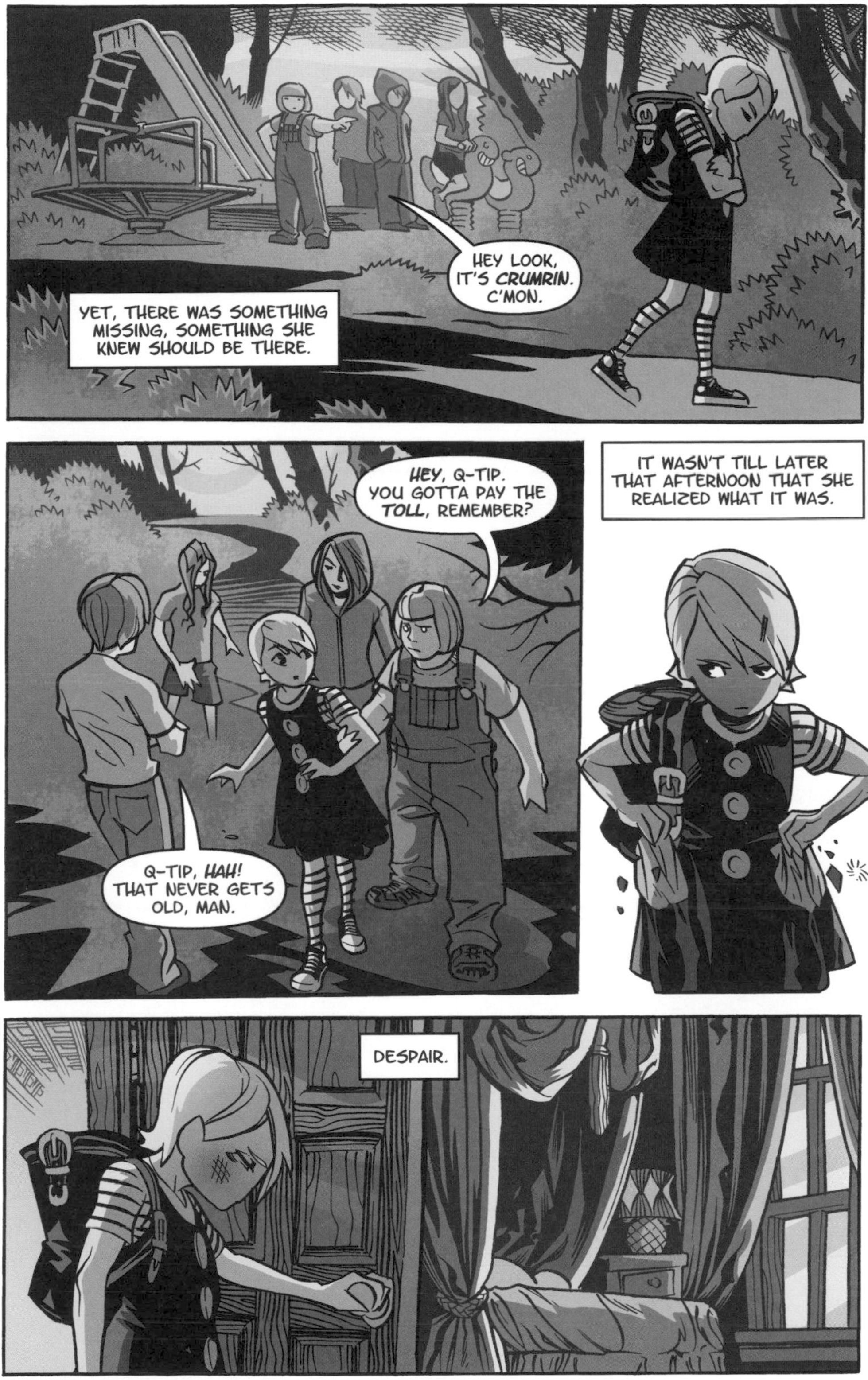
YET, THERE WAS SOMETHING MISSING, SOMETHING SHE KNEW SHOULD BE THERE.
HEY LOOK, IT'S CRUMRIN. C'MON.
HEY, Q-TIP. YOU GOTTA PAY THE TOLL, REMEMBER?
Q-TIP, HAH! THAT NEVER GETS OLD, MAN.
IT WASN'T TILL LATER THAT AFTERNOON THAT SHE REALIZED WHAT IT WAS.
DESPAIR.

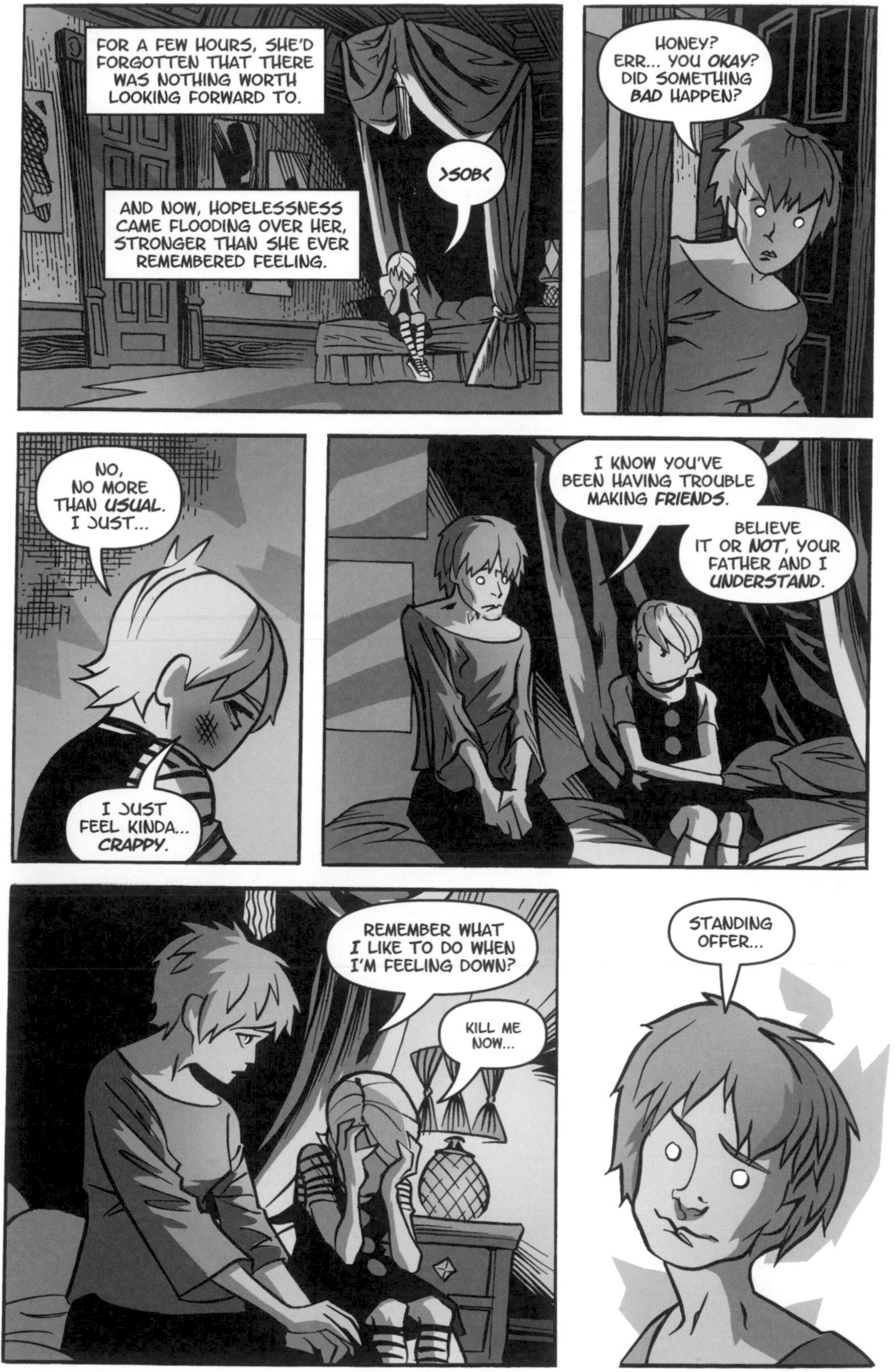
FOR A FEW HOURS, SHE'D FORGOTTEN THAT THERE WAS NOTHING WORTH LOOKING FORWARD TO.
AND NOW, HOPELESSNESS CAME FLOODING OVER HER, STRONGER THAN SHE EVER REMEMBERED FEELING.
>SOB<
HONEY? ERR... YOU OKAY? DID SOMETHING BAD HAPPEN?
NO, NO MORE THAN USUAL. I JUST...
I JUST FEEL KINDA... CRAPPY.
I KNOW YOU'VE BEEN HAVING TROUBLE MAKING FRIENDS.
BELIEVE IT OR NOT, YOUR FATHER AND I UNDERSTAND.
REMEMBER WHAT I LIKE TO DO WHEN I'M FEELING DOWN?
KILL ME NOW...
STANDING OFFER...

THERE'S NOTHING LIKE A NEW *DRESS* TO CHASE THE *OOGIE FEELINGS* AWAY.

USUALLY, COURTNEY WOULD RATHER RUB SAND IN HER EYES THAN GO SHOPPING WITH HER MOTHER.

HOW CAN I *YOUTHENIZE* YOU TODAY?

YOUTHENIZ

FABULOIDE

Fairy Ladd

BOOK E

OH, YOU'LL JUST LOOK *DARLING* IN THIS.

UUUUH...

BUT TODAY...

WANNA TRY IT ON? FOR *ME*?

SHE JUST COULDN'T SEE THE POINT OF RESISTING ANYMORE.

OKAY, MOM.

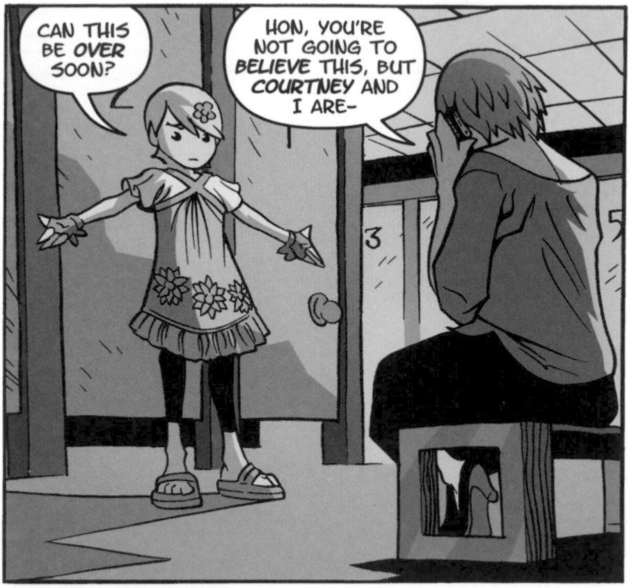
CAN THIS BE OVER SOON?
HON, YOU'RE NOT GOING TO BELIEVE THIS, BUT COURTNEY AND I ARE-
3

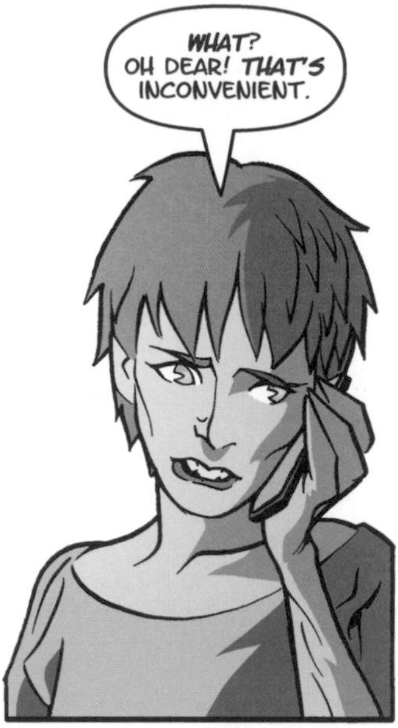
WHAT? OH DEAR! THAT'S INCONVENIENT.

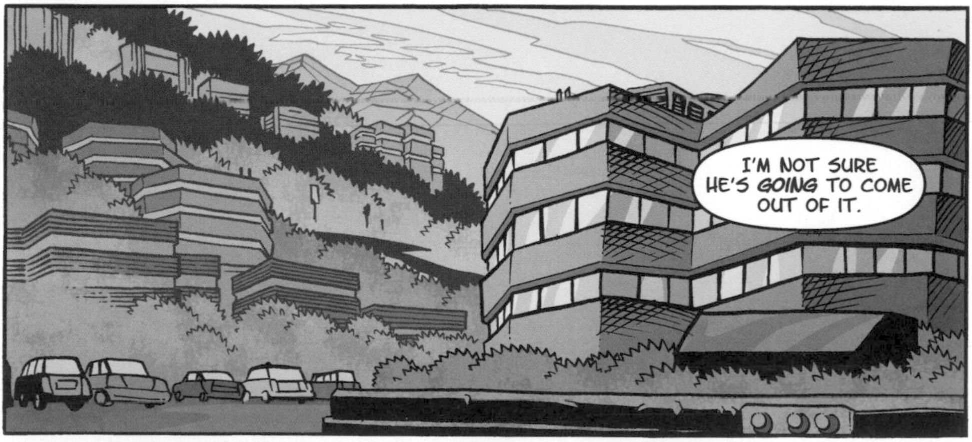
I'M NOT SURE HE'S GOING TO COME OUT OF IT.

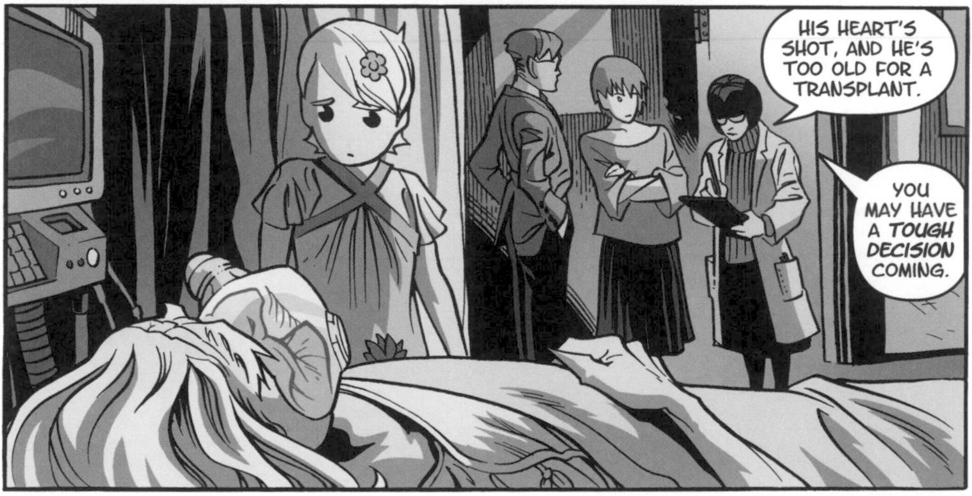
HIS HEART'S SHOT, AND HE'S TOO OLD FOR A TRANSPLANT.
YOU MAY HAVE A TOUGH DECISION COMING.

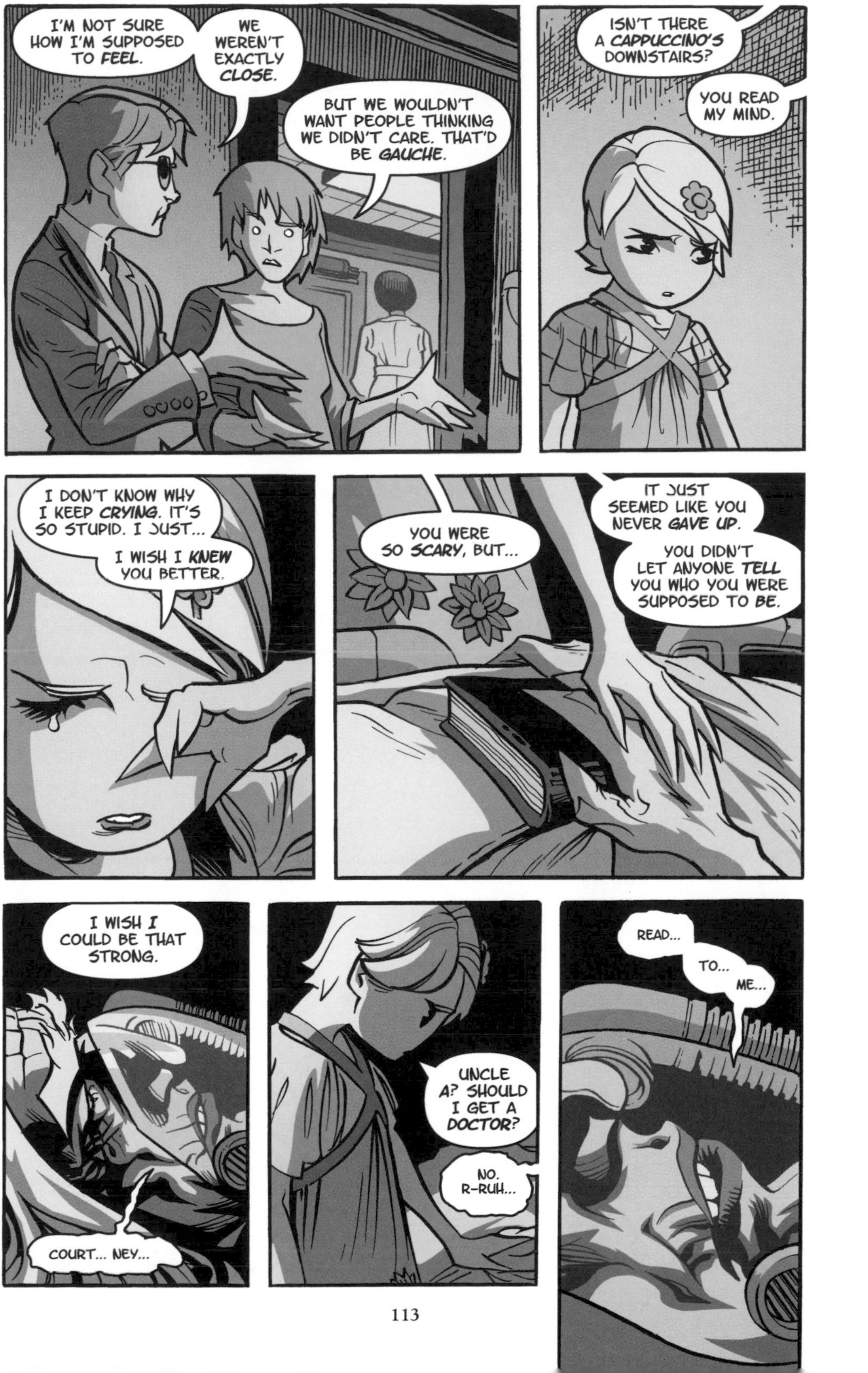
I'M NOT SURE HOW I'M SUPPOSED TO FEEL.
WE WEREN'T EXACTLY CLOSE.
BUT WE WOULDN'T WANT PEOPLE THINKING WE DIDN'T CARE. THAT'D BE GAUCHE.
ISN'T THERE A CAPPUCCINO'S DOWNSTAIRS?
YOU READ MY MIND.
I DON'T KNOW WHY I KEEP CRYING. IT'S SO STUPID. I JUST...
I WISH I KNEW YOU BETTER.
YOU WERE SO SCARY, BUT...
IT JUST SEEMED LIKE YOU NEVER GAVE UP.
YOU DIDN'T LET ANYONE TELL YOU WHO YOU WERE SUPPOSED TO BE.
I WISH I COULD BE THAT STRONG.
COURT... NEY...
UNCLE A? SHOULD I GET A DOCTOR?
NO. R-RUH...
READ...
TO...
ME...

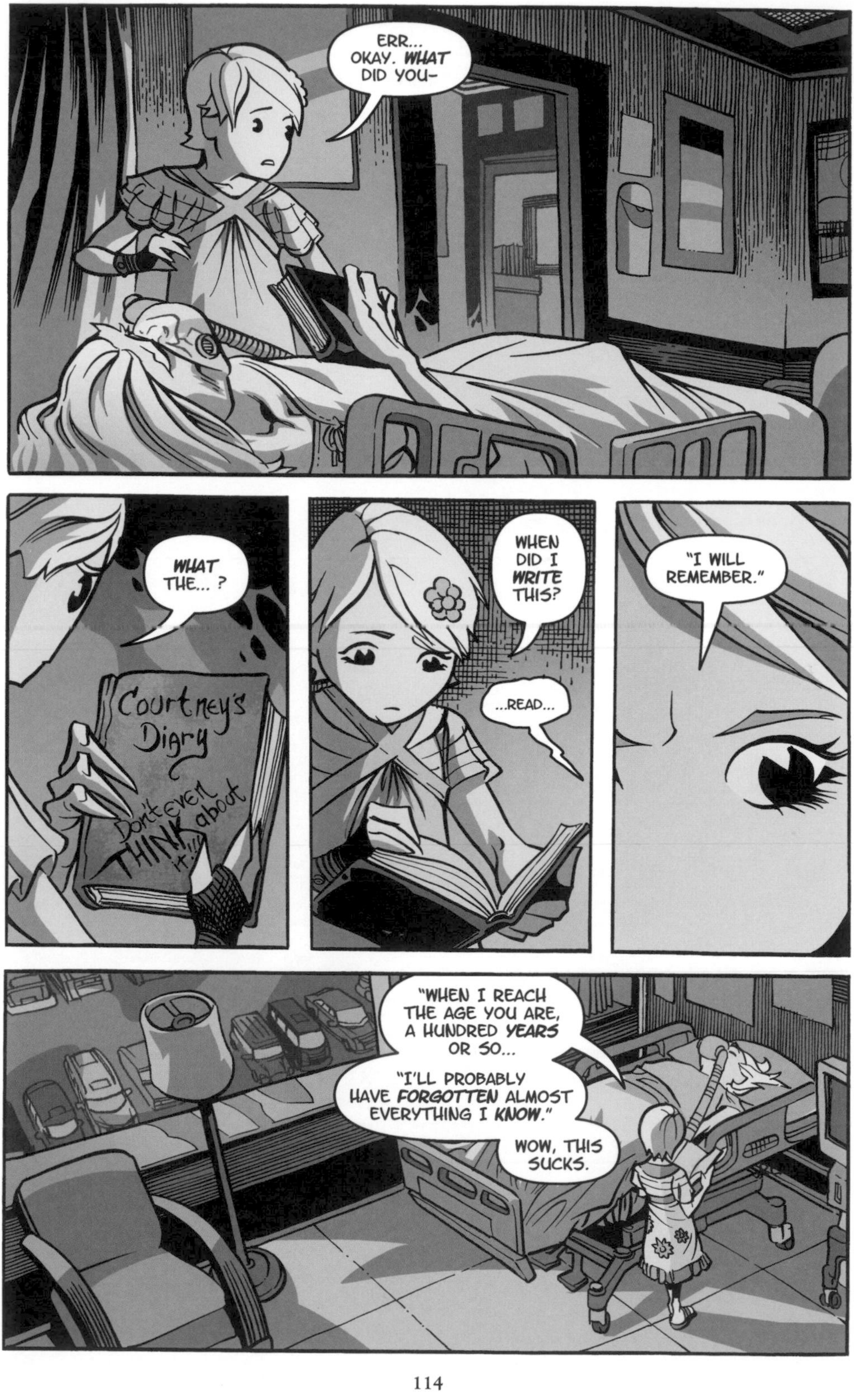
ERR... OKAY. WHAT DID YOU-
WHAT THE... ?
Courtney's Diary
Don't even THINK about it!!!
WHEN DID I WRITE THIS?
...READ...
"I WILL REMEMBER."
"WHEN I REACH THE AGE YOU ARE, A HUNDRED YEARS OR SO...
"I'LL PROBABLY HAVE FORGOTTEN ALMOST EVERYTHING I KNOW."
WOW, THIS SUCKS.

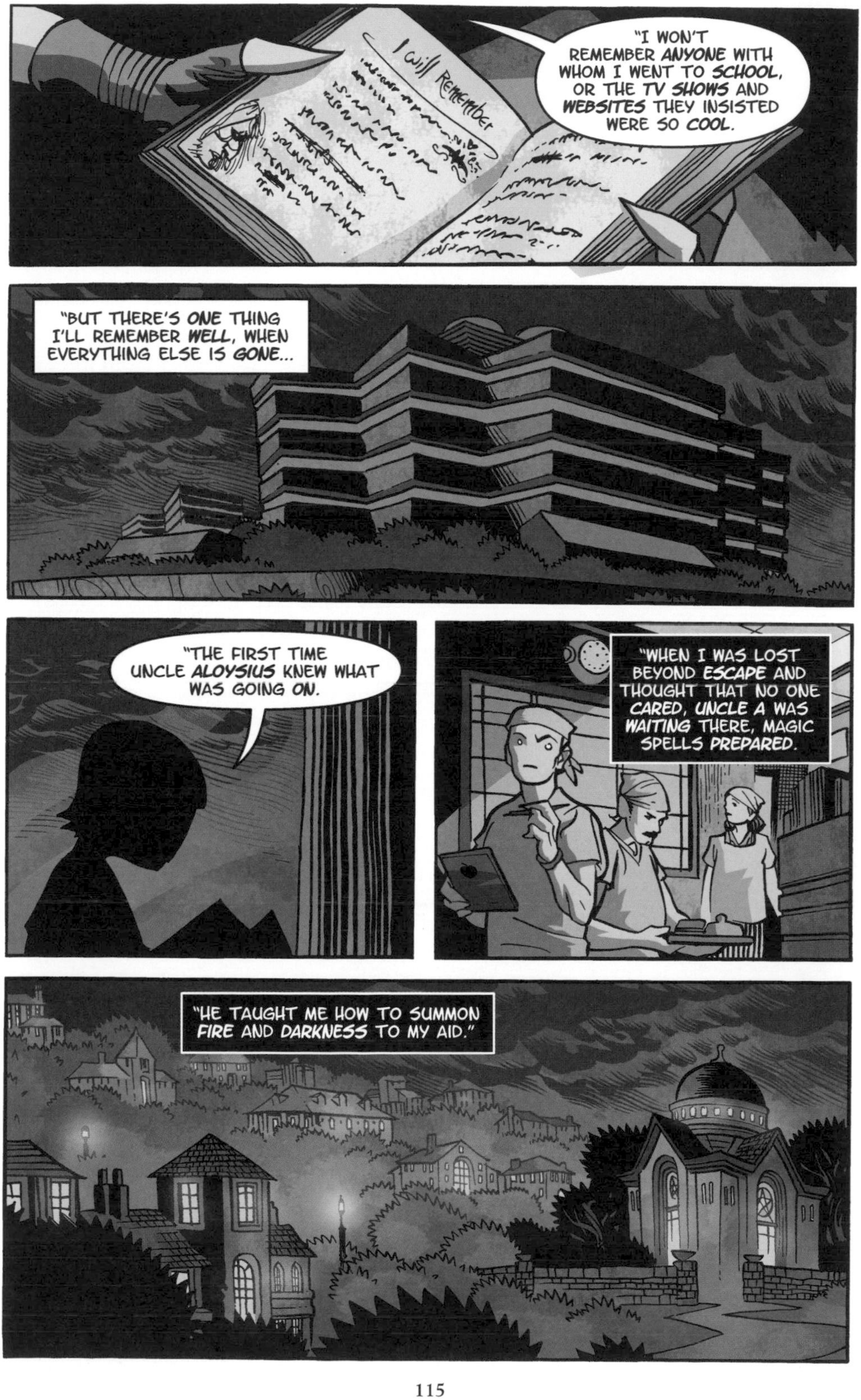
I will Remember
"I WON'T REMEMBER ANYONE WITH WHOM I WENT TO SCHOOL, OR THE TV SHOWS AND WEBSITES THEY INSISTED WERE SO COOL.
"BUT THERE'S ONE THING I'LL REMEMBER WELL, WHEN EVERYTHING ELSE IS GONE...
"THE FIRST TIME UNCLE ALOYSIUS KNEW WHAT WAS GOING ON.
"WHEN I WAS LOST BEYOND ESCAPE AND THOUGHT THAT NO ONE CARED, UNCLE A WAS WAITING THERE, MAGIC SPELLS PREPARED.
"HE TAUGHT ME HOW TO SUMMON FIRE AND DARKNESS TO MY AID."

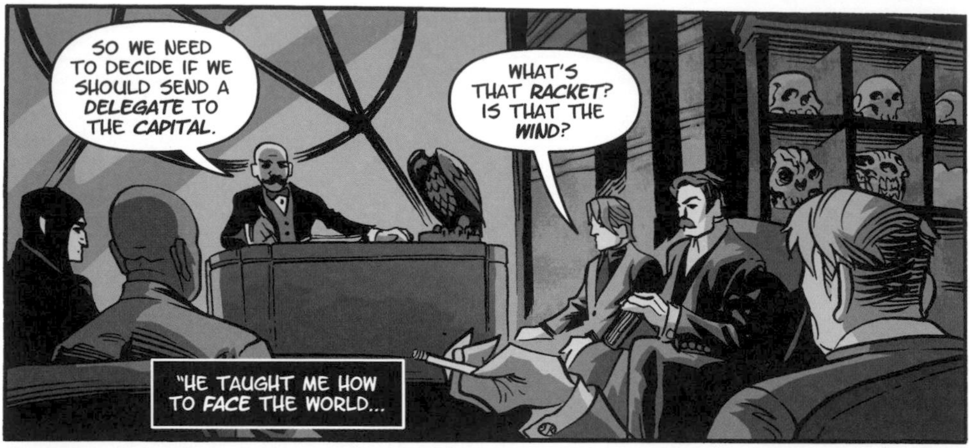
SO WE NEED TO DECIDE IF WE SHOULD SEND A DELEGATE TO THE CAPITAL.
WHAT'S THAT RACKET? IS THAT THE WIND?
"HE TAUGHT ME HOW TO FACE THE WORLD...

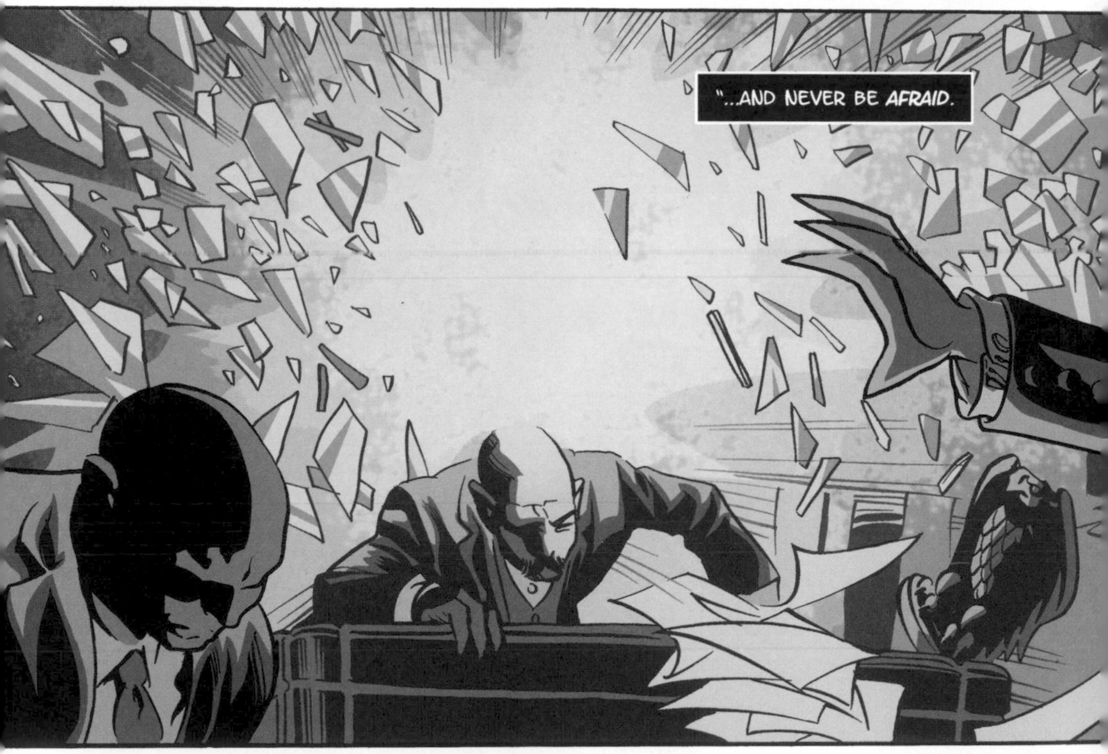
"...AND NEVER BE AFRAID.

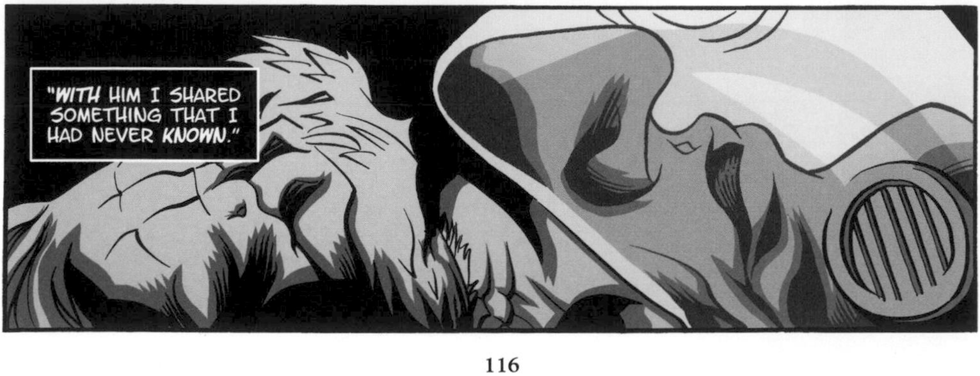
"WITH HIM I SHARED SOMETHING THAT I HAD NEVER KNOWN."

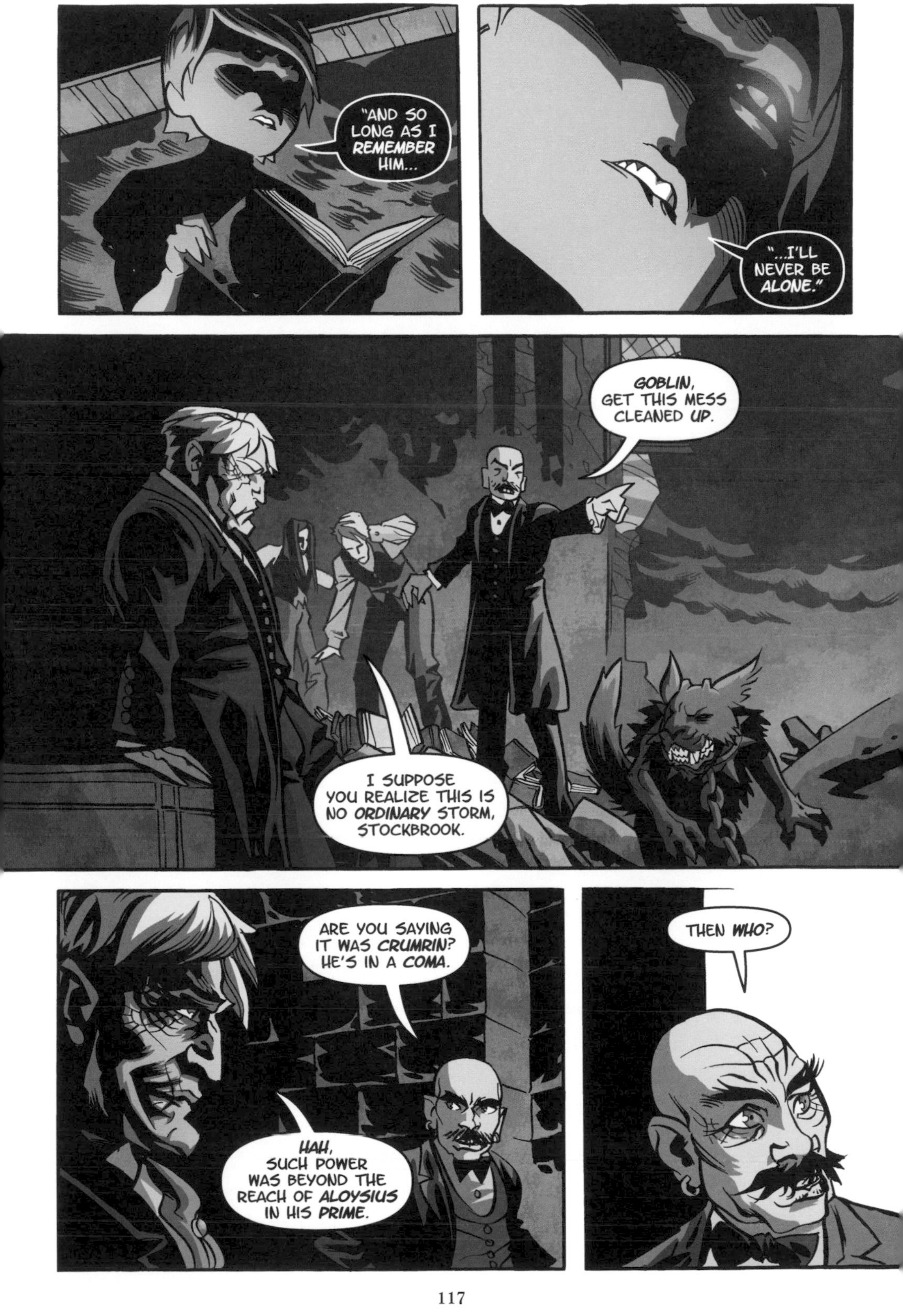
"AND SO LONG AS I REMEMBER HIM...
"...I'LL NEVER BE ALONE."
GOBLIN, GET THIS MESS CLEANED UP.
I SUPPOSE YOU REALIZE THIS IS NO ORDINARY STORM, STOCKBROOK.
ARE YOU SAYING IT WAS CRUMRIN? HE'S IN A COMA.
HAH, SUCH POWER WAS BEYOND THE REACH OF ALOYSIUS IN HIS PRIME.
THEN WHO?

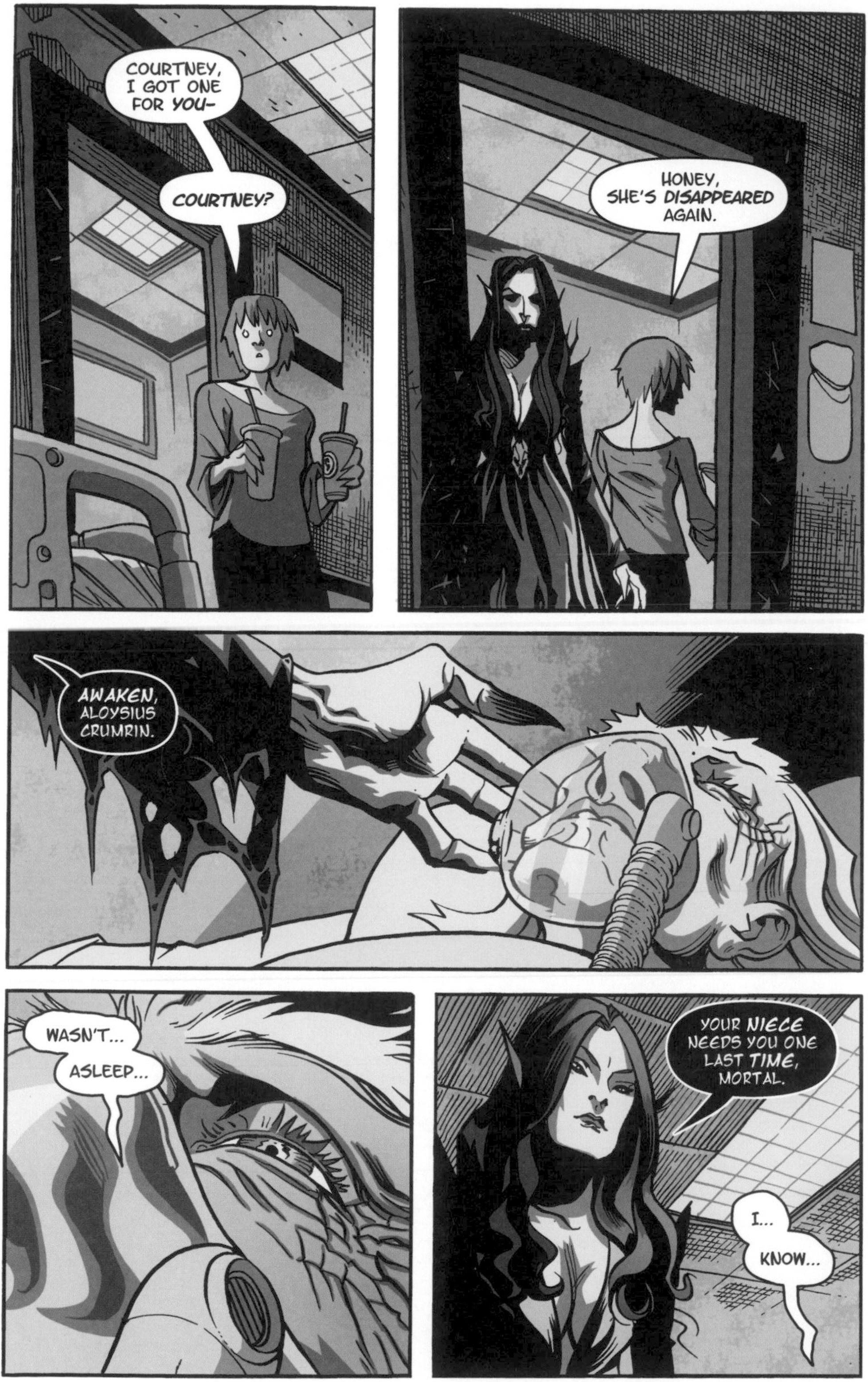
COURTNEY, I GOT ONE FOR YOU-
COURTNEY?
HONEY, SHE'S DISAPPEARED AGAIN.
AWAKEN, ALOYSIUS CRUMRIN.
WASN'T...
ASLEEP...
YOUR NIECE NEEDS YOU ONE LAST TIME, MORTAL.
I...
KNOW...

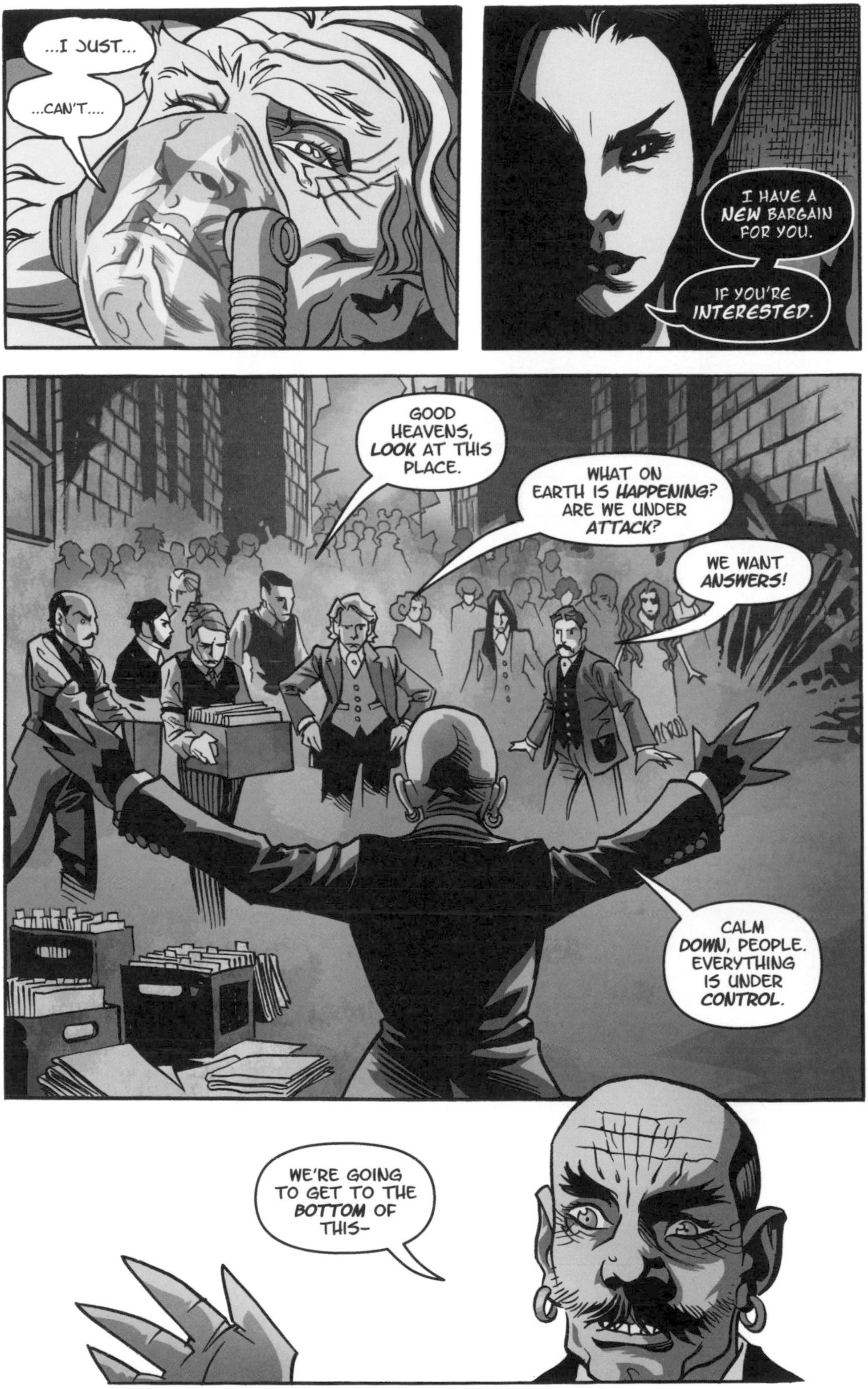
...I JUST...
...CAN'T....
I HAVE A NEW BARGAIN FOR YOU.
IF YOU'RE INTERESTED.
GOOD HEAVENS, LOOK AT THIS PLACE.
WHAT ON EARTH IS HAPPENING? ARE WE UNDER ATTACK?
WE WANT ANSWERS!
CALM DOWN, PEOPLE. EVERYTHING IS UNDER CONTROL.
WE'RE GOING TO GET TO THE BOTTOM OF THIS-

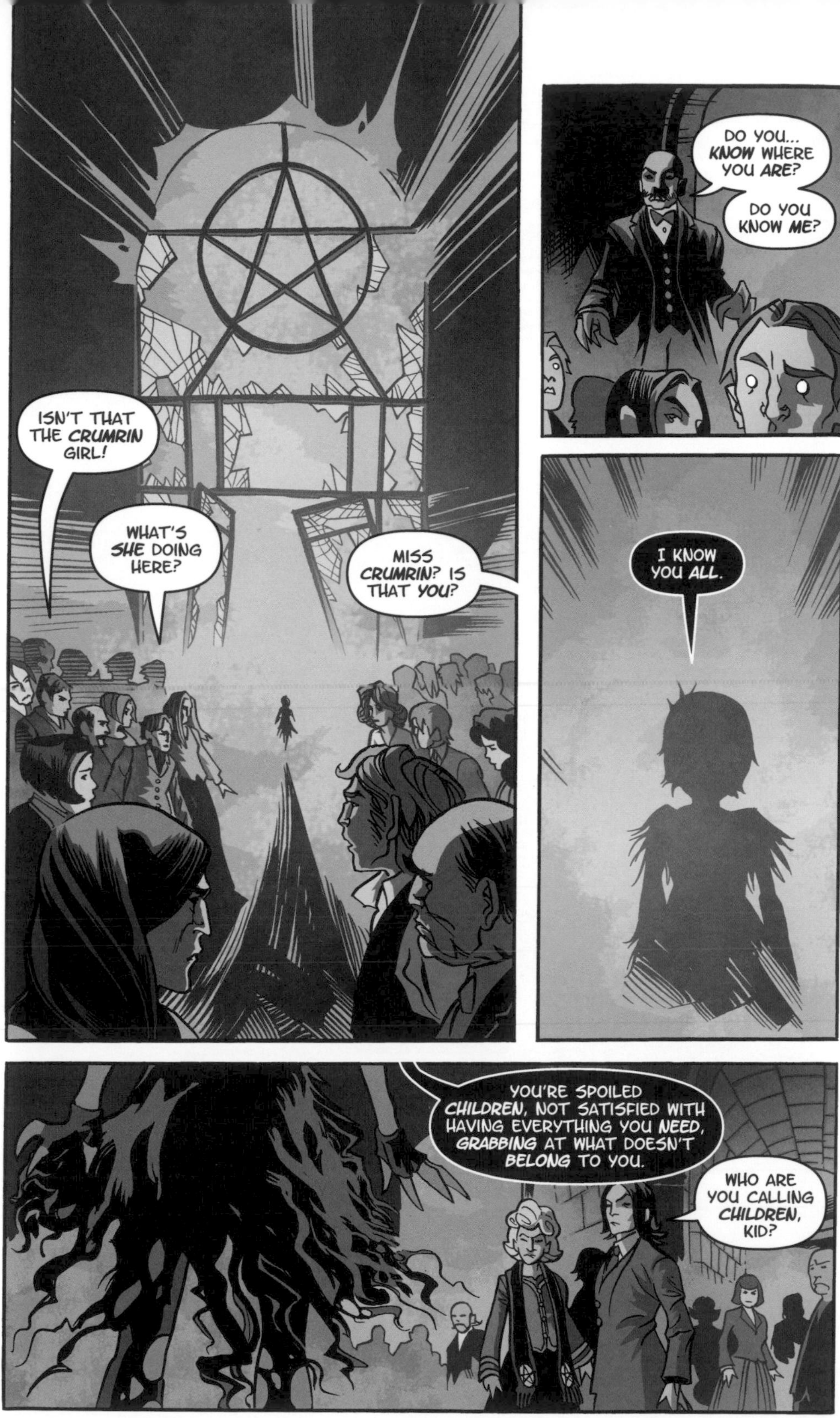
ISN'T THAT THE CRUMRIN GIRL!
WHAT'S SHE DOING HERE?
MISS CRUMRIN? IS THAT YOU?
DO YOU... KNOW WHERE YOU ARE?
DO YOU KNOW ME?
I KNOW YOU ALL.
YOU'RE SPOILED CHILDREN, NOT SATISFIED WITH HAVING EVERYTHING YOU NEED, GRABBING AT WHAT DOESN'T BELONG TO YOU.
WHO ARE YOU CALLING CHILDREN, KID?

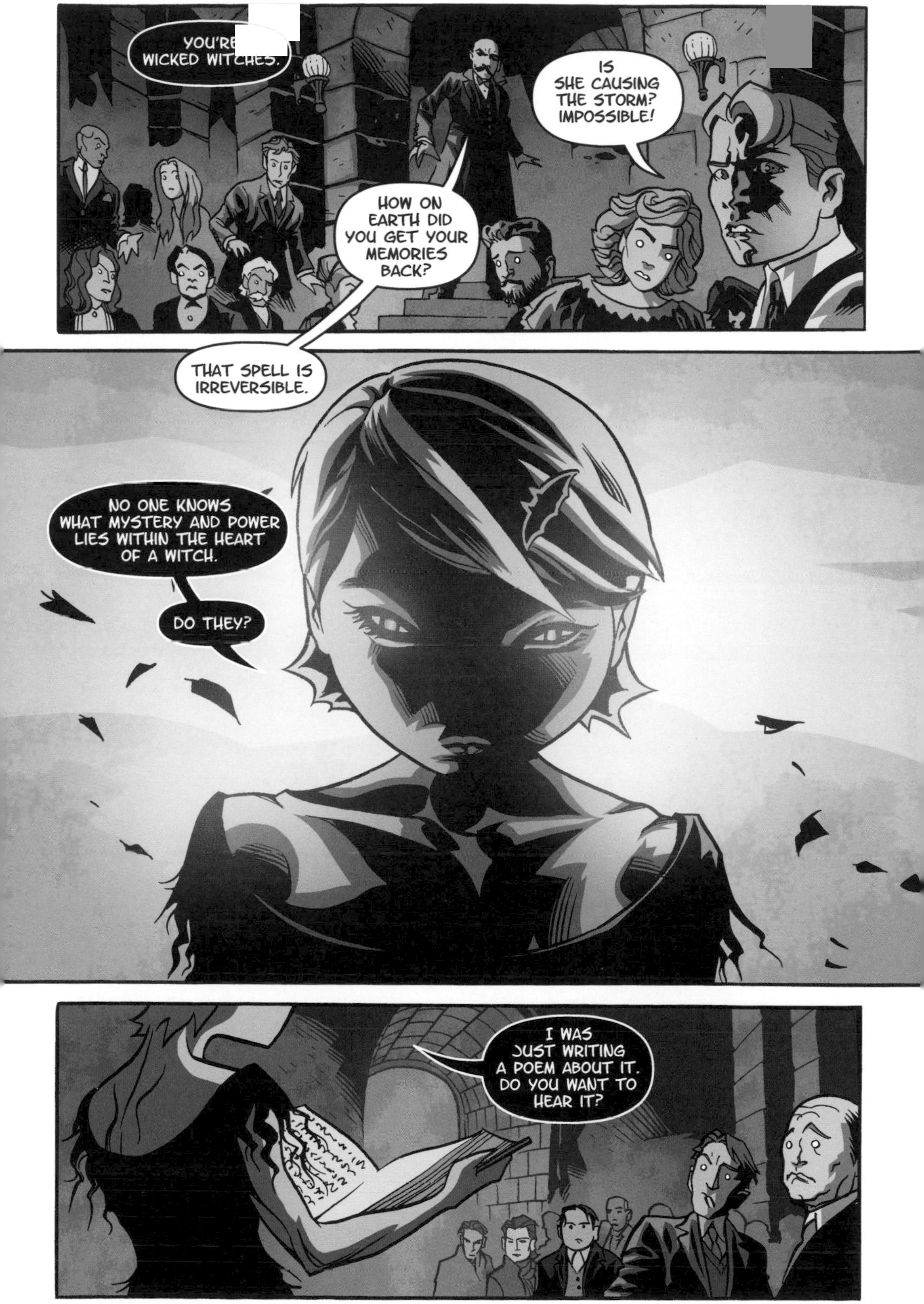
YOU'RE WICKED WITCHES.
HOW ON EARTH DID YOU GET YOUR MEMORIES BACK?
IS SHE CAUSING THE STORM? IMPOSSIBLE!
THAT SPELL IS IRREVERSIBLE.
NO ONE KNOWS WHAT MYSTERY AND POWER LIES WITHIN THE HEART OF A WITCH.
DO THEY?
I WAS JUST WRITING A POEM ABOUT IT. DO YOU WANT TO HEAR IT?

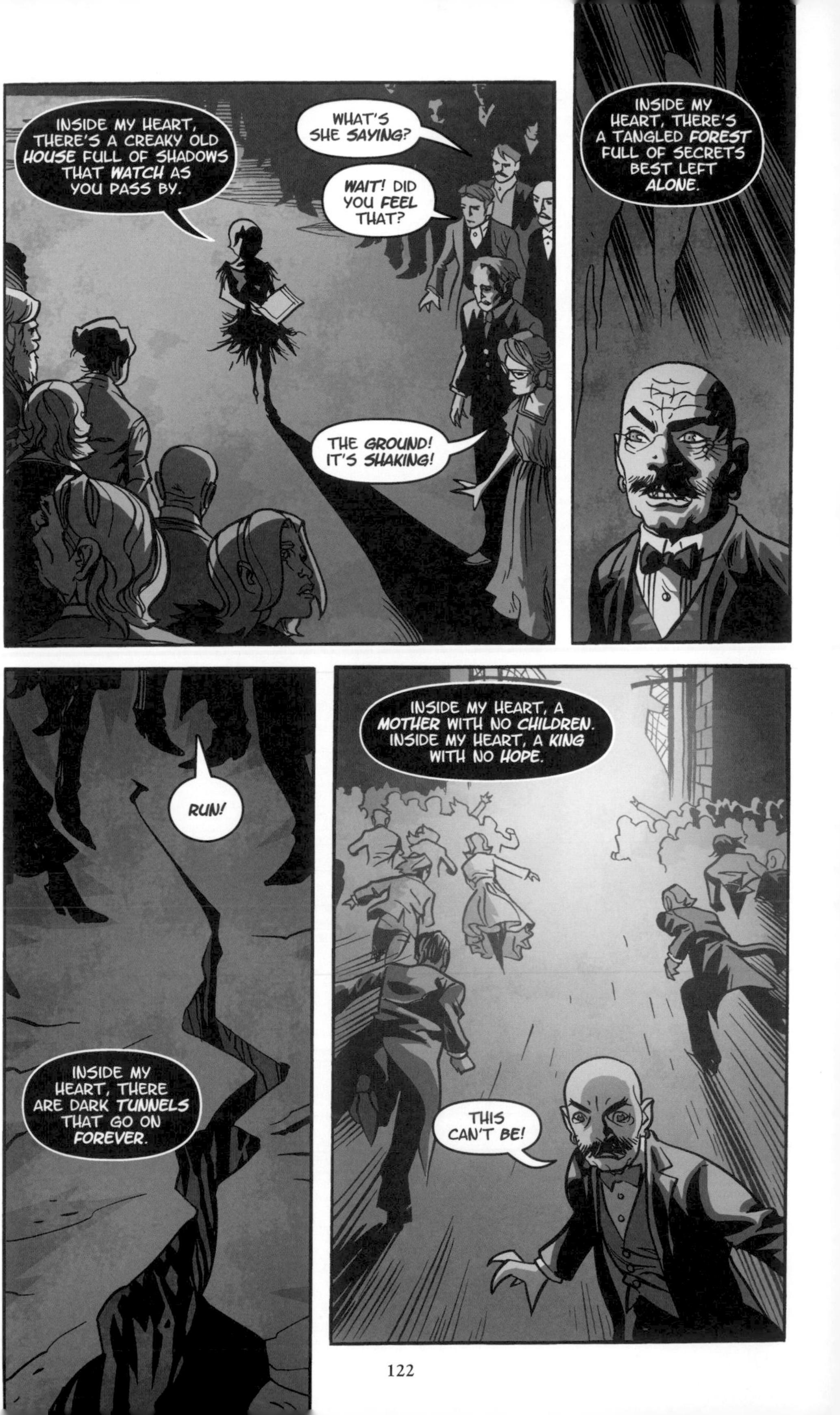
INSIDE MY HEART, THERE'S A CREAKY OLD HOUSE FULL OF SHADOWS THAT WATCH AS YOU PASS BY.
WHAT'S SHE SAYING?
WAIT! DID YOU FEEL THAT?
THE GROUND! IT'S SHAKING!
INSIDE MY HEART, THERE'S A TANGLED FOREST FULL OF SECRETS BEST LEFT ALONE.
RUN!
INSIDE MY HEART, THERE ARE DARK TUNNELS THAT GO ON FOREVER.
INSIDE MY HEART, A MOTHER WITH NO CHILDREN. INSIDE MY HEART, A KING WITH NO HOPE.
THIS CAN'T BE!

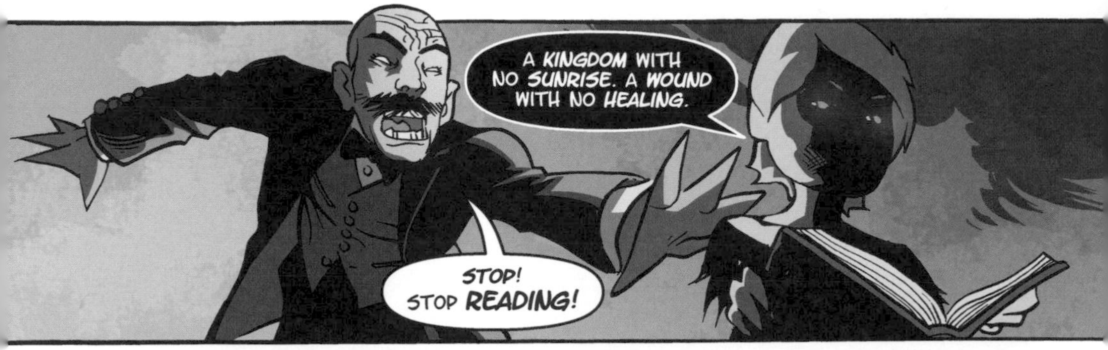
A KINGDOM WITH NO SUNRISE. A WOUND WITH NO HEALING.
STOP! STOP READING!

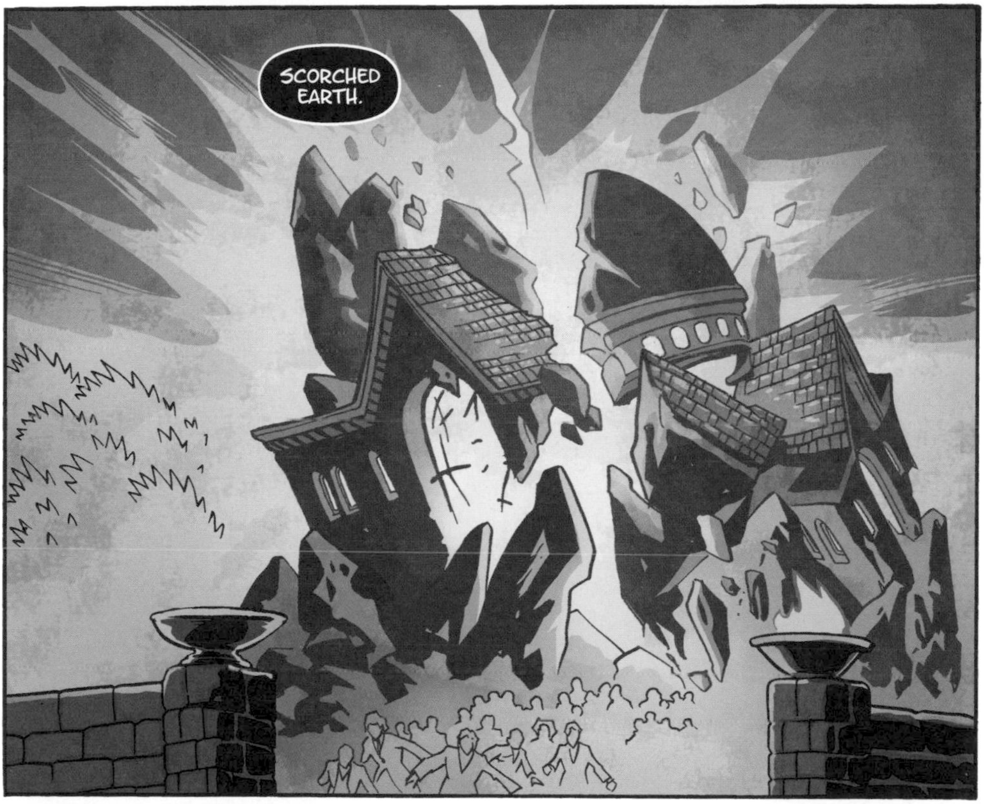
SCORCHED EARTH.

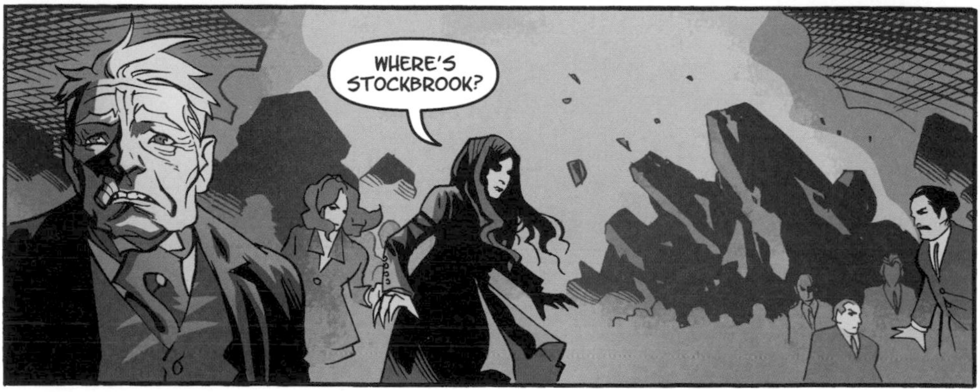
WHERE'S STOCKBROOK?

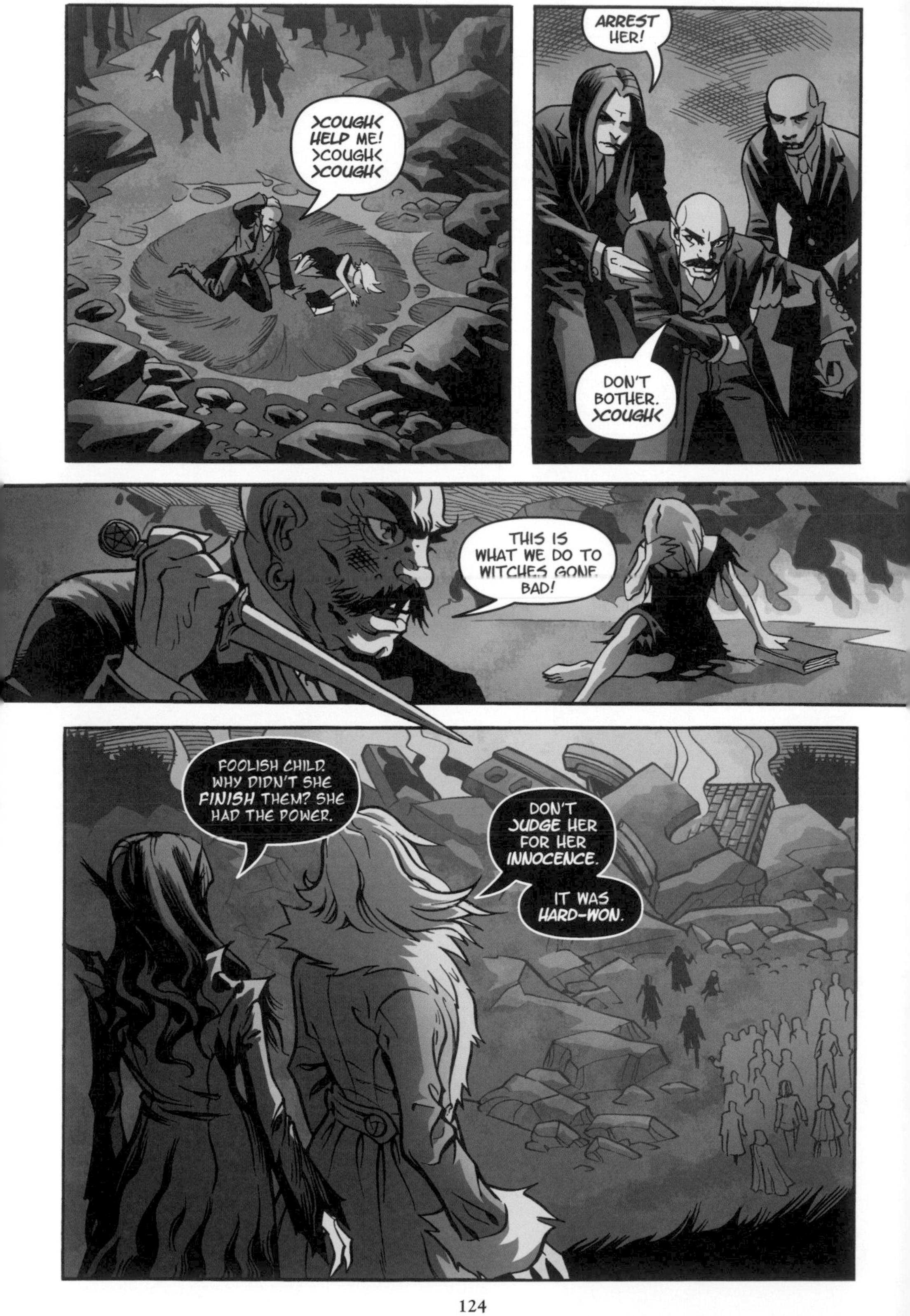
>COUGH< HELP ME! >COUGH< >COUGH<
ARREST HER!
DON'T BOTHER. >COUGH<
THIS IS WHAT WE DO TO WITCHES GONE BAD!
FOOLISH CHILD. WHY DIDN'T SHE FINISH THEM? SHE HAD THE POWER.
DON'T JUDGE HER FOR HER INNOCENCE.
IT WAS HARD-WON.

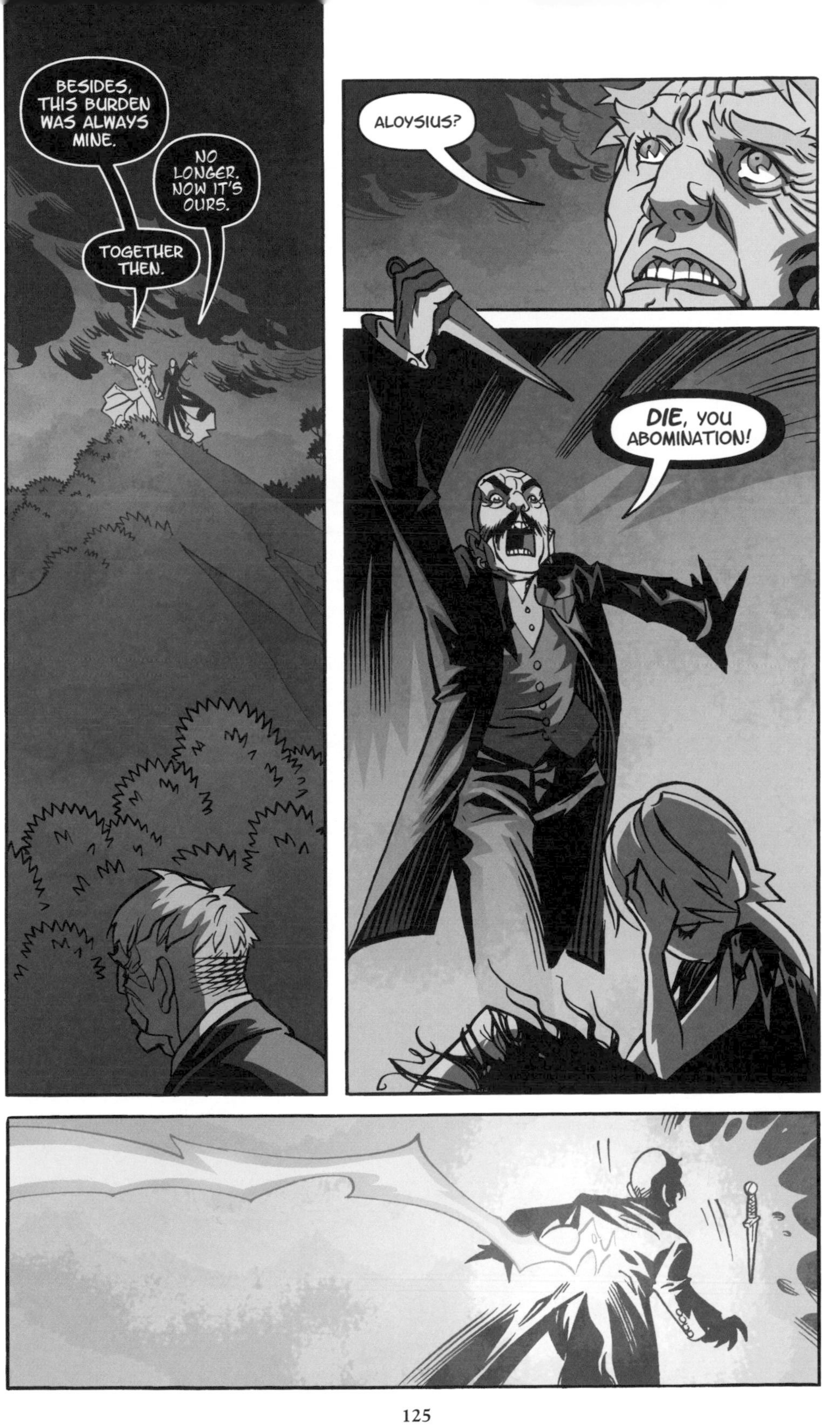
BESIDES, THIS BURDEN WAS ALWAYS MINE.
NO LONGER. NOW IT'S OURS.
TOGETHER THEN.
ALOYSIUS?
DIE, YOU ABOMINATION!

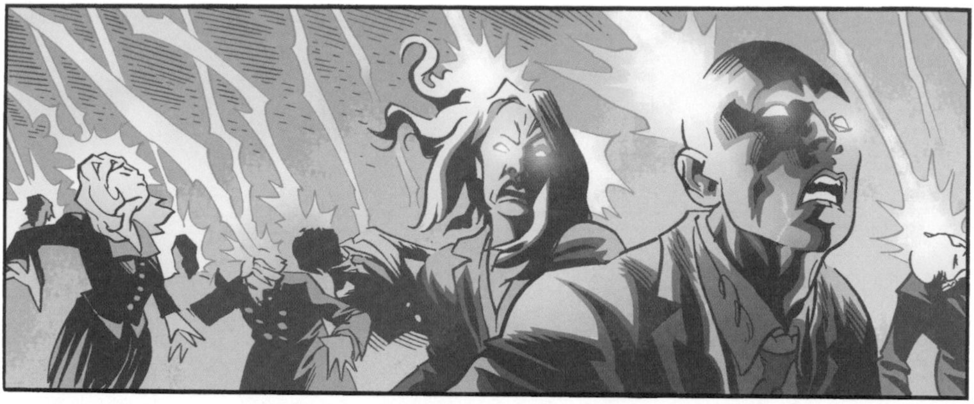

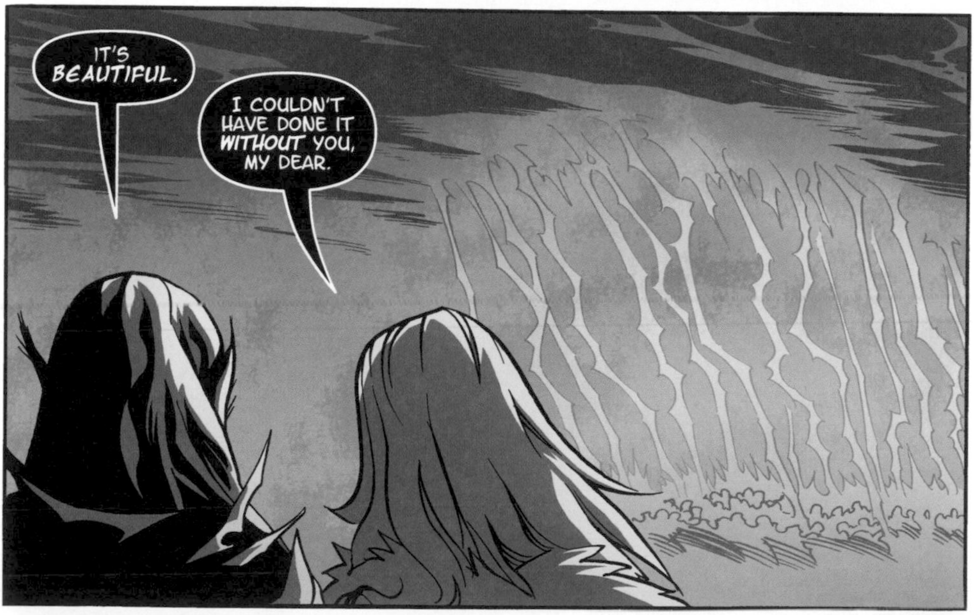
IT'S BEAUTIFUL.
I COULDN'T HAVE DONE IT WITHOUT YOU, MY DEAR.

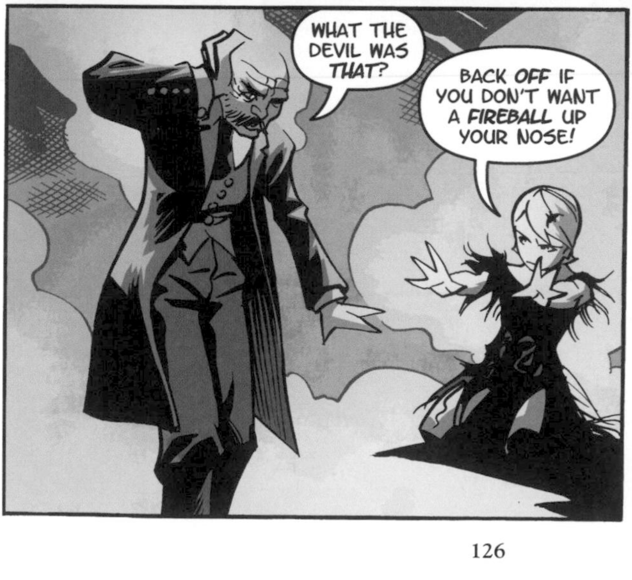
WHAT THE DEVIL WAS THAT?
BACK OFF IF YOU DON'T WANT A FIREBALL UP YOUR NOSE!

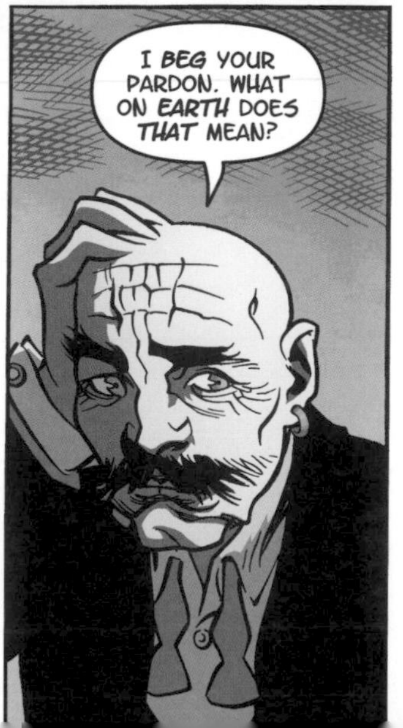
I BEG YOUR PARDON. WHAT ON EARTH DOES THAT MEAN?

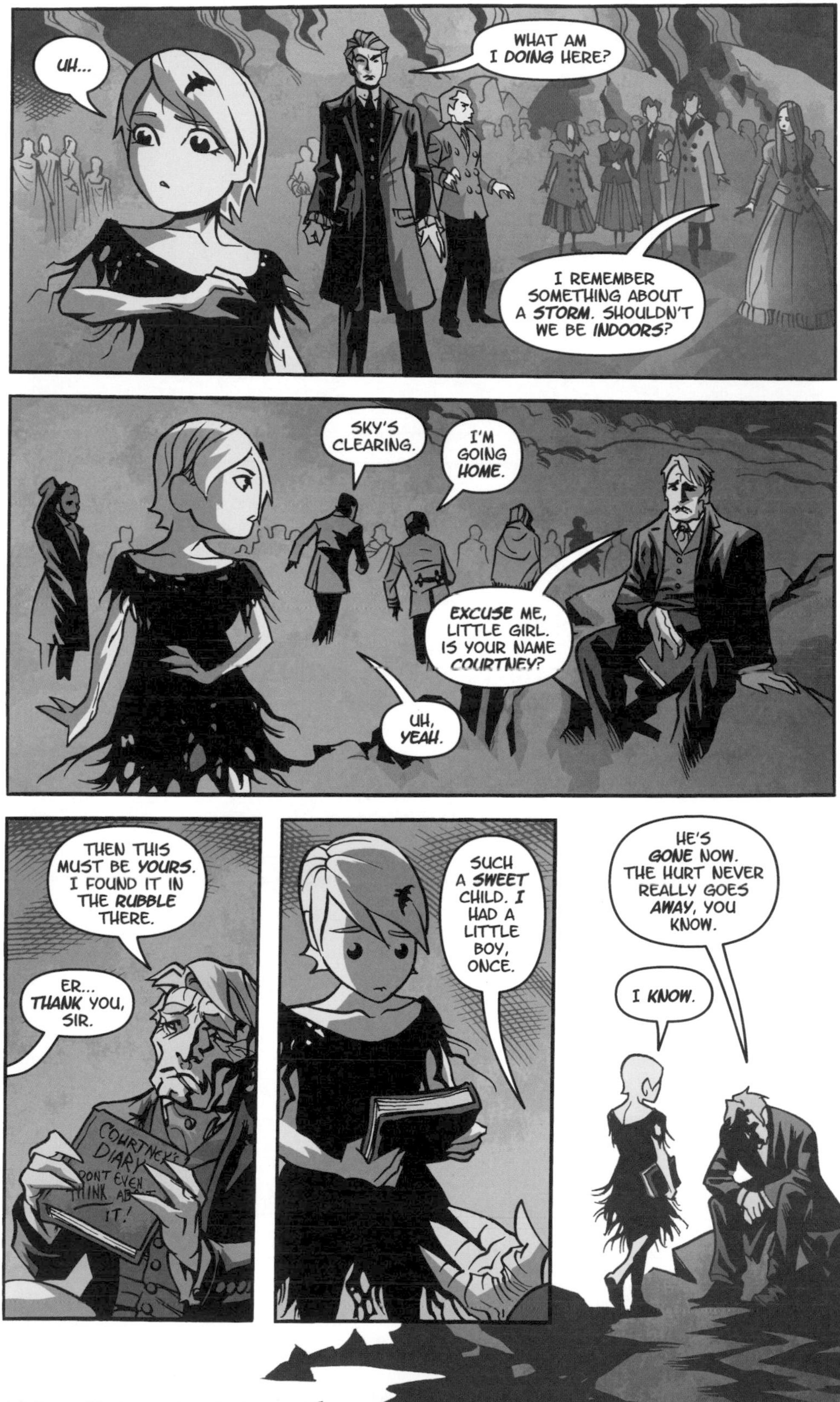
UH...
WHAT AM I DOING HERE?
I REMEMBER SOMETHING ABOUT A STORM. SHOULDN'T WE BE INDOORS?
SKY'S CLEARING.
I'M GOING HOME.
EXCUSE ME, LITTLE GIRL. IS YOUR NAME COURTNEY?
UH, YEAH.
THEN THIS MUST BE YOURS. I FOUND IT IN THE RUBBLE THERE.
ER... THANK YOU, SIR.
COURTNEY'S DIARY
DON'T EVEN THINK AB IT!
SUCH A SWEET CHILD. I HAD A LITTLE BOY, ONCE.
HE'S GONE NOW. THE HURT NEVER REALLY GOES AWAY, YOU KNOW.
I KNOW.

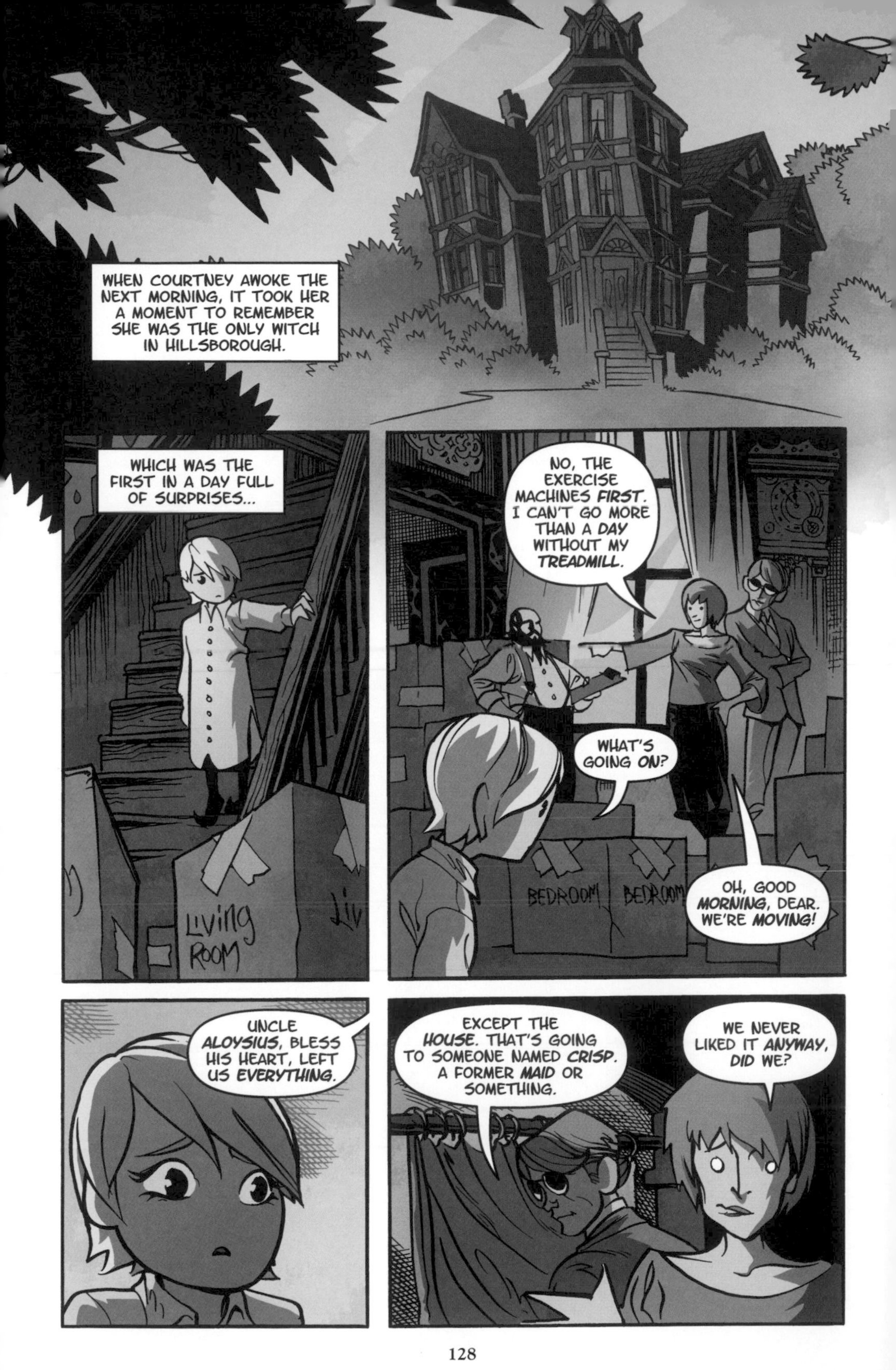
WHEN COURTNEY AWOKE THE NEXT MORNING, IT TOOK HER A MOMENT TO REMEMBER SHE WAS THE ONLY WITCH IN HILLSBOROUGH.
WHICH WAS THE FIRST IN A DAY FULL OF SURPRISES...
LIVING ROOM
NO, THE EXERCISE MACHINES FIRST. I CAN'T GO MORE THAN A DAY WITHOUT MY TREADMILL.
WHAT'S GOING ON?
BEDROOM
BEDROOM
OH, GOOD MORNING, DEAR. WE'RE MOVING!
UNCLE ALOYSIUS, BLESS HIS HEART, LEFT US EVERYTHING.
EXCEPT THE HOUSE. THAT'S GOING TO SOMEONE NAMED CRISP. A FORMER MAID OR SOMETHING.
WE NEVER LIKED IT ANYWAY, DID WE?

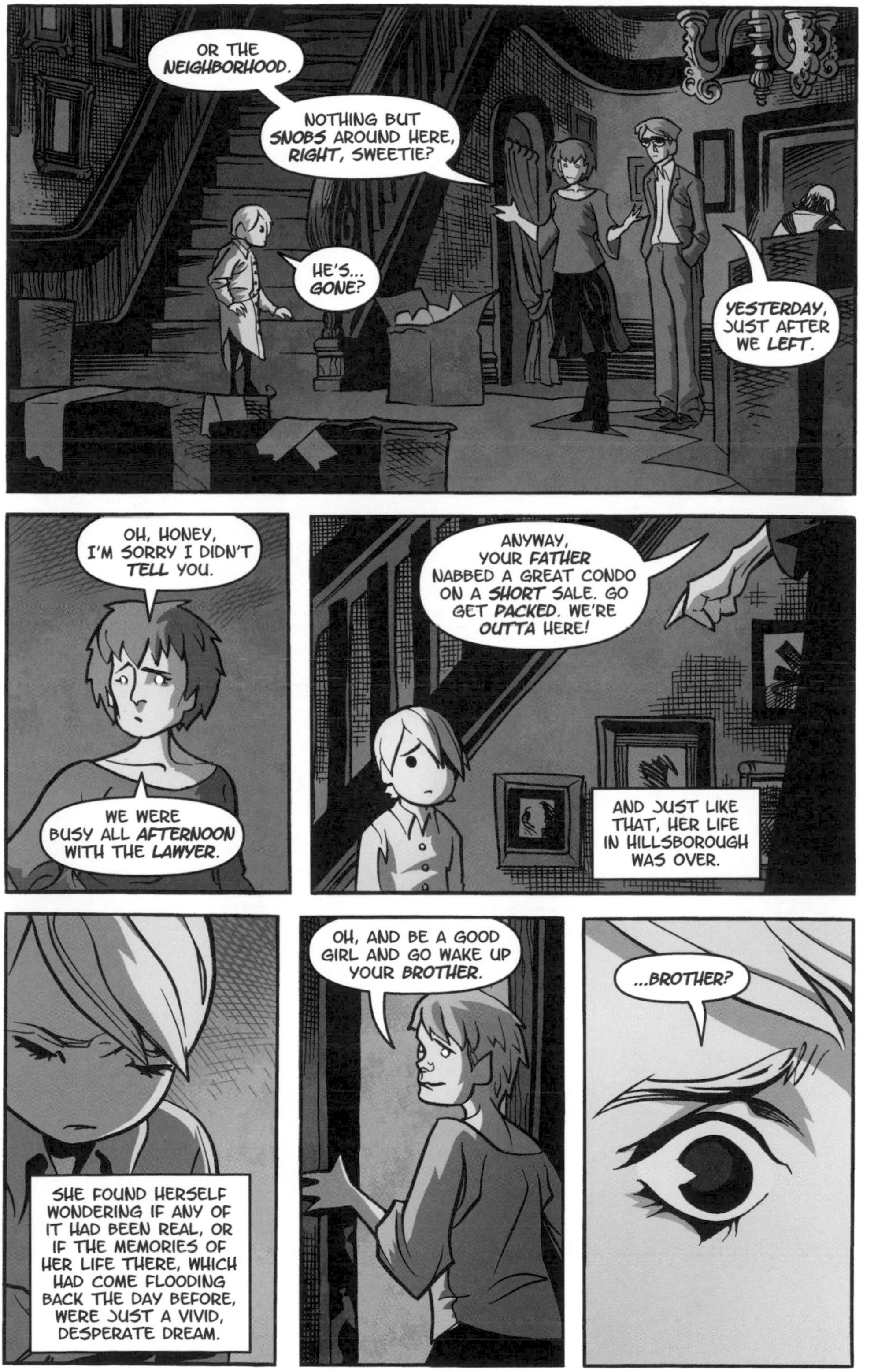
OR THE NEIGHBORHOOD.
NOTHING BUT SNOBS AROUND HERE, RIGHT, SWEETIE?
HE'S... GONE?
YESTERDAY, JUST AFTER WE LEFT.
OH, HONEY, I'M SORRY I DIDN'T TELL YOU.
WE WERE BUSY ALL AFTERNOON WITH THE LAWYER.
ANYWAY, YOUR FATHER NABBED A GREAT CONDO ON A SHORT SALE. GO GET PACKED. WE'RE OUTTA HERE!
AND JUST LIKE THAT, HER LIFE IN HILLSBOROUGH WAS OVER.
SHE FOUND HERSELF WONDERING IF ANY OF IT HAD BEEN REAL, OR IF THE MEMORIES OF HER LIFE THERE, WHICH HAD COME FLOODING BACK THE DAY BEFORE, WERE JUST A VIVID, DESPERATE DREAM.
OH, AND BE A GOOD GIRL AND GO WAKE UP YOUR BROTHER.
...BROTHER?

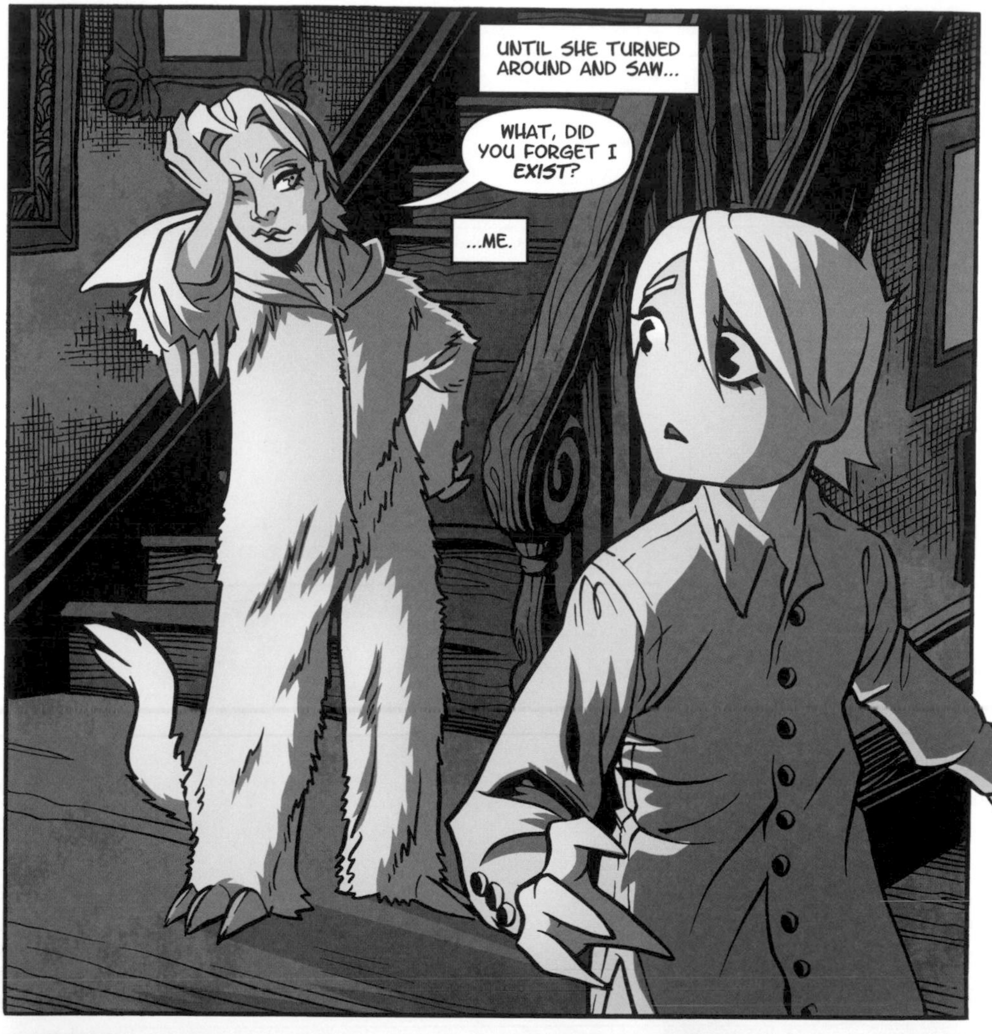
UNTIL SHE TURNED AROUND AND SAW...
WHAT, DID YOU FORGET I EXIST?
...ME.
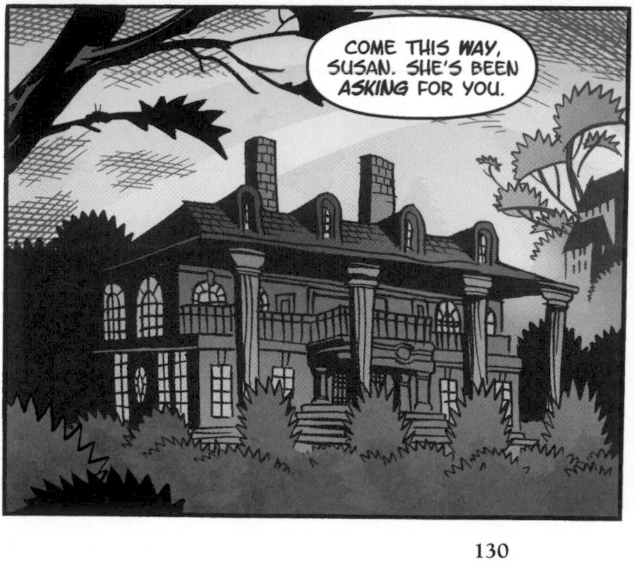
COME THIS WAY, SUSAN. SHE'S BEEN ASKING FOR YOU.
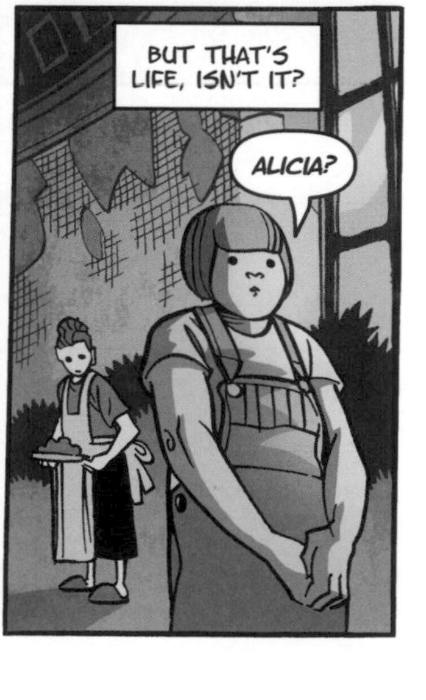
BUT THAT'S LIFE, ISN'T IT?
ALICIA?

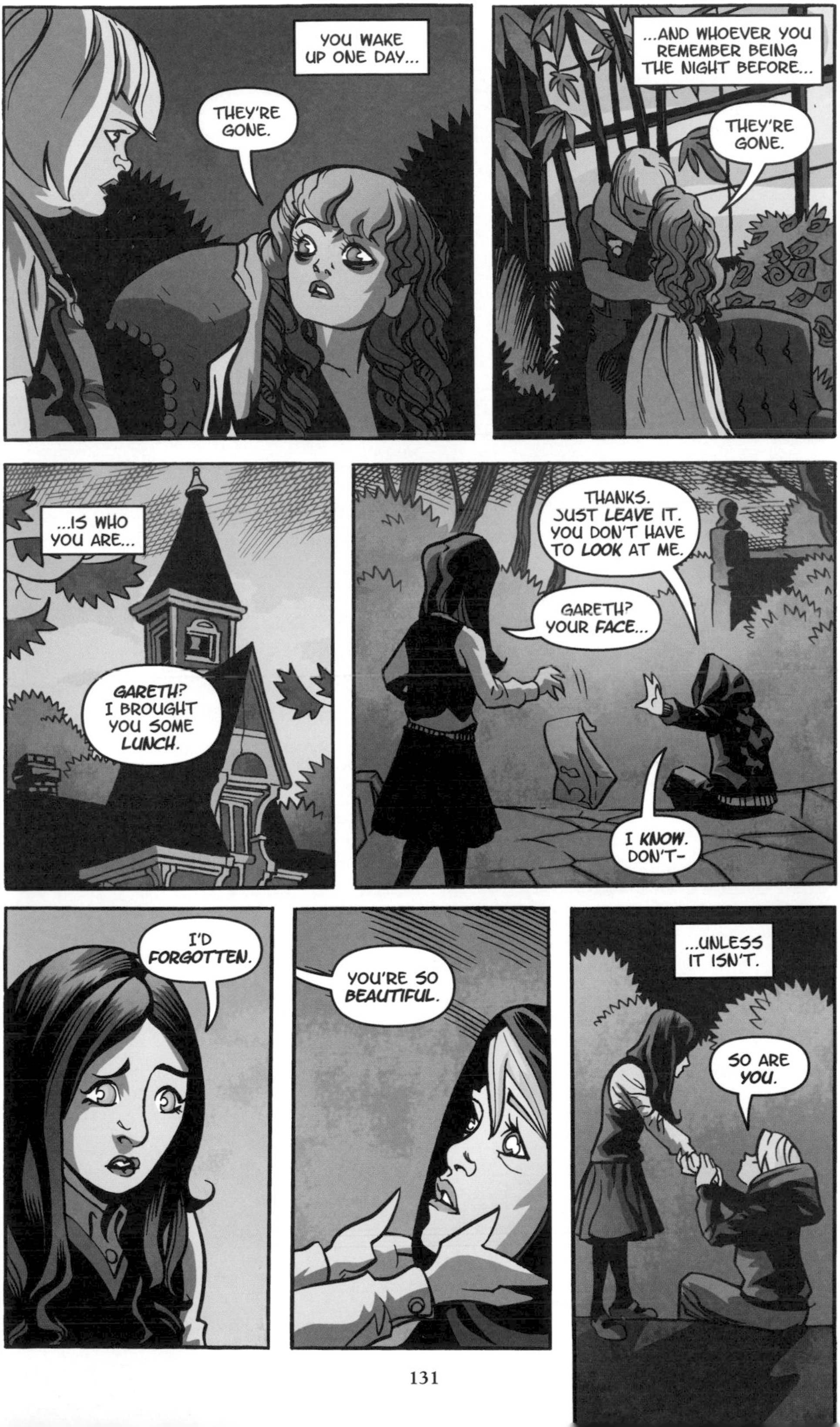
YOU WAKE UP ONE DAY...
THEY'RE GONE.
...AND WHOEVER YOU REMEMBER BEING THE NIGHT BEFORE...
THEY'RE GONE.
...IS WHO YOU ARE...
GARETH? I BROUGHT YOU SOME LUNCH.
THANKS. JUST LEAVE IT. YOU DON'T HAVE TO LOOK AT ME.
GARETH? YOUR FACE...
I KNOW. DON'T-
I'D FORGOTTEN.
YOU'RE SO BEAUTIFUL.
...UNLESS IT ISN'T.
SO ARE YOU.

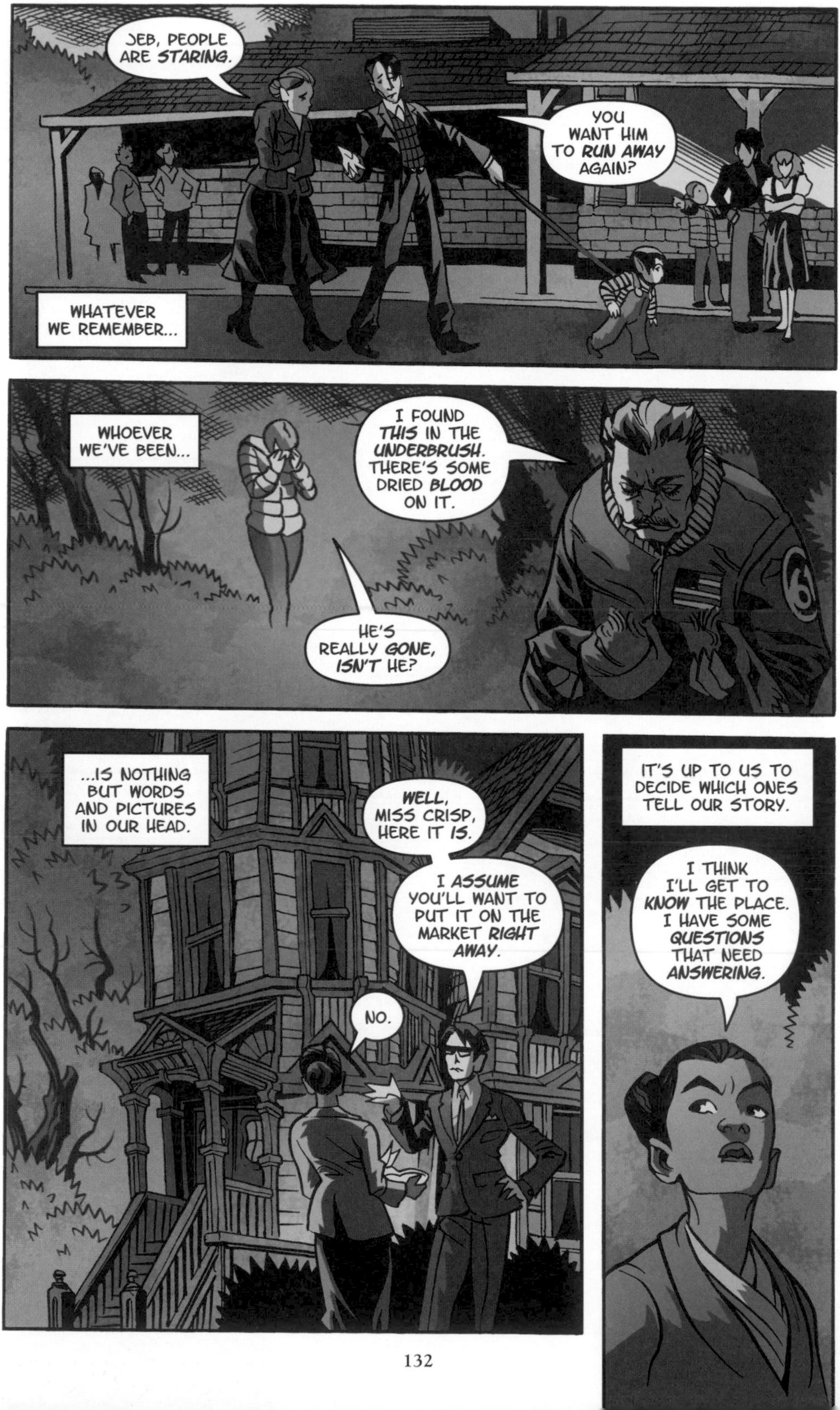
JEB, PEOPLE ARE STARING.
YOU WANT HIM TO RUN AWAY AGAIN?
WHATEVER WE REMEMBER...
WHOEVER WE'VE BEEN...
I FOUND THIS IN THE UNDERBRUSH. THERE'S SOME DRIED BLOOD ON IT.
HE'S REALLY GONE, ISN'T HE?
...IS NOTHING BUT WORDS AND PICTURES IN OUR HEAD.
WELL, MISS CRISP, HERE IT IS.
I ASSUME YOU'LL WANT TO PUT IT ON THE MARKET RIGHT AWAY.
NO.
IT'S UP TO US TO DECIDE WHICH ONES TELL OUR STORY.
I THINK I'LL GET TO KNOW THE PLACE. I HAVE SOME QUESTIONS THAT NEED ANSWERING.

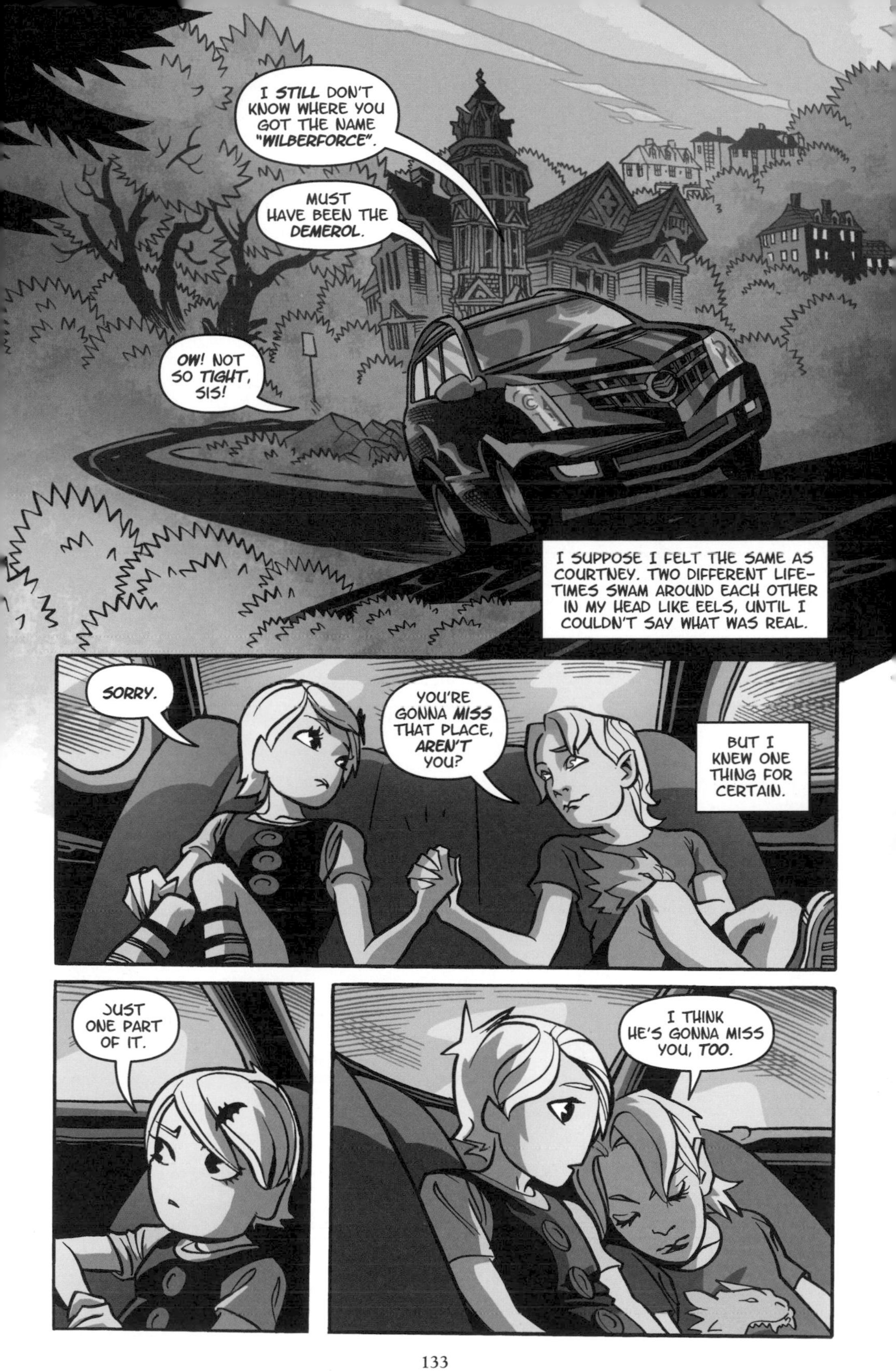
I STILL DON'T KNOW WHERE YOU GOT THE NAME "WILBERFORCE".
MUST HAVE BEEN THE DEMEROL.
OW! NOT SO TIGHT, SIS!
I SUPPOSE I FELT THE SAME AS COURTNEY. TWO DIFFERENT LIFE-TIMES SWAM AROUND EACH OTHER IN MY HEAD LIKE EELS, UNTIL I COULDN'T SAY WHAT WAS REAL.
SORRY.
YOU'RE GONNA MISS THAT PLACE, AREN'T YOU?
BUT I KNEW ONE THING FOR CERTAIN.
JUST ONE PART OF IT.
I THINK HE'S GONNA MISS YOU, TOO.

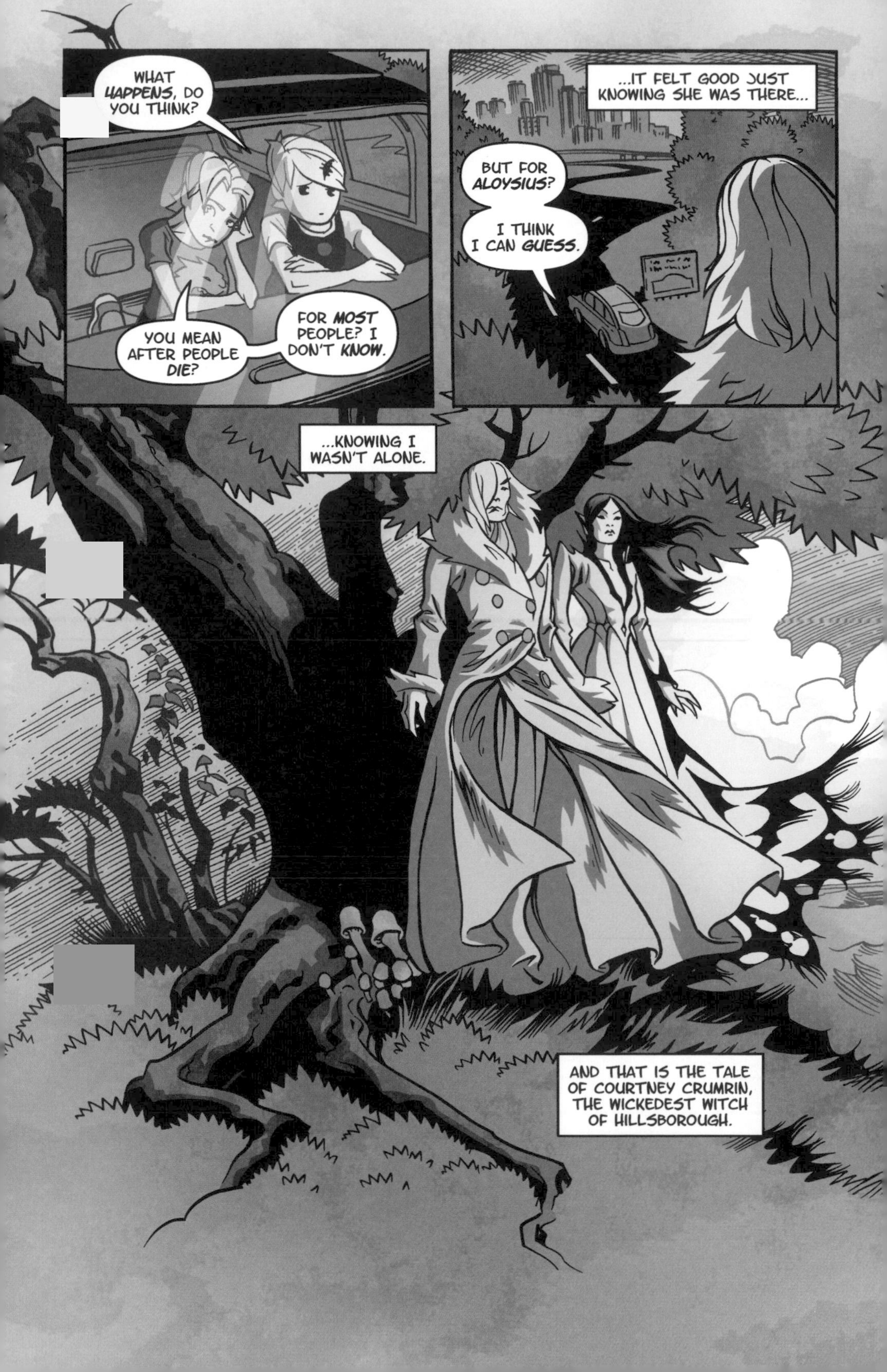
WHAT HAPPENS, DO YOU THINK?
YOU MEAN AFTER PEOPLE DIE?
FOR MOST PEOPLE? I DON'T KNOW.
...IT FELT GOOD JUST KNOWING SHE WAS THERE...
BUT FOR ALOYSIUS?
I THINK I CAN GUESS.
...KNOWING I WASN'T ALONE.
AND THAT IS THE TALE OF COURTNEY CRUMRIN, THE WICKEDEST WITCH OF HILLSBOROUGH.

Courtney Crumrin

Volume Six

Crumrin

The Final Spell

Cover Gallery

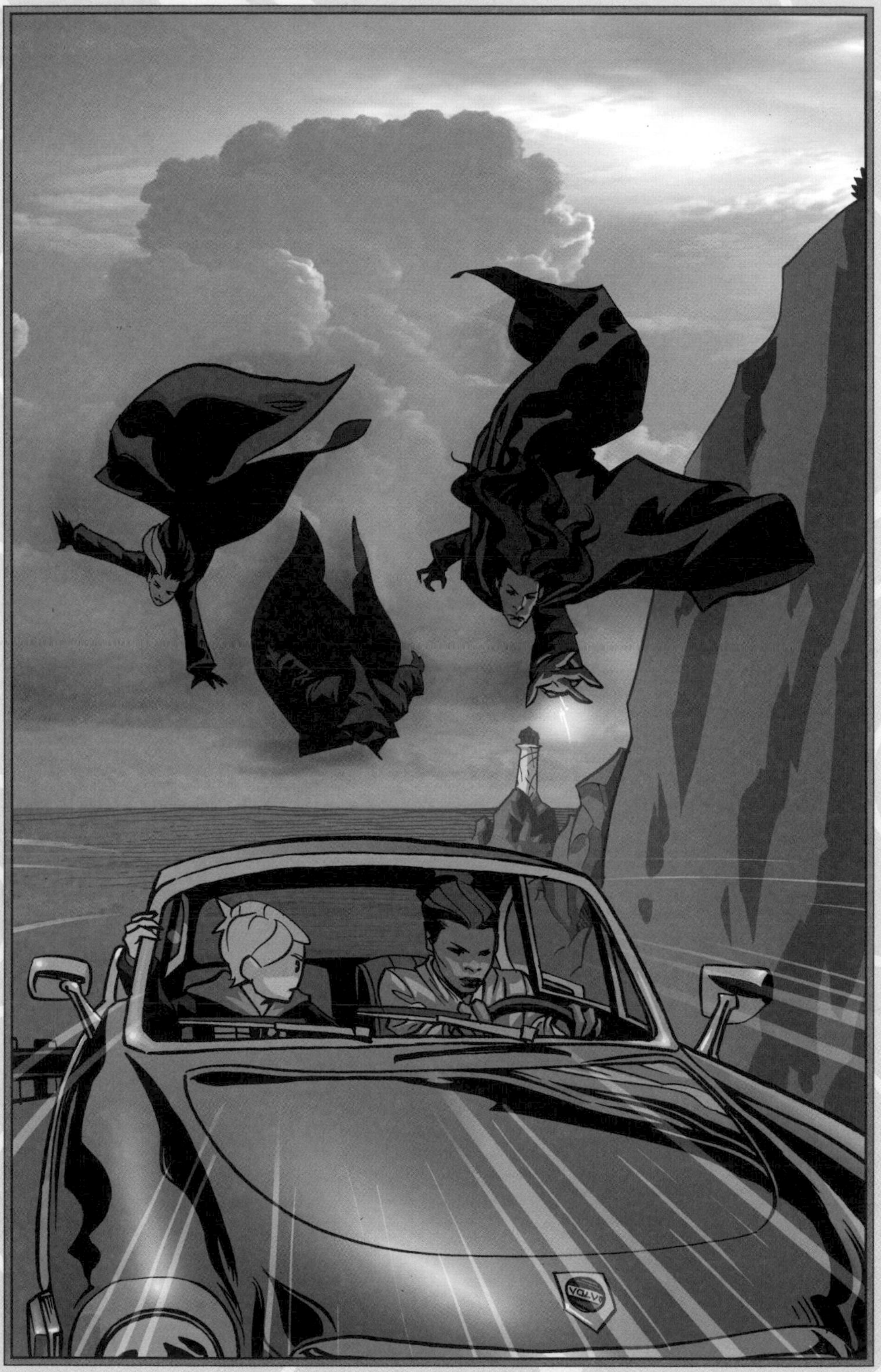
VOLVO

Cover artwork for *Courtney Crumrin* issue #6.

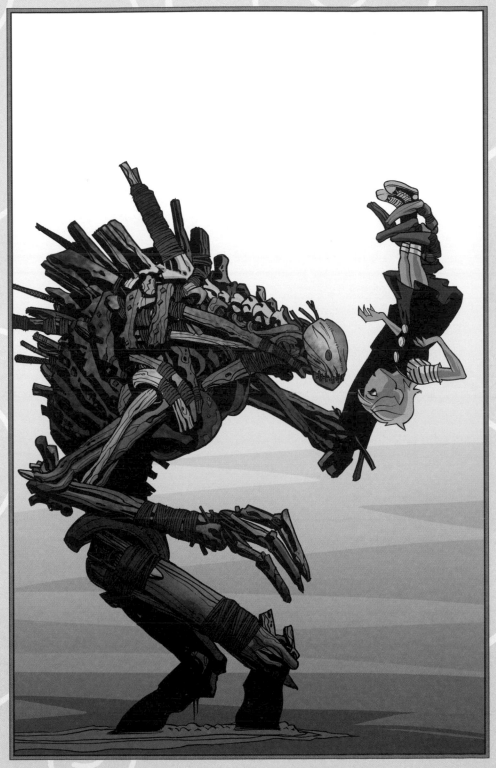

Cover artwork for *Courtney Crumrin* issue #7.

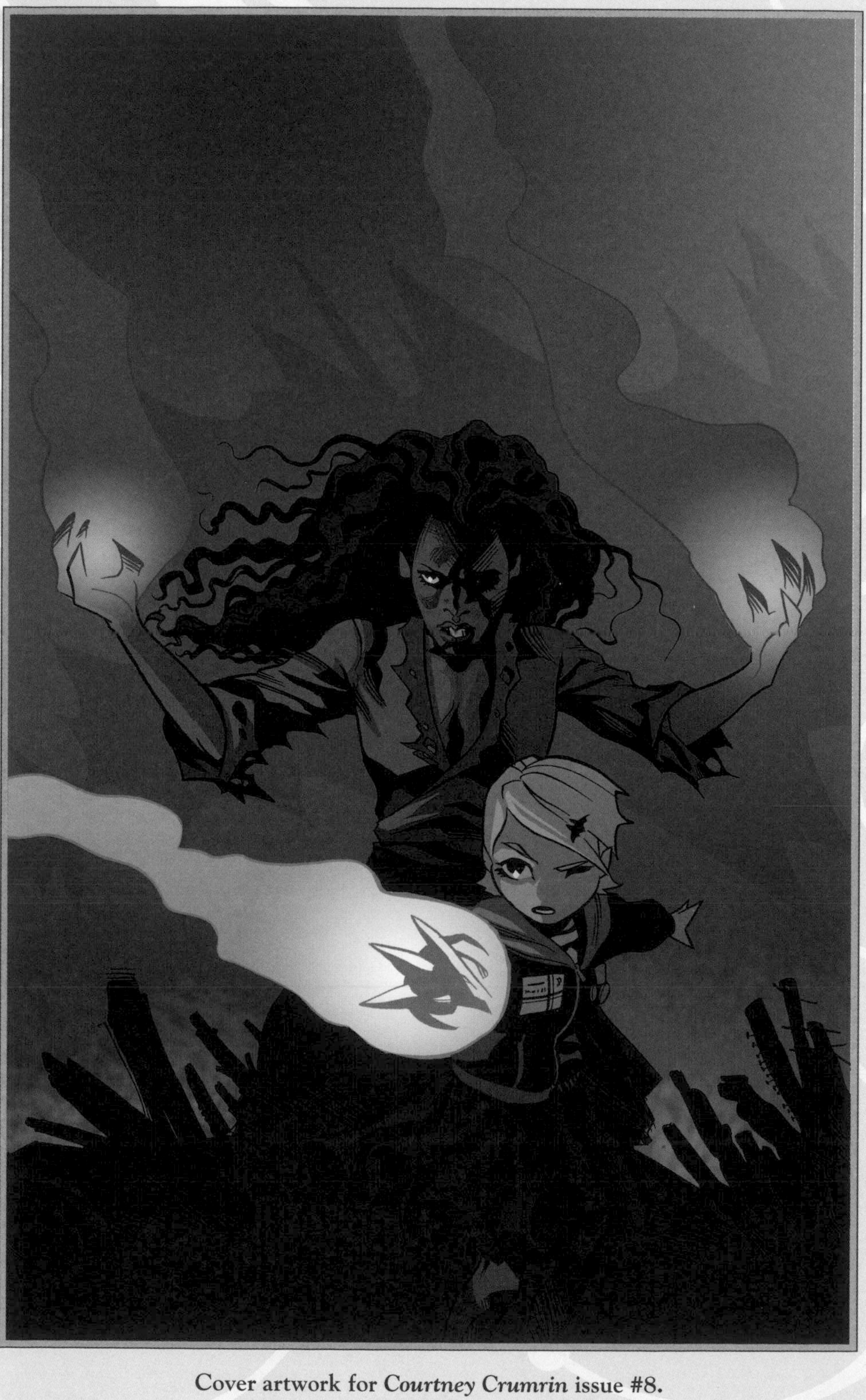

Cover artwork for *Courtney Crumrin* issue #8.

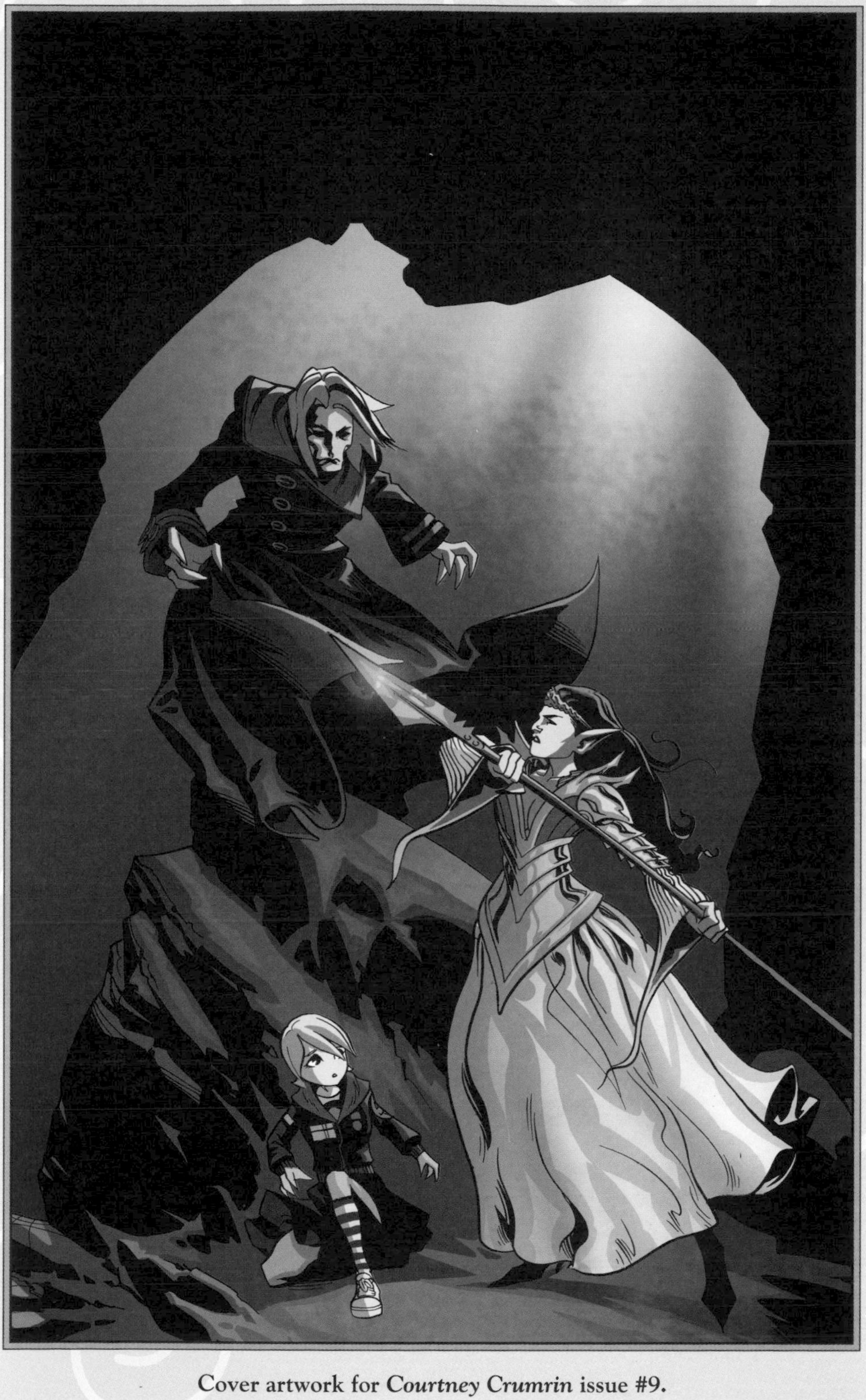

Cover artwork for *Courtney Crumrin* issue #9.

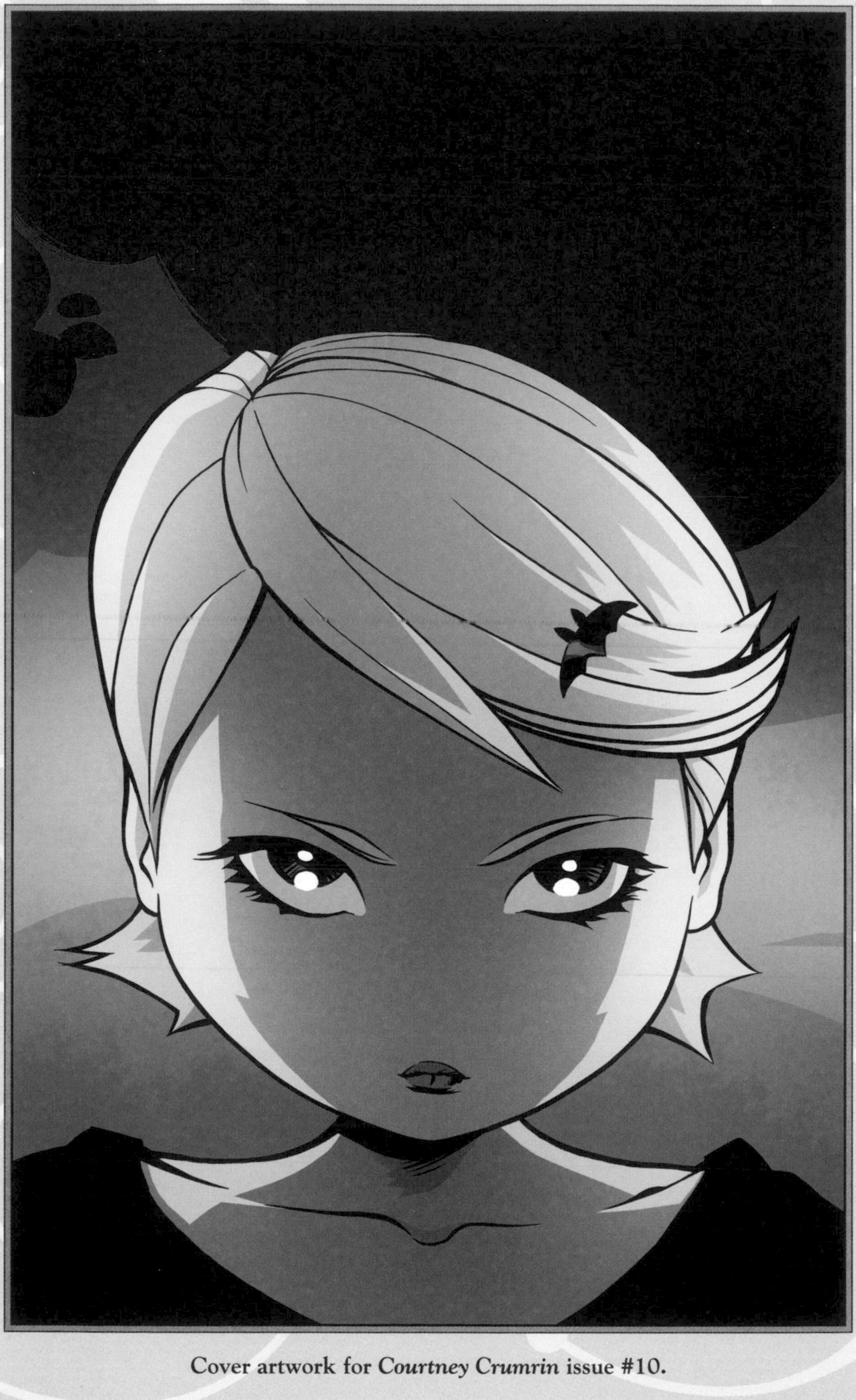

Cover artwork for *Courtney Crumrin* issue #10.